Greenberg's GUIDES

LIONEL TRAINS

1945 - 1969
Volume VI: Accessories

SECOND EDITION

Alan Stewart

KALMBACH
BOOKS

Printed in China

01 02 03 04 05 06 07 08 09   10 9 8 7 6 5 4 3 2 1

Visit our website at
http://kalmbachbooks.com
Secure online ordering available

Publisher's Cataloging-in-Publication
Prepared by Quality Books, Inc.

Stewart, Alan, 1939-
    [Guide to Lionel trains, 1945-1969]
    Greenberg's guide to Lionel trains, 1945-1969.
  Vol. VI, Accessories / Alan Stewart. — 2nd ed.
    p. cm.
    Includes index.
    ISBN 0-89778-475-8 (soft)
    ISBN 0-89778-476-6 (hardbound)

    1. Railroads—Models. 2. Lionel Corporation
I. Johnson, Kent. II. Title. III. Title: Accessories
IV. Title: Guide to Lionel trains, 1945-1969. V. Title:
Lionel trains, 1945-1969.

TF197.S84 2001   625.1'9
                        QBI01-700517

Art director: Kristi Ludwig
Book design: Sabine Beaupré

Table of Contents

Dedication

This book is dedicated to the memory of Joshua Lionel Cowen and the thousands of men and women of the Lionel Corporation whose labor and imagination created perhaps the greatest toy of all time. Their efforts shine like a beacon through the years, brightening the lives of all that choose to preserve and enjoy Lionel trains.

This book is also dedicated to the memory of John H. Van Slyke, a wonderful friend for 30 years and an authority on the Lionel showroom in New York. John's knowledge and enthusiasm for Lionel trains have inspired the author and contributed greatly to the content of this volume.

Acknowledgments

It is impossible to list all the friends and acquaintances who have shared information and enhanced the author's knowledge over his many years of collecting and operating Lionel trains, but this book would not have been possible without them. Special thanks go to those who made major contributions to the actual preparation of this volume by supplying information and pictures or lending items to be photographed. The author extends his heartfelt thanks to Joe Algozzini, Paul Ambrose, Ron Antonelli, Ed Barbret, Ernie Chornyei, Don Corrigan, Gary Holick, Virginia Ingling, Barry Keener, Terral Klaassen, Jeff Lampert, Terry Olexsy, Buz and Norma Ray, Mo Rose, Dick Sanford, Don Simonini, Mark Stephens, Dr. Charles Weber, and John Wickland.

An outstanding crew at Kalmbach Publishing Co. helped make this revised edition possible. Leading the way was Roger Carp, who edited and organized the manuscript and became somewhat of an expert on Lionel accessories along the way. Mary Algozin did her usual superb job of copy-editing and proofreading the text. Sabine Beaupré handled the attractive layout of the book, while Kristi Ludwig designed the neat cover. William Zuback and Jim Forbes, two of the finest photographers around, took the pictures that fill every page with color and interest. Overseeing final production of the book were Helene Tsigistras and Annette Wall. All of them have the author's utmost gratitude.

Foreword

Welcome to the second edition of *Volume VI: Accessories,* in *Greenberg's Guide to Lionel Trains, 1945-1969*. Thanks to the many Lionel enthusiasts who made the first edition an outstanding success. Despite so many knowledgeable collectors reviewing the manuscript, only the inadvertent omission of the 321-100 Trestle Bridge and a few minor corrections were brought to our attention. Thus we can conclude the first effort was a satisfyingly thorough treatment of the subject.

Nevertheless, research has continued and some exciting finds have come to light. Noted in the first edition were a few items that were cataloged but could not be verified as having been produced. At least, no sample could be found to photograph. Happily, a few of these have been located and are brought to you in this new edition. The list of items unaccounted for has been greatly reduced, but there remain one or two elusive items.

In addition, a number of new details and even a few new variations have surfaced through the ongoing efforts of a dedicated collecting fraternity. Entries for almost all the major accessories and those for many of the minor ones have been rewritten to include the new information and to improve the descriptions. Finally, several new and revised photographs are included to show some of the new "finds" and better illustrate the fascinating array of hardware that makes up the family of Lionel accessories.

CHAPTER 1

Operating Freight-Handling Accessories

Two of Lionel's most innovative and exciting postwar accessories, the 345 Culvert Pipe Unloader (left) and 342 Culvert Loader (right). They are linked in operation by a 345-10 Bridge included with the unloader.

Among the most exciting Lionel accessories are those that actually load or unload freight. Whether handling coal, steel, culvert pipes, barrels, truck trailers, lumber, or even atomic waste, these accessories add another dimension to the play value of Lionel trains. Given space constraints, most beginning operators are faced with running trains in an endless loop. Lionel sought to improve this scenario by introducing a variety of action-packed accessories to place along the track and give purpose to the train's movements.

While some were introduced late in the prewar era, remote control operating accessories reached their zenith during postwar production. These accessories inspired budding railroad tycoons to expand their creative potential. Union Carbide, an industrial materials producer and supplier to Lionel, captured the essence of this spirit in an advertisement that featured a young boy gazing longingly at the likeness of a Lionel 97 Coal Elevator. Perhaps Lionel's own advertisements best reflected the significance of operating accessories by proclaiming, "No model railroad is complete without at least one automatic accessory."

97 ELECTRIC, REMOTE CONTROL COAL ELEVATOR, 1938–42, 1946–50

The 97 was the first of Lionel's remote control freight loaders/unloaders and the first in an extensive line of coal-handling accessories. Used in conjunction with Lionel's automatic dump cars, the 97 provides a continuous cycle of operating action.

An automatic dump car, such as Lionel's 3459, positioned on a remote control track section at the conveyor side of the 97, unloads coal into the receiving bin. Turning the knob on the controller starts the conveyor chain and tips the receiving bin so that a series of tiny buckets can carry coal up to the tower bin, which has a capacity of several carloads. Pressing the button on the controller sends coal cascading from the tower, through a chute, and into a waiting hopper or dump car (or all over the track, depending on the skill and presence of mind of the operator).

As first depicted in the 1938 catalog, the 97 lacked a tilting bin to hold the coal at the base of the conveyor apparatus. The same illustration also portrayed a two-lever control unit. However, all known production units have the tilting bin and use Lionel's 97C Controller, which has a knob and a button.

Two other prewar coal elevators resemble the 97 but lack certain operational features. The 96 Coal Elevator uses a hand crank conveyor to carry the coal to the tower bin. The 98 Coal Bunker has no conveyor, just a chute for manually filling the tower and an electric remote control for releasing the coal. These economy versions were introduced in 1939 and came with a 96C Single Button

Five coal elevator variations. Upper left: 98. Upper middle and right: Two versions of the 96. Lower left: 97 with gray tower and elevator from 1942. Lower right: Common 97 from 1938-41 and 1947-50.

Controller. 1940 was the last production year for these affordable alternatives; only the 97 was reissued in the postwar years.

Over the 10 years the 97 was cataloged, eight printings of the 97-60 instruction sheet are known. The issues of 11-38, 3-39, 4-40, 3-41, 1-42, and 1-46 are printed in the typical prewar and early postwar colors of dark blue ink on lighter blue paper. Two different paper sizes have been found or reported for the issues of 3-41 and 1-42. Black ink on white paper was used for the final two issues, dated 3-48 and 8-49.

Each 97 has a yellow metal bunker with red metal roof, a black unpainted Bakelite base, and a silver-painted (except painted gray in 1942 only) metal tower and conveyor structure. This accessory included a 97C Controller with approximately 3 feet of 3-conductor wire, instruction sheet, and bag of 206 Artificial Coal. The 97 was designed to be placed between either O or O27 gauge straight tracks spaced approximately 15″ apart (center rail to center rail). Prices shown are for the postwar loader only. Dimensions: 11½″ x 6″ base, 12″ high.

Gd	VG	Ex	LN
125	170	215	300

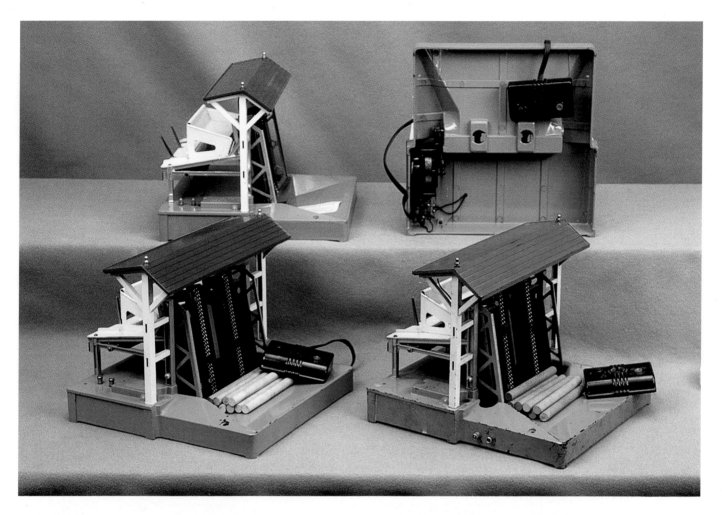

164 OPERATING LOG LOADER, 1940–42, 1946–50

Designed as a companion to Lionel's previously released remote control operating lumber cars, the 164 added even more action and could store logs in two locations. An operating lumber car, such as Lionel's 3451, positioned on a remote control track section at the conveyor side of the 164, unloads logs into the receiving bin, where they can be stored. Turning the knob of the 97C Controller (common with the 97 Coal Elevator) starts the chain conveyor (along with plenty of noise), which carries the logs to a holding tray on the upper level, the second storage location. Each press of the controller "unload" button releases two logs from the holding tray and into a waiting car on the adjacent track. Thanks to the storage feature, this can even be the same car that originally unloaded the logs, a handy feature for pikes with limited rolling stock.

Over the eight years it was cataloged (no train catalogs were issued for 1943 or 1944, and 164 was not in the 1945 flyer), six printings of the instruction sheet are known. Prewar and early postwar issues were on lighter blue paper with dark blue ink. The first was 164-65 dated 9-40. Then, for some reason, the part or form number became 164-80 for the issue of 10-40. Thereafter, the number returned to 164-65 for all remaining issues. Completing the list of blue-on-blue issues are those of 3-41, 1-46, and 11-46. The final issue of 7-49 changed to black ink on white paper.

Lower right: Earliest 164, probably initial 1940 production, with side-mounted power terminals. Lower left: Late 1941 or 1942 vintage with gray-painted conveyor and rack supports and terminals in more common location. Upper left: Postwar 164. Upper right: Underside of postwar 164, which is distinguished from prewar model by round holes in the log hook wells.

Two L430 (27-3) lamps just under the roof illuminate the action for night operation, but they are energized whenever power is applied to the 164. Each 164 has a Bakelite base painted green, die-cast roof supports painted yellow, silver-painted (except gray in 1942) conveyor frame and supports, and a red-painted Bakelite roof. Came with a 97C Controller pre-wired to the loader, instruction sheet, and 12 sticks of 164-64 "lumber." Dimensions: 11¼" x 10¾" base, 9" high.

(A) 1940. Earliest version of the 164, with power terminals on the side of the base and a cutout for the conveyor gear shaft to pass through during assembly. Although eliminated after 1940, this cutout and the side-mounted terminals continued to be shown in the consumer catalog picture every year this item appeared. Only in the photograph of the boy operating a 164 in the 1940 catalog are the terminals shown on the top surface of the base, where they actually were for all except early 1940 production! This version has two motor-mounting screws. A few of the earliest of these early models have been observed with conical chain take-up wheels on either side of each chain where they wrap around the top axle. These were the same take-up wheels used on the 97 at the top of that conveyor chain. They evidently were not needed on the 164 and were quickly eliminated, making for a rare and interesting variation! There are no holes in the

182 Triple-Action Magnet Crane. Note the black controller buttons; many were green or red. J. Algozzini Collection.

bottom "wells" in the base where the lumber hooks come up beneath the logs to lift them. Silver-painted support structure for the conveyor.   **160   200   280   370**

(B) Extensively redesigned base without the cutout for the conveyor gear, power terminals moved to the top surface of the base, and a single motor-mounting screw. No holes in the conveyor "wells." Silver-painted conveyor support structure.
160   200   280   370

(C) 1942 production only. Same as (B) except gray-painted conveyor support structure. No holes in conveyor "wells."
130   180   255   340

(D) Same as (B) except dime-sized holes in the bottom of the two conveyor "wells" in the base where the lumber hooks come up beneath the logs to lift them. This is the most common variation, and all examples are probably postwar. The holes were most likely added to facilitate cleaning debris from the wells that might interfere with operation of the conveyor.
100   160   225   310

182 TRIPLE-ACTION MAGNET CRANE, 1946–49

The illustration in Lionel's 1946 Advance Catalog indicated that the prewar 165 crane would be reissued for the first full year of postwar production. But by the time production started, Lionel had made substantial changes to the crane and renumbered it as 182. The 1946 consumer catalog nevertheless included a picture of the earlier 165.

Loading and unloading scrap metal are the 182's primary functions, and it accomplishes these tasks in a realistic though somewhat noisy manner. Pressing either of two buttons (one for up, the other for down) on the 165C Controller (carried over from the prewar crane) causes a hook (equipped with an electromagnet and powered by a motorized hoist) to raise or lower. Two other buttons on the controller rotate the cab and boom in either direction in a full circle. The instruction sheet cautions the operator not to simultaneously press the "up" and "left" or "down" and "right" buttons because doing so causes the motor to try to run in opposite directions at the same time. Pressing the "up" and "right" or "down" and "left" buttons simultaneously is all right. Red (most common), black, and green button

colors have been observed on the four-button, one-knob controller.

One other caution is not to rotate the cab continuously in either direction. As the cab rotates, it also winds or unwinds the hook cable from its drum. So a continuous rotation in the direction causing the hook to rise will eventually cause the hook to jam in the full up position. Continuous rotation in the other direction will cause the cable to fully unwind, and then commence winding in the opposite direction. This will have the effect of reversing the "up" and "down" control buttons, an undesirable result that can also be achieved by continuing to hold the "down" button beyond the point where the hook reaches the full down position. An on/off knob energizes the electromagnet that picks up, holds, and, when de-energized, drops steel scrap into a waiting gondola or other receptacle. A manually operated hand wheel at the rear of the cab raises or lowers the boom.

Compared to the 165, the 182 is fitted with a new die-cast cab platform, a new plastic cab, and a detailed plastic boom that replaces the Bakelite boom on the 165. This gave a distinctly more realistic, if not quite true-to-scale, appearance. The 182's cab and boom are shared with the 2460 Operating Crane Car, but the magnet crane's cab is enhanced by the addition of a clear molded smokestack, usually painted light gray. Lionel's engineers installed a red light inside the cab to illuminate the interior when the magnet is turned on so operators remembered to turn it off. This light was not a problem in the metal cab of the 165, but if left on in the plastic 182 cab, it softened or even melted the area above the bulb. To alleviate this problem in later production, Lionel applied silver paint on the inside of the cab above the lamp. Unfortunately, this did not entirely resolve the problem, as some painted examples still have distorted plastic above the lamp. Operators may need to install a small piece of aluminum foil above the lamp to effectively deflect the heat.

A motor, originally designed for Lionel's OO gauge Hudson, powers the 165 and 182 cranes. Two solenoids control the cab rotation and hoist clutches. Both cranes are equipped with a black electromagnet marked "Cutler Hammer." Note that the cabs from Lionel's 2460, 6460, and 6560 crane cars fit on the 182. However, cabs with a molded-in stack, or without any stack, were not used on the magnet crane and are not considered to be original. Some individuals have drilled 2460 cabs and added a stack (the graphics on the 2460 and the 182 cabs are identical). Collectors should be aware of this modification.

Each 182 has a black-painted plastic cab, black Bakelite base, gray-painted glue-in stack (although a few examples have been noted with a black glue-in stack), and an aluminum-painted metal tower structure. Instruction sheets are part number 182-35, dated 7-46 or 12-46, with dark blue printing on light blue paper. Replacement lamp is L1458-R (165-53). Each 182 included a bag of 182-22 Steel Scrap (actually punched-out scrap from forming track ties), 160 Bin, instruction sheet, and 165C Controller pre-wired to the crane. Dimensions: 6" x 6½" base, 10" high.

(A) As described above.   **120   160   230   310**

(B) Same as (A) except black stack. These might be late production, as it appears the stack was glued in prior to painting and decorating the cab. This might have been a cost savings from avoiding scrap, if gluing in the gray stack damaged some of the

264 Operating Fork Lift Platform with original box. J. Algozzini Collection.

otherwise finished cabs, and from avoiding a separate paint operation for the gray stacks. C. Rohlfing Collection.

	Gd	VG	Ex	LN
	120	160	230	310

264 OPERATING FORK LIFT PLATFORM, 1957–60

This accessory is somewhat similar to the operating milk car because both involve men at work who have repetitive jobs to do and perform operations that cannot continue without a manual reload once they are done. The 264 was one of the last of the motorized remote control freight-handling accessories built by Lionel in the postwar period.

In operation, the forklift platform is unsophisticated but great fun to watch! First, a special 6264 Flatcar (included with the set) must have at least one of its twin bays loaded with 264-11 Timbers. Side stakes on this car hold the timber in place for transport; however, the operator must manually remove the stakes on the unloading side (and only on the unloading side!) before the forklift truck can perform any work. Once the railcar is in position with the stakes removed, pressing the 90 Controller button energizes the vibrating motor, which causes the forklift to shuttle back and forth along its short route. Jaws on the forklift grip the first piece of timber and transport it to the platform, where the jaws open and allow the timber to fall. The forklift then returns for a second timber and so on. A spring in the mechanism allows the forklift to pick up timber in any position across the width of the flatcar. After the last timber in the first bay is unloaded, the 6264 Flatcar must be repositioned so that the second bay can be unloaded. Then the operator must manually gather and stack the timbers on the racks of the 6264 in preparation for the next operation.

A special instruction sheet, labeled "IMPORTANT," was included with the 264. This sheet, numbered 1733, printed both in black on yellow paper and in blue on white paper, and dated 9-57, noted the need to correctly position the side stakes on the 6264 and maintain the cleanliness of the forklift's underside and the platform surface on which it traveled. The flatcar stakes must be positioned with the tapered side facing out so the timbers rest against a vertical rather than a tapered surface. This prevents the timbers from riding up the stakes as the forklift picks them up. If the truck hesitates or stops in its travel, the instruction sheet recommends cleaning the sliding surfaces. No lubricant of any type should be used on these surfaces.

Each 264 has a black painted steel frame, brown molded superstructure, orange molded plastic forklift body, and the white simulated crane as used on the 464 Operating Lumber Mill. Known instruction sheets carry part number 264-28, dated 7-57 or 8-58, with the first printed with brown ink on yellow paper, while the later one has been reported with both blue ink and black ink on white paper. Included special 6264 Flatcar with 264-11 Timbers and 90 Controller. A replacement envelope (264-151) of 12 Timbers was available as catalog number 264-150. Dimensions: 10" x 10⅝" base, 5½" high.

Gd	VG	Ex	LN
175	235	295	380

282/282R PORTAL GANTRY CRANE, 1954–57

This accessory was manufactured in two distinct versions: an earlier 282 and a later 282R. While they are almost identical in outward appearance and operation, the 282R is arguably the better of the two because of its redesigned mechanical components. It is, however, harder to find than the 282 and may not always be marked with an "R" on the side of the cab. The key to distinguishing one from the other is to look for a cab that snaps on (282R) rather than one held by screws (282).

The 282 and 282R differ in appearance and in some operational characteristics from the 182. They are perhaps more realistic and imposing, a result of the intricate structure and detailing of Lionel's "heavy bridge construction" gantry frame. While the 182 requires an open hopper car or gondola to be spotted adjacent to one of its sides for loading, the 282's open gantry superstructure enables a railcar to pass directly under the accessory itself.

Functionally, the 182, 282, and 282R perform the same type of operations in much the same manner. The OO gauge locomotive motor used in the 182 was not used in the 282 or 282R. Instead, Lionel installed an O gauge locomotive motor with a different wiring scheme. While the earlier 165 and 182 cranes used black, six-conductor wire to connect the accessory to its controller, the 282 was supplied with gray, five-conductor wire whose insulation tends over time to become brittle, crack, and fall off. Replacement wire is available and is a "must" if you intend to operate a 282 or 282R.

Most 282 cranes use a blackened electromagnet housing, while 282R cranes have a silver-colored magnet. These magnet housings are plain stamped steel, not the detailed die-cast housings used on the 165 and 182, but they have the handy feature of a hook on top so they can be stowed out of the way on a pin (included in the boom) when the operator wants to use the hook for lifting. According to the Lionel Service Manual, a properly functioning 282 should be able to lift a weight of approximately four ounces. Where the 165 and 182 employed two solenoids to control cab rotation and the hoist clutches, the 282 uses one with a spring to accomplish the same tasks. Nevertheless, the earlier two-solenoid approach was apparently more reliable because the 282 had to be extensively redesigned during its four-year run.

In the course of its transition from a 282 to a 282R, the screw-on cab mounting changed to snap-on mounting secured by three tabs, and the glued-on gray stack became a molded-in black stack. The 182's cab light to indicate that the magnet was ener-

282 with glued-on stack (left) and 282R with integral stack (right). Note stowed position of the magnet on the 282R when hook is used for lifting. Crane rails were not made by Lionel.

	Gd	VG	Ex	LN

gized was eliminated in the 282 cranes. Unfortunately, the problem remained of the magnet overheating if left on too long. Transitional changes most likely occurred over time and perhaps in somewhat irregular fashion, so some contradictory features may be found in transition pieces. Still, it is likely that the 282's mechanical components were redesigned at the same time as the change to the snap-on cab. If you intend to operate your crane, the 282R is preferable to the 282.

All these cranes have a gray molded gantry superstructure, a black or red cab with white lettering ("LIONEL" arched, "LINES" straight across), glued-in smokestack on cab (282 only) or molded-in stack (282R only), a maroon plastic cab base with simulated tread pattern, and a black molded boom. The 282 and 282R came with a three-lever 282-200 Controller, pre-wired to the crane. Use of lever controls eliminated the possibility, presented by the 165C Controller, of pressing an incorrect combination of buttons and causing the motor to stall. Known instruction sheets are all part number 282-99 with dates of 10-54 (blue ink on white paper), 2-55 (black ink on white paper), and 7/55 (reported with blue or black ink on white paper). When new, each 282 came with envelope 282-27 containing the instruction sheet, two 81-32 Connecting Wires, and four pieces of iron "scrap." These pieces of scrap were actually small sintered-iron idler gears used in locomotive drive trains. Dimensions: portal 5½" x 7½", span 3½", height to top of stack 10½".

(A) 1954. Screw-mounted cab with glued-on gray stack, black magnet housing.

	Gd	VG	Ex	LN
	100	125	175	260

(B) 1955 and later. Snap-on cab secured by three tabs. Watch for signs of repair on the rear tab slot. Cab usually has "282R" on each side, but later versions may have a red or black unpainted cab, the same as the cab on the 6560 crane car. Molded in stack matching cab color, usually black. Silver magnet housing.

	Gd	VG	Ex	LN
	125	150	210	290

342 CULVERT PIPE LOADER, 1956–58

This accessory and its companion, the 345 Culvert Pipe Unloader, were introduced a year apart: the 342 in 1956, and the 345 in 1957. Together, they were the last of Lionel's great freight-handling accessories that could complete a full loading and unloading cycle completely by remote control. They were cataloged together for only two years, 1957 and 1958, with the 345 carried over to 1959, perhaps to sell off remaining inventory.

When the 342 is operated independently, the operator must manually load the seven 342-40 Culvert Pipe sections onto the inclined loader ramp platform. The action begins after the special 6342 Culvert Car (included in the set) is positioned with the highest part of its inclined ramp directly beneath the traveling crane. Pressing the 90 Controller button starts the vibrating motor that powers the crane. As each culvert section is picked off the accessory's loader ramp, gravity causes another to roll down into the loading position. The same effect takes place as the culvert sections drop into the waiting car, with gravity pulling each

The overstamped gondola box used for the separate-sale 6342 Culvert Car.

An example of a 346 renumbered as 348. The car is in a box that also has been renumbered. This suggests a conversion by Madison Hardware Co., but no conclusive proof has surfaced.

successive section to the low end, thereby accommodating additional sections.

As much fun as the 342 is by itself, operators experience a real delight when they use it in conjunction with the 345. Then an endless sequence of remote control action can occur. The 345 supplies culvert sections to the 342 over the 345-10 Bridge (included with the 345) while switch engines shuttle filled and empty Culvert Cars into their proper positions. The 342 and 345 are finicky to adjust (mechanically and electrically) as each requires different transformer voltage settings to operate properly. It helps to have a separate voltage control for each. Still, once tuned, they operate well.

The 6342 Culvert Car packed with each 342 and 345 did not have a separate box because the packing was designed to accommodate this car without one. However, these cars were sold separately, in which case they came packaged in a rare over-stamped 6462 Gondola box. Each 342 has a black-painted metal base with a tan superstructure, gray loading platform, and red building with dark gray roof. Two 342-46 instruction sheets are known: issues of 9-56 (bright blue ink on white paper) and 4-57 (black ink on yellow paper), the latter depicting the 342/345 combination. A complete 342 set included the loading station, 6342 Culvert Car, 90 Controller, instruction sheet, connecting wires, and seven 342-40 Culvert Pipe sections. Dimensions: 11½″ x 10″ base, 6″ high.

| | 130 | 190 | 250 | 320 |

345 CULVERT PIPE UNLOADER, 1957–59

Many of the comments for the 342 apply to the 345. With this accessory, a traveling crane with a permanent magnet lifts metal 342-40 Culvert Pipe sections off the 6342 Culvert Car and places them on a holding ramp. If used in conjunction with the 342 Culvert Pipe Loader, the ramps of each accessory can be connected by a 345-10 Bridge section that came with the 345. This permits culvert sections to roll freely onto the 342's holding ramp. Reproductions of the 345-10 Bridge are readily available. The 345 is similar in appearance to the 342, but features an elevated control tower structure on its platform. Like the 342, the 345 is difficult to keep in proper adjustment, but it works well when set at the correct operating voltage.

A 345 you acquire may have tape on the face of the magnet. The Lionel Service Manual suggests adding tape as a means of tempering the strength of the magnet enough to pick up a culvert section yet release it cleanly when the crane reaches the loading ramp wall. If the magnet is too strong, the mechanism may fail to release the culvert. An important note regarding the counterweight used to pull the crane in the direction of the gondola is included in instruction sheet 345-7.8 (dated 10-57, printed in bright blue ink on white paper). It has a screw that is used to lock it to its guide in the crane support for shipping. This screw must be loosened for operation so the counterweight slides freely in the guide. Unfortunately, the counterweight is prone to rust, so it may take more than loosening the screw to get it to move freely.

	Gd	VG	Ex	LN

Two versions of the magnet holder have been observed: one with only plastic visible on each side and the other with what appears to be a pick-up roller inserted crossways. The latter seems more common and may have been a factory modification to add weight so the magnet would lower more reliably. This accessory included a 6342 Culvert Car, seven 342-40 Culvert Pipe sections, 90 Controller, instruction sheet, and 345-10 Bridge. Dimensions: 12¼" x 9½" base, 8¼" high.

	175	250	325	400

346 OPERATING CULVERT UNLOADER, 1964–65 (uncataloged)

Uncataloged in Lionel's consumer catalogs, the 346 is shown as a component of one set in the 1964 Sears, Roebuck Christmas Catalog and as a component of two sets in the 1965 Sears Christmas Catalog. This accessory is identical to the 345, except that it uses a hand crank in place of the vibrating motor. Even the plastic platform retained the molded-in number 345. The description in the 1964 Sears catalog led many to believe that the accessory was a remote control culvert loader rather than the hand-operated unloader that was pictured and sold.

The packaging tells an interesting story about this budget accessory made for the cost-conscious mail-order and department-store trade. All Sears sets containing the 346 included a 6342 Culvert Car, but the boxes indicate that this car was packaged with the other set contents and not with the unloader. This increased the piece count of the set and may have led customers to believe they were getting more for their money. It is also possible, perhaps probable, that other stores besides Sears received sets containing this accessory.

The first volume of *Greenberg's Guide to Lionel Trains, 1945–69* notes that the 6342 Culvert Car included in sets with

Two variations of the 352 Ice Depot: Brown platform is the earlier production (left); red is the more common.

	Gd	VG	Ex	LN

the 346, as well as with the separately sold 348, was different from the 6342 Culvert Car included with the earlier 342 and 345. The body type is IIb rather than IIa, which means that the earlier metal frame was eliminated and the trucks were fastened directly to the plastic body with rivets. The trucks were changed to the plastic AAR type, and all cars examined with new unloaders had one dummy coupler and one operating coupler. This car has also been reported with two dummy couplers. Finally, the graphics no longer displayed the "NEW 2-49" found on the earlier cars.

Four new unloaders, including examples of the 346 and the 348 (described below) were examined to determine variations based on the packaging. The 346 has a Z-type liner without provision for a car. The 348 reverts to the 345-style box liner with a special cardboard pocket made to accommodate the car. One example even had the "6" in 346 made into an "8," and the car was simply placed on the unloader platform. The 348 with the car packaging has a printed, paste-on 348 label applied over the 346 conventionally printed on the box. Two 346-21 instruction sheets are known, dated 8/64 and 8/65, both using black ink on white paper. A third issue, dated 6/66, is mentioned in the 348 entry below. Dimensions: 12¼" x 9½" base, 8¼" high.

	70	115	160	250

348 OPERATING CULVERT UNLOADER, 1966–69

The 348 was offered as a separate-sale version of the 346, with the box liner reverting to the 345-type so the car could be accommodated inside the accessory box. Evidently Lionel had a few leftover 346s from the department-store specials. As noted in the description of the 346, one set has been found with the "6" in 346 on the box label made into an "8." In that set, no provision was made for the car in the box liner, and the car was placed on top of the unloader ramp. Without the packaging, there is no way to distinguish a 346 from a 348. Most 348 boxes have a pasted-on 348 label applied over the 346 marking printed on the box.

Of special interest is the 348 instruction sheet, part number 346-21, dated 6/66, and printed in black ink on white paper. It is the same as the sheet included with the 346, except that all reference to the number 346 has been removed (not counting the sheet part number). Also, the warranty and return statement were expanded, and a Postal Service ZIP code was shown for the Lionel Service Department. Dimensions: 12¼″ x 9½″ base, 8¼″ high.

| | 70 | 120 | 170 | 260 |

352 ICE DEPOT, 1955–57

This is a really "cool" accessory! The operator manually inserts plastic 352-29 Ice Blocks into an inclined loading chute at the top of the structure. One ice block is permanently glued at the bottom of the chute to serve as a bottom stop. The other blocks (eight initially came with the accessory) are manually loaded ahead of the bottom stop. Then the chute must be manually tipped up, causing the ice blocks to slide down into the icehouse and out the loading chute, ready for the figure to push them into a waiting refrigerator car. Pushing the button on the 90 Controller causes a metal plate to extend from the platform, opening the top hatch of a 6352 Ice Car positioned alongside the accessory. Almost simultaneously, the iceman uses his paddle to sweep ice blocks, one by one with each press of the controller button, into the car's open hatch. When all the blocks are loaded, the operator must manually retrieve them from the car and reload the depot.

To keep the figure moving at a slower and more realistic pace, Lionel incorporated a dashpot like one used on the 3662 Automatic Refrigerated Milk Car for the same purpose. A dashpot is a type of shock absorber, a piston that moves air out of a cylinder. Lionel designers used a dashpot because it permitted the use of a rapid-acting but inexpensive electrical solenoid for power. The Lionel Service Manual included the following message regarding the dashpot for the 3662 Milk Car: "The effectiveness of the dashpot depends on the air seal between the cylinder and piston which is maintained by means of a mixture of oil and Molykote applied to the edge of the piston. Other parts of the mechanism, however, such as the two moving levers should be lubricated only with Molykote powder." Molykote, a brand name for powdered molybdenum disulfide, is a dry lubricant still available that lasts longer than oil, will not "gum," and does not attract dirt or dust.

The 352 was cataloged for three years and was shown each year with a brown 352-3 Platform Structure and a blue 352-11 Ice House Roof. The platform was indeed made in brown-molded, unpainted plastic. Based on catalog illustrations and collector observations, this color was the first version; it is less common than the later red structure. The icehouse roof has not been observed in any color but red. The platform and roof colors were never updated in the catalog to reflect production changes. Only the 6352 Ice Car illustration was changed each year. For 1955, the car was shown painted white and with graphics that never appeared in actual production. The next year the car color and left-side graphics are as produced, but the 6352-14 Ice Compartment Door is depicted without graphics. Finally, in the 1957 catalog, the car was shown as having three lines of data and a lower black line on the ice compartment door. The common production ice car has four lines of data on this door, and the entire door graphic is rubber-stamped, while the rest of the car is heat-stamped. Only toward the end of the production run did the lettering on the ice compartment door change to heat-stamped lettering, including only three lines of data. Today, this last variation is hard to find.

When purchased new, the 352 included the 6352 Ice Car nestled in a pocket of the inner packing, without a separate box. For 1955, 1956, and 1957, this car was available for separate sale in a rare 6352-25 Classic box. Included in instruction sheet 352-44 is a warning not to load more than five ice blocks into the car's ice compartment or turn a loaded car upside down, lest the ice blocks jam in the ice compartment and make the door difficult to open. Envelope 352-45 containing the ice blocks and other small parts has been found with the "8" blanked out and "5" substituted for the quantity of ice blocks enclosed. Extra ice blocks were offered as part number 352-55 in a small envelope containing seven blocks. The ice blocks, figure, and arms/paddle piece have been reproduced and are so small that they cannot be properly marked as being reproductions.

Each 352 has a white shed, red roof, blue figure with orange arms and paddle, and a brown or red plastic support structure. Known instruction sheets are part number 352-44, dated 9-55 (black ink on white paper), and 10-55 (reported in both black and dark blue ink on white paper). Dimensions: 11¾″ x 4″ base, 8½″ high.

(A) Brown unpainted plastic platform structure. 6352 Ice Car has ice compartment door with rubber-stamped lettering and four lines of data.

| | 130 | 170 | 260 | 320 |

(B) Red unpainted plastic platform structure. 6352 Ice Car has ice compartment door with rubber-stamped lettering and four lines of data.

| | 130 | 170 | 240 | 310 |

(C) Same as (B) except that 6352 Ice Car has ice compartment door with three lines of lettering; door graphics are heat-stamped.

| | 150 | 190 | 285 | 350 |

362 BARREL LOADER, 1952–57

When the 362 was introduced, the catalog description claimed that the "active little workman superintends the whole operation." The writer of this copy exaggerated, since the workman is neither active nor little! At ¼″ to the foot, which is correct O scale, the figure on this accessory stands about 8′-3″ tall, certainly the Paul Bunyan of the barrel industry. The worker is inanimate, although he is located so that an observer can imagine that he (and not a dip formed into the ramp) causes the barrels to tip over for their ride up to the loading chute. In 1954, when a companion barrel car was introduced, the figure sent aboard to handle that part of the operation was a more realistic 6 scale feet tall.

In operation, flipping the 364C On/Off Switch energizes the vibrating action that causes upright or horizontal barrels on the lower platform to move to the 362's inclined ramp. At the base of the ramp, upright barrels tip over for the ride up the ramp to the elevated deck. Horizontal barrels glide right over the tip-over

Early (front) and late variations of the 362 Barrel Loader.

feature. From the elevated deck, the barrels roll over a tilting gate and drop into a waiting gondola or barrel car.

The 362-48 Tilting Gate has been expertly reproduced, differing only slightly in color and fine detail from the original. This part is easily broken, so reproduction gates are common. Grades of Excellent and Like New require all original parts. A railcar was not included with this accessory, but it did include six brown-stained wooden barrels.

Although the 362 enjoyed a relatively long run, it changed very little over the years. The color of the figure is the most visible variation. He was molded in white (or cream color) as well as the more common dark blue. Blue workmen came with or without a painted face. Two new-in-the-box examples of the 362 were studied. One was a 1952 version that had a white workman, and the other was a 1954 model with a blue, unpainted figure. In 1952 production pieces, all eight baseplate screws must be removed to reach the two mechanism-mounting screws. In 1953, two holes were added to the bottom plate so the two mounting screws could be reached and the whole ramp and vibrator assembly removed without having to disturb the baseplate.

Also of interest is the redesign of the box used to pack the 362. For 1952, the box was part number 362-90, and it opened on the two ends. By 1954, it had changed to part number 362-104, which opened on the top and bottom (lengthwise). The early box had only blue printing, including the OPS (Office of Price Stabilization) ceiling price of $7.75; the later box used red and blue ink and did not have a price on it. A third box, part no. 362-103 dated 1955, opens lengthwise but only on one side. Further reports are needed to determine when the switch in boxes was made and whether other variations exist.

The 3562 Operating Barrel Car did not appear until the 362

had been on the market for two years. Consequently, some of the special items Lionel made so that the two could work together came along with the car and not with the loader. Among these items is the 3562-48 Ramp Clip, which clips to the 362's lower ramp to bridge the gap between the car and the loader and allow barrels to reach the ramp.

Instruction sheets are 362-96, dated 10-52, 4-53, 4-54, and 4-55, all printed in blue ink on white paper except the 4/54 version, which had black ink on white paper. Later versions reflect the introduction of the 3562 Operating Barrel Car. Supplementary notice, Form 1267, dated 11-52, indicated that for some loaders a voltage slightly above or below the recommended 12–14 range might work best. The notice also suggested connecting the accessory to variable, rather than fixed, voltage posts of a transformer.

Each 362 has a gray plastic base, yellow ramp, and brown plastic fence. The fence usually has "LIONEL" in gold on the trackside, but a few, probably very early, examples have this in red. There were several variations in the color and stamping of the steel base plate, including cadmium-plated with black rubber-stamping, black-painted with silver rubber-stamping, black-painted with nomenclature stamped in the metal, and cadmium-plated with nomenclature stamped in the metal. The set came with a 362-94 envelope, dated 10-52 or 3-54, packed with wire, instructions, 364C On/Off Switch, and two 362-82 Track Clips for holding the loader in proper relation to the track when it could not be attached to a table with screws. A 362-78 Set of 6 Barrels in a small Classic box was included with the 362 and offered for separate sale. Prices listed are for the

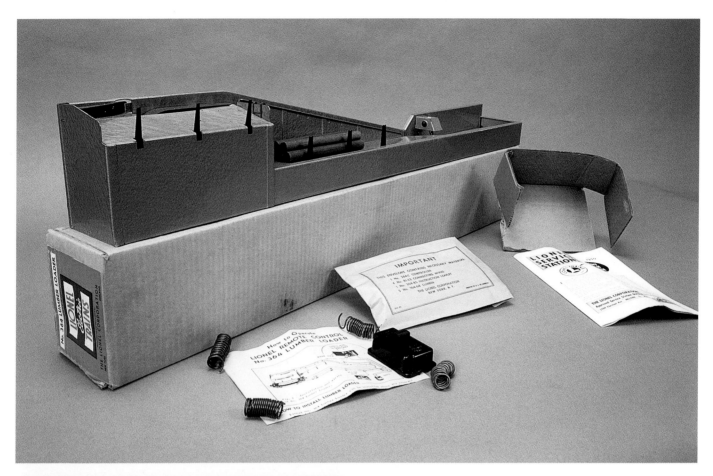

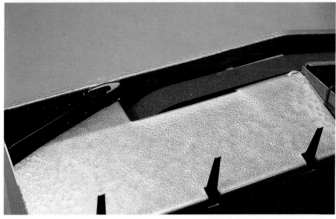

This close-up of a 364 shows the improved guide at the top of the conveyor.

This 364 Conveyor Lumber Loader has the common hammertone finish and minimal interior packaging. Note the stained logs; they came unstained until 1954. M. Stephens Collection.

	Gd	VG	Ex	LN
(B) 1953–57 version with two access holes in the baseplate, allowing the two mechanism screws to be reached without removing the baseplate. Baseplate cadmium-plated. Blue figure with painted face.	45	75	105	150
(C) 1953–57. Same as (B) except bottom plate has black-painted finish. Plain blue workman.	45	75	105	150

(B) 1953–57 version with two access holes in the baseplate, allowing the two mechanism screws to be reached without removing the baseplate. Baseplate cadmium-plated. Blue figure with painted face.

(C) 1953–57. Same as (B) except bottom plate has black-painted finish. Plain blue workman.

364 CONVEYOR LUMBER LOADER, 1948–57

The 364 was among the first of Lionel's all-new postwar designs. In terms of both size and years cataloged, it was one of the firm's "longest" accessories at nearly 28 inches and a decade, respectively. And it operates quite reliably. Logs are either manually placed or dumped by a log dump car, such as Lionel's 3461, at the lower receiving end of the 364. Flipping the 364C On/Off Switch starts the conveyor belt that transports the logs, end to end in single file, up the ramp. The logs ascend to the loading platform, where they roll off over tilting stakes and into another waiting lumber car.

	Gd	VG	Ex	LN

barrel loader only, without a barrel car. Dimensions: 19″ x 4⅛″ base, 4″ high.

(A) 1952 version with cadmium-plated base plate without two access holes for mechanism screws. While the figure is easily changed, a white one is more likely correct for 1952, followed in later years by a blue one with a painted face and then a plain blue one. A few of these came with the "LIONEL" on the trackside fence done in red, rather than the usual gold color. These are NRS items.

	Gd	VG	Ex	LN
	50	85	115	165

The Conveyor Lumber Loader has illumination at the bottom of the ramp provided by an L53 clear bulb under a spotting lamp cover with red and green lenses. Lamp L363 will fit, but draws 0.2 amps current rather than 0.1 for the L53. Extra heat generated by the hotter bulb can melt the colored lenses in the lamp cover. The unloading and loading activity take place on the same side of the accessory and along the same stretch of track, somewhat diminishing the effect of seeing a load transfer from one location to another.

Few changes were made in the 364 over the years. The earliest version had a dark gray crackle finish that feels rough. Later versions, including those made in 1949 and perhaps some from late 1948, switched to a smooth, silver-gray hammer-tone finish. The only other significant change was the motor brushplate, which was redesigned in 1949 or 1950. An identical change was made in the 397 Diesel-Type Coal Loader. Precise dating of the change is unknown, but it is safe to say that all original crackle-finish 364s should have the 364M-24 Brush Plate with tubular brush holders. An interesting operational feature is the cam-operated 364-50 Flapper Plate. This is simply the floor of the log-receiving bin. When the conveyor is operating, a cam on one of its rollers causes this floor to move up and down slightly to help free any logs that might have been unloaded crossways.

One operational problem with the 364 involves the triangular 364-23 Guide Block at the top of the conveyor. This piece is supposed to nudge logs off the conveyor belt and start them rolling down to the waiting car. On early models, a slightly protruding vertical edge of the block tended to snag logs riding the rear edge of the belt. This jammed the works, and logs would line up until the top one was freed by hand. Lionel corrected the problem by bending a metal tab out of the rear surface of the loader, providing a seamless transition to the guide block. Loaders with the crackle finish and the early hammer-tone models were most prone to jam. The corrective tab was not introduced until 1950 or 1951.

Right: Earliest and most desirable variation of the 397 Operating Diesel-Type Coal Loader had a painted red tray and came with 206 Artificial Coal. Left: Common version had unpainted tray and usually came with a smaller bag of 207 Artificial Coal.

	Gd	VG	Ex	LN

When the 364 was introduced in 1948, it was a budget log loader at $12.50 compared to the 164, which retailed at $21.50. These two items shared log-loading duties in the catalog for three years. Instruction sheets are 364-85, dated 10-48, 1-49, 7-49, 4-50, 10-53, 8-54, 2-55, and 8-57, all with black ink on white or buff paper except the 8-54 sheet, which used blue ink, and the 8-57 sheet, which used brown ink on yellow paper. Each 364 included five 164-64 logs (unstained until 1954 during and after which they were stained brown), instructions, hookup wire, and 364C On/Off Switch. Dimensions: $27\frac{7}{8}$" x $3\frac{3}{16}$" base, $4\frac{1}{8}$" high.

(A) 1948 version with dark gray crackle finish. Motor brushplate with tubular brush holders.

	Gd	VG	Ex	LN
	90	110	140	180

(B) 1949–57 versions with smooth, silver-gray hammer-tone finish. Top guide block has metal guide tab on later production. This version may be found with either type brushplate on the motor, although one with tubular brush holders would not be correct on a version with the metal guide tab.

	Gd	VG	Ex	LN
	85	100	120	160

397 OPERATING DIESEL-TYPE COAL LOADER, 1948–57

Operating the 397 is simple and straightforward. Flipping a 364C On/Off Switch starts the loader transporting coal from a receiving bin into a waiting hopper, such as Lionel's 3456, or a coal dump car (and all over the surrounding area) by means of a conveyor belt.

Over the decade of its catalog appearances, nearly every part of the 397 was changed at some point, resulting in an extensive array of variations. Compounding the problem, many variations are easily re-created by interchanging one or more of the primary components (several of which have a number of variations of their own). Because so many "variations" are known to exist, only the two primary versions are addressed here. All versions are valued about equally, except the original 1948 model.

For the operator, the 397s built after 1949 tend to function best, have more durable colors, and are less prone to coal jamming. For the collector, the early 1948 production is preferable because it is scarcer and more colorful (if the paint is still intact!) and has a 70 Yard Light attached to the base.

With a cataloged life of 10 years, several instruction sheet variations could be expected, and the 397 did not disappoint. Probably first was 397-49, dated 12/48. Then the part number changed to 397-64 for an undated issue, followed by dated issues of 2/49, 11/49, 8-52, 4-53, and 5-55. All are known in black ink on white paper. In addition, the issue of 2/49 is known with dark blue ink on lighter blue paper, while the issues of 8-52, 4-53, and 5-55 are also available with blue ink on white paper.

Each 397 has a motor cover molded in light-colored, dark-colored, or red-marble plastic painted yellow (earliest) or blue (most common), scoop assembly molded of black plastic painted red-orange (earliest), or molded in unpainted red plastic (most common), and die-cast base assembly painted gray (earliest), or a hammer-tone finish (most common). When new, this accessory included a bag of 206 (1948-49) or 207 Artificial Coal, instructions, hookup wire, and 364C On/Off Switch. Dimensions: 10⅛" x 7⁷⁄₁₆" base, 6" high.

(A) 1948. Yellow-painted motor cover with General Motors decal on side, 70 Yard Light mounted on a dark-gray painted die-cast base, black molded receiving tray painted red (very prone to paint flaking). Came with instruction sheet 397-49, dated 12/48, which depicts the 70 Yard Light, or the undated 397-64. Enough of these have been observed with a hammer-tone painted base to conclude that this combination is also original. Some sellers have been known to strip the paint from the tray and sell this accessory with a black tray.

	125	225	325	400

(B) 1949–57. Blue-painted motor cover with GM decal, light silver-gray painted base with a hammer-tone pattern, unpainted red receiving tray. In 1949 production, a mixture of parts can be found. Almost any combination can be assembled (as Lionel appears to have done), so no exceptional value ascribed to transition pieces.

	90	110	160	200

Note: See the December 1991 issue of *Classic Toy Trains* for a comprehensive treatment of 397 variations.

456 OPERATING COAL RAMP AND HOPPER CAR, 1950–55

It was described in the 1950 consumer catalog as "by far the most unusual, most fascinating of all Lionel rail side accessories." That may have been stretching things a bit, but the 456 is an innovative and impressive addition to any layout. It performs three separate actions, all by remote control. First, the 3456 Operating Hopper Car is shunted (as the last of at least three cars in a train) to the top of the inclined ramp, where it automatically couples to the ramp. Pushing the first of three

buttons on the 456-100 Controller uncouples the hopper from the train, which allows the train to pull away. A second controller button opens the doors beneath the hopper and dumps the coal into a bin below. Pressing the third button uncouples the hopper from the ramp so it can roll down to re-couple with its train.

The first Operating Coal Ramps were dark gray, rather than the more common light gray. The Lionel Service Manual pages for this accessory, dated 1-52, mention the two shades of gray. An "X" suffix is assigned to the dark gray (early) version. The "X" was apparently Lionel's means of tracking superseded parts that were still made for service when a new part could not be substituted for the old part. Later parts lists dropped the X-designated parts. One example studied has a light gray 456-35 Ramp End Assembly riveted to a dark gray ramp, with no evidence of tampering. Packaged in a box with a 1950 date on the box maker's certificate, this is most likely a transitional piece. Considering that there is a picture in the 1951 catalog of a light gray ramp, the transition probably took place during 1950 production.

Early dark gray ramp versions used braided wire for the handrails, while later versions and all the light gray versions used fishing line. The braided wire is similar to light-gauge picture-hanging wire. This change was not mentioned in the Lionel Service Manual, perhaps because the later fishing-line handrail would also work for the earlier model. The handrails are often broken or missing on 456s offered for sale. They can be repaired with fishing line but should include the correct eyelet, washer, and handrail spring in the end tower. The spring keeps the handrails tight while allowing "give" if they are accidentally snagged. Sometimes, a quick repair meant simply tying the line without using the spring. At the bottom of the ramp, the handrail was secured by an ordinary carpet tack, which had an official 456-64 Lionel part number!

Each 456 came with a special 3456 Operating Hopper Car, which was packed in an orange, blue, and white Middle Classic box. As explained in the first volume of *Greenberg's Guide to Lionel Trains, 1945–1969*, there are at least two variations of the car's body mold as well as differences in the trucks.

Seven issues of the instruction sheet, part number 456-93, are known. All were printed in dark blue ink on white or buff paper. These sheets are dated 10-50, 11-50, 3-51, 5-52, 8-53, 8-54, and 4-55. Note that the first revision is dated only one month after the initial publication. In that revision, two notes of interest to the operator were added. The first stated that "coupling is easiest when bumper coupler is open and car coupler is closed." (The 456-25 Knuckle on the bumper coupler differed from that on Lionel's truck-type coupler.) The second helpful hint was "if your floor or platform is not level, insert a small spacer under the ramp to help the car roll down easier."

The 456-5 parts envelope contained two 456-85 Coal Bin Mounting Posts (for use when the 456 and 397 are operated together), an instruction sheet, two 4-40 x ³⁄₁₆" binding head screws, and two 2-56 x ³⁄₁₆" roundhead screws. These screws came in a small, plain envelope packed inside the main envelope and are used to attach the track to the end of the ramp. The instructions do not state that the 2-56 screws go with O27, while the 4-40 screws are for O track, but it is fairly easy to determine

| | Gd | VG | Ex | LN |

which screw size to use with what type of track. Replacement lamp for the bumper pilot light is L363 (151-1) or L53.

In addition to the small parts envelope, each 456 came with a three-button 456-100 Controller, bag of 206 Artificial Coal, and 456-83 maroon-molded plastic Coal Bin with a 456-84 blackened metal Coal Bin Door. Using the Coal Bin Mounting Posts, the bin can be placed on top of the 397 Coal Loader and positioned under the unloading section of the coal ramp. When the Coal Bin Door is hooked in its open position, coal from the hopper car can cascade down into the 397 Coal Loader for immediate transfer to another car.

Of interest is the illustration of the 456 in Lionel's 1950 Advance Catalog, where the wiring connections are shown on an angled panel at the back of the ramp, rather than hidden underneath, as they were on all known ramps actually produced. Even the 1950 consumer catalog illustrated what is most likely a pre-production sample. The piers, or ramp support columns, are pictured as olive drab rather than gray, the ramp handrails appear to be solid wire instead of flexible wire, and the car is a standard Lehigh Valley hopper instead of the operating Norfolk & Western hopper with a plunger on the bottom and opening bottom hatches. However, by 1951 the artist had a production model to work with and the picture is more representative of what was actually produced. Dimensions: 35⅛" x 3⅜" base, 6⅞" high, to top of lamp cover.

(A) 1950. Dark gray ramp, braided wire handrails (early) or fishing line handrails.

	Gd	VG	Ex	LN
	110	160	225	310

(B) 1951–55. Light gray ramp, fishing line handrails.

	Gd	VG	Ex	LN
	95	150	200	260

This 456 Operating Coal Ramp from 1950 had dark gray-painted surfaces on its ramp. Although it came in a 1950 box (orange-printed background on the label), it remained unsold long enough to be given a 1951 OPS price sticker. M. Stephens Collection.

460 PIGGY BACK TRANSPORTATION SET, 1955–57

This is another item whose name and catalog depictions reflect an interesting history of development. For the three years that this accessory was listed, the catalog identified it as the "No. 460 PIGGY BACK TRANSPORTATION SET." However, the only known instruction sheet, part number 460-70, dated 10-55 (blue ink on white paper), calls it "No. 460 TRUCK TRANSPORT SET." The Lionel Service Manual refers to it as "PIGGYBACK PLATFORM." The 460 lacks the excitement of remote control, but at $12.95 it was a bargain.

With a fair amount of skill, manipulation of a hand crank and lever allows an operator to imagine operating a forklift truck and maneuvering heavy trailers on and off a railcar. The crank pivots the lift truck 360 degrees about a fixed point at the center of the platform, while the lever raises and lowers the lifting arms. A skillful combination of these actions moves the trailers between the platform and the 3460 Flat Car included in the set.

The first appearance of the 460 in Lionel's 1955 advance catalog shows a design quite different from what was produced. The platform, as shown, had ramps at either side rather than at the rear. Two hand wheels were depicted, instead of a single hand wheel and lever, and the trailers were shown loaded straight out to the railcar by some unknown mechanism, each activated by its own hand wheel. The forklift truck was absent. The railcar pictured was similar to a 3461 Log Dump Car, without the stakes or a tray, and looked too short to accommodate both trailers. The trailers in the catalog picture had Lionel billboards covering their sides.

Cataloged from 1955 through 1957, the 460 Piggy Back Transportation Set used the hand-eye coordination of an operator rather than electrical remote-control to move trailers onto the 3460 Flatcar packed with the set. J. Wickland Collection.

Even though the picture in the subsequent consumer catalog was closer to what was produced, discrepancies remained. For example, while the production platforms had depressions to accommodate the trailer wheels, two bumper stops are illustrated in the catalog. Even the instruction sheet shows these bumpers rather than the depressions. The lift truck is shown in yellow (instead of the produced red) and is out of position. Neither the correct red 3460 Flatcar nor the trailer retainer rack on the railcar was ever shown. The most accurate depiction of the trailers appeared in 1956, when they were pictured as dark green with "Lionel Trains" tags. In 1957, the trailer picture was changed to depict Cooper-Jarrett signs, but they incorrectly covered most of the trailer side. In all catalog illustrations, the railcar stayed the same as in the first advance catalog picture: too short to accommodate two trailers. Assuming the catalog artist used a prototype as a model, these pictures provide interesting glimpses of what might have been.

The major variation is in the ROSS/TRAILOADER lettering on the lift truck. Most likely, the common thin metal stick-on tag with black background and silver lettering was first, followed by the less common white rubber-stamped label. Otherwise, the 460 appears to have gone unchanged over the three years it was cataloged. This fact and the existence of only one instruction sheet suggest that it probably did not sell well and was most likely pro-

duced for only one or two years, with excess inventory being depleted by cataloging the item for an additional year or two.

The lift-truck driver is frequently on a coffee break when this accessory is acquired today. He is a tiny blue man approximately 4 scale feet tall and was evidently too small to get his face painted. Only a small tab molded into his bottom keeps him in place, so it is not surprising to find him missing. Unmarked reproductions of this figure are available and are distinguishable only in side-by-side comparisons with an original. The steering column in the lift truck is always a silver-colored die-cast metal piece, with the column angled and exposed all the way to the floorboard. (This was changed for the uncataloged rerun numbered 461, described below.) Note that the blackened-metal 460-26 Base Plate Assembly on the platform bottom has "PIGGYBACK / NO.460 /," etc., embossed on it. This lettering is missing on the 461.

The first vans used were labeled "LIONEL LINES." Cooper-Jarrett tags for the trailers were introduced in 1956, but the 460's catalog picture does not show them until 1957. Trailers are easily changed; however, there are no substantiated reports of any 460 that originally came with Cooper-Jarrett trailers. This tends to substantiate the theory that the 460 was actually produced only in 1955. The 3460 Flatcar included with all 460s is described in the first volume of *Greenberg's Guide to Lionel Trains, 1945–1969* and is not mentioned with anything other than LIONEL LINES trailers.

The thin, metal stick-on signs on these trailers for "Fruehauf" and "Duravan" are the same type as those used for most of the lift trucks. Of interest is that two versions of these signs are known. The most common, and most legible, has a black background with silver lettering and borders. The other version appears to be a bad batch of the same thing. The lettering and borders are weak and the whole sign appears almost entirely black, which makes it hard to read. These tags were not carried over on later vans, except the very early gray Cooper-Jarrett vans.

Early versions of these dark green molded-plastic vans have two red spotting marks on the lower edge on each side. They assist the operator in positioning the forklift so the conical projections on the lifting arms will enter the mating holes molded into the trailer's underside. This stabilizes the trailer while it is being moved and ensures that it is positioned properly to fit on the railcar or in the wheel wells on the platform.

The 3460 came nestled in the packing of new 460s and did not have its own box. It was listed for separate sale in 1955 only, but no example in an original box had been documented until collector Barry Keener acquired one in 1999. Unlike the over-stamped gondola box used for the 6342 Culvert Car, Lionel printed a special classic box for separate-sale 3460s. And this box was for just the flatcar, with no vans! The 6430 Flatcar with Cooper-Jarrett Vans, introduced in 1956, is the same car with a new number and can also be used with a 460. Dimensions: 8⅝" x 11" base, 1¾" high; car is 11¼" long.

(A) Probable 1955 early and more common version with thin, metal stick-on signs with a black background with silver ROSS/TRAILOADER. Excellent or Like New condition requires the presence of original lift-truck operator and all signs on the lift truck and on the dark green vans. Vans may have "Fruehauf" and "Duravan" signs with black background and silver letters and borders or the less common predominantly black version with poorly defined letters and borders. Earlier vans also have two red spotting marks on the lower edge on each side.

| 75 | 90 | 130 | 160 |

(B) Probably late 1955 (possibly later) version with less-common white rubber-stamped ROSS/TRAILOADER on sides of lift truck. Excellent and Like New condition requires the presence of original lift-truck operator and all signs on the dark green vans.

| 85 | 100 | 150 | 180 |

460P PLATFORM, 1955–57

The original box is required to identify this accessory correctly. Without that box, the platform is just an orphan from a regular 460. All observed examples of this box have a "No. 460P PLATFORM" label printed in blue on a brown paper tape strip applied to a regular 460 carton. The author's 460P also contains a lift truck with white rubber-stamped lettering, but others have been reported with the stick-on tag. Values indicated are for the box and contents of equivalent condition. However, if you find a box in good condition, don't worry too much about what, if anything, is in it! The box is a rare and desirable collectible.

| 300 | 500 | 700 | 900 |

461 PLATFORM WITH TRUCK AND TRAILER, 1966 (uncataloged)

Of the numerous examples of this accessory observed over the years, none has included an original instruction sheet. Even two sealed examples opened for research purposes contained no printed matter whatsoever. However, another 461 contained an original 461-13 instruction sheet, dated 7/66, printed black on white paper, about 5½" x 8½". This sheet contains the explanation of its own rarity, as it reads, ". . .the Transport Set consists of a special flat car, a pair of truck trailers and a loading and unloading platform."

Only one example with two trailers and a flat car has been reported, and it also contains a Midgetoy tractor. Yet that 461 has standard packaging with no special provision for the flatcar or tractor, and it contains no instruction sheet! Apparently, Lionel made a last-minute decision to change the content (and reduce the cost) of this accessory by substituting the Midgetoy tractor for one trailer and eliminating the flatcar. All other known examples of this accessory come with only one white van and the red tractor to pull it. With this change just at the start of production, there was no time to reprint the inaccurate instruction sheet, so they left it out of most 461s. The wording on the observed version of this instruction sheet is identical to the 460-70 sheet, except that "The" is substituted for "No. 460" in two places.

Also of interest is the existence of a Lionel Service Manual page for the 6431 (dated 11-66) but not one for the 461. Also introduced in 1966, 6431 is just a 6430 flatcar with two white trailer vans packaged in a special Cellophane-front box to make room for the Midgetoy tractor. Complete details on this car appear in the first volume of *Greenberg's Guide to Lionel Trains, 1945–1969*.

The undated box for the 461 is labeled with the Hillside, New Jersey, address rather than the Hagerstown, Maryland, address used for 1968 items. This is a substantial cardboard carton, which indicates that the 461 was initially intended as a separate-sale item. However, it has been reported as a component of the uncataloged Montgomery Ward set 19546 (Ward's product number 48-21303). Perhaps it was intended to complement the 6431 or be something different for a minimal investment during the waning years of Lionel.

The die-cast metal cab-over truck tractor, painted bright red, was made by Midge Toy Co. of Rockford, Illinois. It also made a die-cast trailer to go with the tractor for its own line, but Lionel bought only the tractor and gave it part number 6431-150. Cast inside in raised letters are the markings "MIDGE TOY, ROCKFORD, ILL. U. S. A. PATENT 2775847." The trailer was

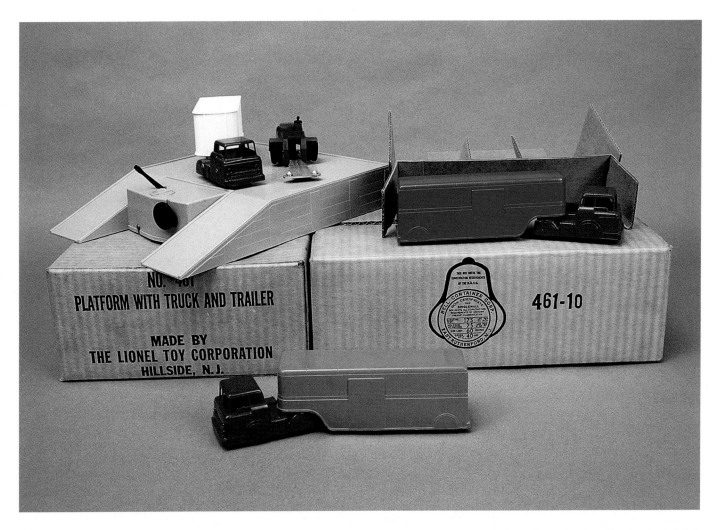

produced by Lionel as part number 6430-150. This time, though, it was molded in white and did not have slots for a nametag on the side. It has only a single rear wheel on each side, rather than the dual wheels used on earlier models that came with the 6430, 460, etc. On the underside, a large hole was drilled to accommodate the pin on the tractor so the two could be coupled. It is interesting to note that in the 1968 Numerical Parts List, the last such publication of the original Lionel Toy Corp., no 461 part numbers are listed for this accessory, a mere two years after it was produced. This was probably due to the fact that there were no unique parts on the 461, at least none that a 460 or 6431 part could not replace.

Besides the van and tractor, there are other differences from the 460. Most notable are the absence of wheel depressions in the platform and a change in the steering column post of the lift truck. Between final production of the 460 and initial production of the 461, Lionel revised the platform mold so it could be used for the 462 Derrick Platform Set. That accessory was designed to load radioactive waste containers instead of trailers, so the depressions for the trailer wheels were removed from the mold. On the underside, the 462 accessory number and Lionel nomenclature were molded in, and guides for the boom and hook operating cables were added. When this mold was resurrected for the 461, the wheel wells were not replaced and the 462 markings were removed, but the cable guide studs remained. Unlike the 460, none of the 461s examined has lettering on the Base Plate Assembly. Thus, a 461 does not have an item number stamped on it and has only the circled "L" to indicate its maker when

461 Platform with Truck and Trailer. The Midgetoy die-cast trailers were not included with this or any other Lionel product. Lionel purchased only the tractor for the 461 and 6431.

	Gd	VG	Ex	LN

separated from the box. This was highly unusual for Lionel and indicative of the "last gasp" nature of this offering.

Lift trucks observed with new-in-the-box 461s have no markings, and the steering columns are different from those supplied with the 460. The redesign provides a vertical column molded as part of the red lift-truck shell, with a tiny blackened die-cast steering wheel affixed to the top. The vertical column retains the driver's legs, making it less likely that he will slide forward and disappear from the lift truck. However, the lift trucks are easily interchanged, and either will do as a replacement for the other. Note that the 460 lift trucks have bright "hubcaps" on the front dual wheels, while those on all 461s observed are blackened. Dimensions: 8⅝" x 11" base, 1¾" high.

(A) Common version described above.

	70	110	150	190

(B) Reportedly came with red 6430 Flatcar, 6511-2 mold and AAR trucks, and yellow Cooper-Jarrett vans with copper and black signs. Unlike normal yellow vans, those with this example have a hole in the bottom to hook up to the truck tractor. H. Powell Collection, original sealed box opened by P. Haffen.
NRS

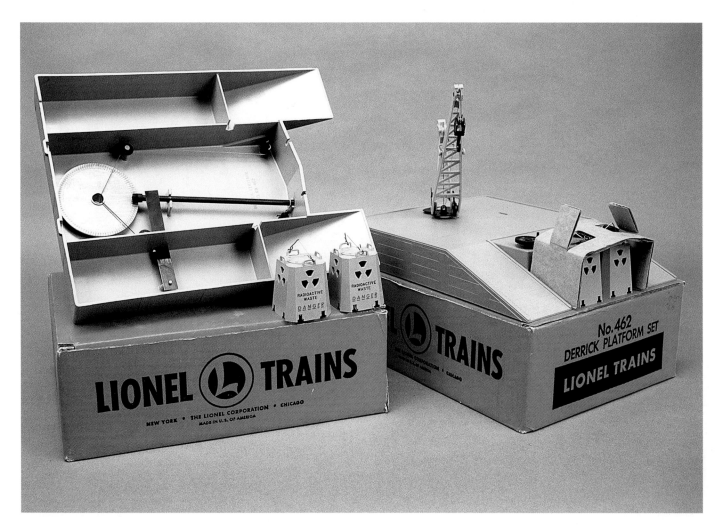

462 DERRICK PLATFORM SET, 1961–62

Similar to the 460 Piggy Back Transportation Set, the 462 Derrick Platform uses three hand cranks to accomplish what is more easily done by hand. One crank rotates the crane, another raises and lowers the boom, and the third raises and lowers the hook. A combination of these actions moves the containers between the platform and a railcar.

Lionel often used existing components to construct new products, and the 462 is a prime example of this practice. Major contributors to this item are the 6805 Atomic Energy Disposal Car, 6660 Boom Car, and 460 Piggyback Transportation Set. This last item supplies the platform for the 462 and required the most modifications. The platform mold was changed to eliminate the wheel depressions for the trailers and the hole for the lever that actuated the lift. Lionel added holes for the derrick-operating crank wheels, two bosses for cable guides, and molded-in nomenclature for the item number and Lionel data.

Unlike the preceding 460 or later 461, the platform was painted tan on the top surface. It was still molded in the same gray plastic as the other two (visible on the underside), but the tan paint was probably used to make it look more like the wood platform that the simulated board detail implies. Why Lionel did not use brown plastic, as it did with the 264 Operating Forklift, remains unknown. The boom is borrowed from the 6660, which borrowed it from the 3360 Burro Crane.

The radioactive waste containers are descendants of the 6805 Atomic Energy Disposal Car load, but they lack an interior red lens housing and light. A unique bail handle was added to give

462 Derrick Platform Set with gray underside and painted tan topside. The packing consists of one cardboard shield for the containers. The hoist has a release lever to allow the boom to lie flat for shipping and storage.

the boom hook something to latch on to. This transformed the shell of the 6805 load into a 462-13 Container, one of the few unique 462 part numbers. The fragile container handles are often found broken. Lionel Trains Inc. has reissued these containers, and they are almost indistinguishable from originals. Even the original molded-in part number remains on some observed examples. Originals are medium gray with heat-stamped "DANGER." The 6805 used the same part, except its color was light tan or sand, as well as the medium gray. The 462 is known to use only gray containers. However, containers are easily interchanged, so price distinctions do not exist for these variations. Reissue containers, at least the few observed, are a lighter gray than the originals.

All observed examples of the 462 came in the solid orange box with black printing that debuted in 1960. The 462 box is unusual because a part number is not printed on it. Each new Derrick Platform set came with a 5½" by 8½" instruction sheet, part number 462-26, dated 10-61 and printed in black ink on white paper. This sheet only illustrated how to raise and lock the short boom in position before operating the 462 and did not describe how to operate the accessory.

A railcar was not included with the 462, and a 6805 will not work with it. That car's containers lack bail handles and grip the rails mounted on the deck of a 6805 too firmly for the 462's

464 Lumber Mill, whose illusion of logs being cut into lumber was somewhat spoiled because the boards were wider than the logs. J. Algozzini Collection.

	Gd	VG	Ex	LN

crane to lift them. A gondola makes the best transport car for the 462 containers, but they barely fit inside, so loading them with the crane is a real challenge! This accessory, being no more exciting to operate than the 460, had a relatively short production span and is somewhat scarce today. Excellent or Like New condition requires the two original containers with perfect handles and the wire bales. Dimensions: 8⅝″ x 11″ base, 1¼″ high.

	155	220	285	350

464 LUMBER MILL, 1956–60

The 464 receives logs from an operating log car, such as Lionel's 3461. Flipping a 364C Controller starts the vibrating motor, which conveys the logs, single file, into one side of the sawmill structure. As the logs enter the structure, they appear to be "cut" lengthwise and subsequently emerge from the other side as dressed lumber. This is just an illusion, of course, as the logs are collected in an interior bin, and the lumber, which must be manually stacked in a hidden chute, is fed out the left side as the logs disappear into the right side. Somewhat marring this illusion is the fact that the lumber emerging from the left is wider than the diameter of the logs from which it appears to be cut! At the conclusion of one operating cycle, the lumber and logs must be manually retrieved and reloaded in their respective locations for the next cycle.

Rube Goldberg would have loved the fishing-line-and-photo-film drive mechanism Lionel used for this item! The vibrating motor simultaneously provides observers with motion and the grating sound of a buzz saw. The Lionel Service Manual pages, dated 2-58, detail the fairly complex procedure of tuning the motor for best operation and recommend a variable voltage source to adjust the mill for optimum performance. They also suggest adding the three major housing assemblies to the base one at a time after tuning, checking operation after each addition. When properly tuned, the 464 is very reliable.

Lights were not provided either on or inside the 464, but the 1956 Lionel Advance Catalog indicates that the original intent was to provide some illumination. That catalog depicts the 464 with two lamp heads from the 395 Floodlight Tower, one mounted on each front corner of the mill roof. The text mentions "powerful floodlights" for use in nighttime operations. Somebody made one of these up a few years ago and passed it off as a prototype for big money!

Included with each 464 was a 464-58 envelope containing a 364C Controller, five 3363-21 Logs, five 464-51 Timbers, three 81-32 Connecting Wires, and instruction sheet 464-57, dated 11-56 (blue ink on white paper). There appears to be no discernable difference between 3363-21 and 164-64 logs. Excellent or

| | Gd | VG | Ex | LN |

497 Coaling Station. The light green roof identifies this as a middle-production version.

Like New condition requires the original simulated crane and roof-mounted dust collector, which have been rerun from the original tooling by Lionel Trains Inc. and reproduced by others. The plastic fence on the left housing is frequently found broken. Note that a 464-151 manila envelope containing six spare Timbers was available for separate sale as catalog number 464-150. Dimensions: 16½″ x 6″ base, 6″ high.

| | **85** | **115** | **160** | **200** |

497 COALING STATION, 1953–58

The last of Lionel's coal handlers, this accessory went virtually unchanged throughout its production run. As pictured in the 1953 Advance Catalog, the 497 had shields on the loading chutes and an access ladder inside one support column. Neither of these features made it into production.

The 497 features four-action remote control operation. A loaded automatic dump car, such as Lionel's 3469, is positioned under the elevated structure of the 497. Care must be taken so the dumping side of the car is on the receiving bin side. Unfortunately, a mistake in dump car orientation will result in the load being deposited in a heap beside the track! Moving the load control lever on the 497-100 Controller to the "dump" position causes a properly oriented car to dump its load into the receiving bin. Holding the bin control lever in the "up" direction hoists the loaded bin to the top of the structure, where it tilts and spills the coal into the storage hopper. Slip clutches

in the lift mechanism prevent damage if the lever is held beyond the point where the bin reaches the limit of its upward travel. Like the 97 elevator, the 497's hopper will hold more than one carload of coal. Holding the controller lever in the down position returns the receiving bin to its trackside position. Holding this lever beyond the full down position produces the undesirable result of starting the bin back up, thus reversing the up and down directions. Selecting the "load" position opens the storage hopper chutes and releases the coal into a waiting hopper or dump car.

For normal production runs of the 497, the roof color is the only significant variation. Both green translucent roofs and dark green opaque roofs have been observed. Reliable reports indicate that dark green roofs were used in 1953 production. Later roofs were a lighter green, except for the last run, when the roof attachment hooks were enlarged and the color reverted to dark green. Since the roof has been reproduced, look for "PART No. 497-63" molded into the underside near the edge of the longest portion to verify authenticity. Also, check the tiny hooks molded into the roof at each end that hold it to the metal sides, as those on all except the last run are often broken.

Two 497-90 instruction sheets are known. The first, dated 12-53, is printed in black ink on white paper and is known in two versions. After Super-O track and the 3359 Twin-Bin Dump Car were introduced, the instructions were revised to include the necessary additional information. Also included are the connections needed for the LW transformer, which was introduced in 1955. The new sheet, dated 11-57, was printed in blue ink on white paper. Contrary to Lionel's usual practice, the instruction sheet was not included in the 497-93 parts envelope, instead being placed loose in the box packing.

Each 497 came with a 497-100 Controller pre-wired to the coaling station, 206 Bag of Artificial Coal, CTC Lockon, 3656-67 (O gauge) and 3657-68 (O27 gauge) power blades, and 3656-66 O gauge grounding clip. As with the 282 cranes, rewired 497s are common, since insulation on the wire to the controller tends to become brittle and crack. A dump car was not included with this accessory. Dimensions: 9½″ x 6″ base, 10″ high.

(A) Yellow-painted metal housing, green metal base. Dick Sanford Collection. **NRS**

(B) 1953. Red-painted metal housing, gray-painted metal base, blackened metal support posts, maroon molded hopper and doors, dark green opaque roof with small latches and correspondingly small square holes in the side housing peaks. Excellent or Like New requires the original roof with intact latches. **110 140 180 240**

(C) 1954–56. Same as (B) except green translucent roof. **100 130 165 225**

(D) 1957–58. Same as (B) except dark green opaque roof, with enlarged latches and enlarged square holes in the side housing peaks. **110 140 180 240**

CHAPTER 2

Operating Structures

The 334 Operating Dispatching Board captured the excitement of a typical passenger station, although its enormous attendant left no doubt that this was a toy.

Operating accessories possess a charm especially associated with Lionel trains. While it is certainly easy to appreciate a well-designed, detailed HO scale layout, somehow the "play value" is lacking. It is much like observing real railroading operations from a low-flying airplane; you can see the trains move, but the element of excitement is missing. Lionel's accessories add that excitement and the feeling that things are truly happening in the miniature world you have created.

Moreover, Lionel's accessories provide operators with an indispensable sense of control that comes only from managing operations surrounding the train. Even settings like oil fields come to life. Rather than leaving the action to the imagination, oil derricks pump oil that seemingly bubbles and flows from the well. Ingenious Lionel accessories like these bring operators and observers right into the action, the type of action that seems to complete a well-designed and landscaped layout. Although many of Lionel's accessories provide action in one form or another, this chapter addresses simple operations other than those related to loading, unloading, or signaling.

| | Gd | VG | Ex | LN |

93 Water Towers. Left: Gray tower from 1941-42 in a box printed in April 1940. Right: Silver tower from 1949-50 in a box printed with names of two cities.

Current and prospective owners of a 38 should first remove the tank and take out the black hoses. Of course, these original hoses should be retained, as they are original Lionel production! After you replace the nipples with aquarium hose couplings purchased from the local pet shop, use surgical tubing to reconnect the pump.

Regrettably, more trouble lies ahead. As a result of the poorly designed pump seal, water frequently leaks from the 38. One solution is to install a redesigned, and hence unoriginal, seal. The alternative is to live with a leak, which quickly damages the pump motor and rusts the mechanism mounting plate. If you actually use a 38, it should be disassembled and thoroughly dried before being stored.

Since most of the parts are common, many comments regarding the 30 Water Tower apply to the 38. A 38-41 Cover Plug came with each 38 Pumping Water Tower to plug the top water-fill hole. Also, a 5CL-73 Funnel from Lionel's chemistry sets was included to use when filling the tower. In addition to the funnel and cover plug, this accessory included a 96C Controller, 38-62 instruction sheet (dated 6-46 and printed in dark blue ink on lighter blue paper), and manila envelope of 38-70 Water Tank Color Tablets. Dimensions: 6¼" x 6¼" base, 10⅞" high to top of fill plug.

(A) Red-painted roof with brown-painted trestle. This is the most common version. However, note that roofs and trestles are easily switched between 30 and 38 towers.

	Gd	VG	Ex	LN
	165	255	350	460

| | Gd | VG | Ex | LN |

(B) Brown-painted roof with black trestle. This has also been observed with a dark gray-painted roof. The less common black-painted, clear-molded trestle is the reason for the higher value.

	Gd	VG	Ex	LN
	180	270	370	480

93 WATER TOWER, 1931–42 and 1946–50

Meant as a "budget" water tower, the 93 lacked remote control features. Only the spout moved, and it required manual lowering and raising. In the postwar years, the tank and trestle were painted silver, with a red base and black spout. Early prewar versions had a green tank with a maroon or terra cotta base. In 1942 the tank, tower, and standpipe were changed to gray, but not all at once. According to the third volume of *Greenberg's Guide to Lionel Trains, 1901–1942*, some examples may have silver and gray parts mixed. With the exception of the green tank version, the 93 had a "LIONEL / TRAINS" decal with red letters outlined in black and a black line around the outer edge of the decal. Values are for the postwar version. Dimensions: 3⅝" x 3⅝" base, 8⅜" high to top of raised spout.

	Gd	VG	Ex	LN
	20	30	40	60

128 Animated Newsstand. Dark green (left) and light green versions.

128 ANIMATED NEWSSTAND, 1957–60

Another of Lionel's ingenious accessories that use the "Vibrotor" mechanism, the 128 uses levers and gears to provide most of the action. A driven pulley moves two levers, the first of which causes the vendor behind the counter to move forward and backward. The second lever, similar to the mechanism that drives the agitator in a washing machine, attaches to a sector gear that pivots the newsboy. It also drives the third lever, which uses a rack-and-pinion arrangement to run the dog back and forth around the hydrant.

Proper operating voltage is 11-13 volts. The Lionel Service Manual warns that too high a voltage may throw the drive line off its pulley and make the mechanism chatter. The 128 is hard to find with an original "newspaper," which is held by friction in a slot on the boy's hand and is easily lost. The dog's black spots appear to be hand-painted, as no two are alike. Many parts of this accessory have been reproduced.

It was originally thought that the 128-84 House Assembly was molded in dark green or a lighter Kelly green. Other examples appeared to be painted in one of these two colors on various other mold colors. Further investigation has revealed that all 128-84 House Assemblies are painted on various colored shells. It is difficult to tell this without removing the house and looking at the unpainted portions of the underside. One example that is painted on a red molded shell has been reported. None of the many examples intently examined have been molded in the final shade of green and left unpainted.

	Gd	VG	Ex	LN

Each 128 has a tan base (various shades are known), painted green stand, red molded roof, red fire hydrant, and hand-painted dog figure. The interior is illuminated by an L53 lamp concealed under the counter. Only a 128-80 instruction sheet dated 10-57 (printed in blue ink on white paper) is known. In addition, a 364C Controller and hookup wire were included. Excellent or Like New condition requires all original parts. Dimensions: 8½" x 6¼" base, 4¼" high.

(A) Bright, almost Kelly green paint on 128-84 House Assembly, which may be molded of most any color plastic. The plastic levers, observed by removing the roof, are black or mixed (i.e., one black and one white). This is probably, but not conclusively, the earliest production. **80 120 175 230**

(B) Dark green paint on 128-84 House Assembly, which may be molded of most any color plastic. Dark green paint seems slightly more common than Kelly green. The plastic levers, observed by removing the roof, are black or mixed (i.e., one black and one white). Since white is the natural color of the nylon used for the levers, they would be less costly to produce and thus likely account for the bulk of production.

80 120 175 230

(C) Two examples reported with roofs containing two molded-in holes for mounting flags. The roof and other parts of the 128 were likely adapted to make an as yet unidentified structure for Lionel's slot car line. Both examples found in excellent condition, one in its original box. **NRS**

138 Water Tower, the last of Lionel's operating water tanks. J. Algozzini Collection.

	Gd	VG	Ex	LN

138 WATER TOWER, 1953–57

This was the successor to the 30 and 38 Water Towers. Although it retained the operating water spout, the 138 had a brown opaque plastic single-walled tank. The plastic roof rests on top, as there are no holes for attaching posts to secure it in position as on the 30 and 38. There is also no center water-fill hole. While the 30 and 38 Water Towers have a die-cast metal base, the 138 came with a gray plastic base with "NO. 138 WATER TANK" molded on its top surface. Lionel changed the base part number from 38-30 on the earlier towers to 138-4. The trestle assembly uses the same design as the 30 and 38. However, while the 30 and 38 trestles were usually molded in clear plastic and painted brown or black, the 138 trestle is unpainted brown plastic.

Because plastic (an electrical insulator) was used to mold the base and the "water standpipe" underneath the tank, the 138 requires two separate metal rods to supply power to the spout solenoid. Connection clips on the bottom replace the two binding posts on earlier tanks for attaching the electrical leads. In the two earlier towers, the metal base and metal water standpipe column provide the electrical ground, while a separate wire, fed through the column, provides the power connection.

Two publication dates for the 138-29 instruction sheet are known: 6-53 and 3-56. Both were done in blue ink on white paper, but the first is also known with black ink. An instruction sheet and 96C Controller (early production) or 90 Controller (starting in 1955) accompanied 138 Towers. Dimensions: 6¼" x 6¼" base, 10¼" high.

(A) 1953 only. Unpainted gray plastic roof.

	80	110	150	175

(B) 1954–57. Unpainted bright orange plastic roof.

	75	100	140	165

	Gd	VG	Ex	LN

161 MAIL PICKUP SET, 1961–63

Fragile and unique, the mail pickup set is the only Lionel accessory that ever attempted transfer of anything to a moving train! By remote control (pressing the 90 Controller button), the signal arm, holding the mailbag, swings close to the side of a passing train. The mailbag is then caught "on the fly" by a magnet glued to one of the cars.

The weak link is the 161-5 Link, which has two tiny teeth that ride in grooves in the center shaft. These grooves are twisted so when the solenoid is activated by the controller, the shaft rises, the link rotates enough to tip the swing-arm support (signal arm), and the weight of the mailbag swings the arm out to the train. Placement of the 161 in relation to the track is critical (instructions specify 2¼"), as is the position of the magnet glued onto the car. Firmly fastening the signal to the layout is recommended. The base may even have to be shimmed so that the signal leans slightly to get the arm to swing properly.

Each 161 has a tan plastic base (containing the solenoid coil), red pole with red-and-white semaphore, red plastic swing arm, and red plastic bag painted gray and hollowed out to carry a magnet. This mailbag should not be confused with the smaller 3428-11 or -22 mailbags without magnets used with the 3428 Operating Mail Car. Only one 161-32 instruction sheet, dated 9-61, is known, and is printed in black ink on greenish-blue paper. To be complete, this accessory must have a 161-23 Magnet, 161-17 Mail Bag, instruction sheet, and 3330-102 Cement Capsule. Dimensions: 4" x 1⅞" base, 8⅝" high to top of raised semaphore arm.

	35	60	90	125

	Gd	VG	Ex	LN

192 RAILROAD CONTROL TOWER, 1959–60

This replica of the towers used to monitor and control the operations of huge railroad yards is yet another accessory that uses a Vibrotor to provide simple action. When wired directly to a variable voltage post on the transformer, this motor causes the two operators to move about the illuminated tower and rotates the anemometer on the roof of the tower. Because this accessory was meant to oversee the operations of a rail yard rather than an airport, it is hard to imagine why it needed an anemometer and a weather vane. However, these additions do provide action and detail.

Fragility and low production combine to make this is a relatively scarce accessory, so locating a complete one in collectible condition is a challenge. Finding a complete original box is even more difficult. This paperboard box with a large cellophane window is one of the flimsiest containers Lionel ever used. Except for color, the tower used on the 192 is the same as the tower on the 197 Rotating Radar Antenna, introduced in 1957. The radar accessory included a 197-24 Whip Antenna, which some people think should also come with the 192, as there is a socket for it. However, the socket was present because the same tower mold was used for both accessories. An antenna can be installed, but it hits the roof and was never included in production.

Often the roof on the 192 is found deformed in the area above the L53 lamp, due to heat. If you intend to operate your 192, a patch of aluminum foil applied to the underside of the roof above the bulb will prevent this. Usually, the weather vane and anemometer are broken or missing. They are available as unmarked reproductions. Finally, the 415-20 Figures are often missing and detail parts of the tower are cracked. Be sure to look for cracks all along the seemingly endless fence, stairs, and cross bracing.

Only one 192-39 instruction sheet, dated 10-59, is known. It is printed in blue ink on white paper. A supplementary 4¼" x 3⅝" special note (numbered 1934) was also included in at least some (probably later) 192s. Printed in black ink on white paper, it shows how to install the four rubber grommets used as "feet" to isolate the base from the train table and minimize vibration. Dimensions: 4" x 5" base, 12" high to top of anemometer.

	105	150	200	250

193 INDUSTRIAL WATER TOWER, 1953–55

The 193 is a reasonably detailed rendition of a 1950s-era water tower for industrial use (as compared with the 30, 38, 93, and 138 water towers for railroad use). An unpainted gray plastic base supports a dark green molded shed (called a "hut" in the Lionel Service Manual), along with a painted metal tower and black-painted cardboard center pipe. The tower is a truncated version of the tower used on the 455 Oil Derrick. The catwalk atop the tower and the lift-off tank are gray plastic painted silver.

Added tank detail consists of a red lens on top and a black metal ladder on the side. A flashing L51 bulb, which is regulated by a bimetallic switch inside the tank, illuminates the red lens. Because the brightness of the light is dimmed by the lens, the effect is somewhat muted. Watch out for a sticking switch, because if it sticks in the "on" position, the constantly illuminated lamp can melt the tank top. Electrical connection is provided

All the pieces of the 161 Mail Pickup Set. Note the unique mailbag on the end of the swing arm and the magnet with its glue capsule in front of the 90 Controller. Yes, some assembly is required!

192 Railroad Control Tower with original box. J. Algozzini Collection.

Early and desirable variation of 193 Industrial Water Tower with black tower (right) and later, more common one with red tower. Note that one box opens from the end and the other from the side. J. Algozzini Collection.

Rear view of the 334 with its Lionel Travel Center storefront and illuminated Airex billboard. J. Algozzini Collection.

	Gd	VG	Ex	LN

through two terminal clips underneath the base. Only a 193-24 instruction sheet, dated 6-53 (black ink on white paper), is known. Dimensions: 6″ x 6″ base, 14¾″ high.

(A) Red-painted metal tower.

	75	95	115	140

(B) Black-painted tower, thought to be earliest production.

	80	100	130	175

334 OPERATING DISPATCHING BOARD, 1957–60

While providing interesting operation, the size of this accessory is out of proportion with most other Lionel accessories. Although smaller than the 1045 Operating Gateman, the dispatching board attendant stands 9 scale feet tall. This accessory apparently did not sell well and is a scarce item today. It was probably cataloged for four years because it took that long to get rid of initial production!

A cleverly designed accessory, the 334 was another application of the Vibrator. The majority of the parts were new and unique to the 334. Pressing a 90 Controller button starts the giant attendant (who has painted hands and face) moving from the left side of the board to the right and then back again, all without holding the controller button. As the attendant reaches the midpoint of his travel from left to right, a pin on the carriage fits into the teeth of the gear-like dial listing train arrival and departure data. As the attendant passes, the dial rotates and changes the

350 Engine Transfer Table (rear) and 350-50 Transfer Table Extension (front).

displayed data. A worm-gear-and-pinion causes the attendant to pivot 180 degrees as he reaches the right side of the platform, so he faces the direction he is moving for the return trip. When the cycle is complete, the action stops automatically and waits for the next command to start.

Whether in action or waiting, the dispatch board is always lit by two interior lamps. Even the simulated clock atop the board is illuminated by optically directing the interior light up to its face. The bulbs are accessed by unscrewing the two ornamental loudspeakers on the top and lifting off the frame. The instruction sheet calls for L53 or L363 bulbs, while the Lionel Service Manual and later replacement lamp charts specify L57. These are all clear, interchangeable, bayonet-base lamps, but the L57 draws 0.1 amps, while the other two draw 0.2 amps, so they burn brighter and hotter.

Only one 334-86 instruction sheet, dated 9-57 (printed in bright blue ink on white paper), is known. It states that the surface of the dispatching board is specially treated so that additional information can be chalked in the lines adjacent to the data windows in the center of the board. Proper operating voltage is 10–14 volts. The Lionel Service Manual warns that too high a voltage may damage the accessory by causing the armature to slap against the coil, possibly throwing the drive belt off its pulley. No variations of the 334 have been reported, offering some support for the idea of limited production.

	Gd	VG	Ex	LN

Each 334 has a gray plastic base, green display board, molded blue attendant with painted hands and face, and lighted billboard on the rear, above a "LIONEL TRAVEL CENTER" insert. A 90 Controller, instruction sheet, and hookup wire were included. Dimensions: 9⅞" x 4⅛" base, 7½" high.

	Gd	VG	Ex	LN
	125	180	235	290

350 ENGINE TRANSFER TABLE, 1957–60

This is one of Lionel's most complex accessories. The table is scaled to the 70-foot average length of the tables used in most railroad yards and will accommodate the largest single power unit made by Lionel as well as short industrial switchers handling one car. To handle double units, it is possible to connect two transfer tables end to end and operate them simultaneously by a single controller. The table and controller are sturdy and trouble-free. The rail bed should be kept flat and level, preferably permanently fixed to the tabletop to assure uniform traction for both table drive wheels. If you want to buy one of these to operate, the instruction sheet is extremely helpful. There is only one known sheet, part number 350-88, dated 11-57. It is printed in black or blue ink on white paper.

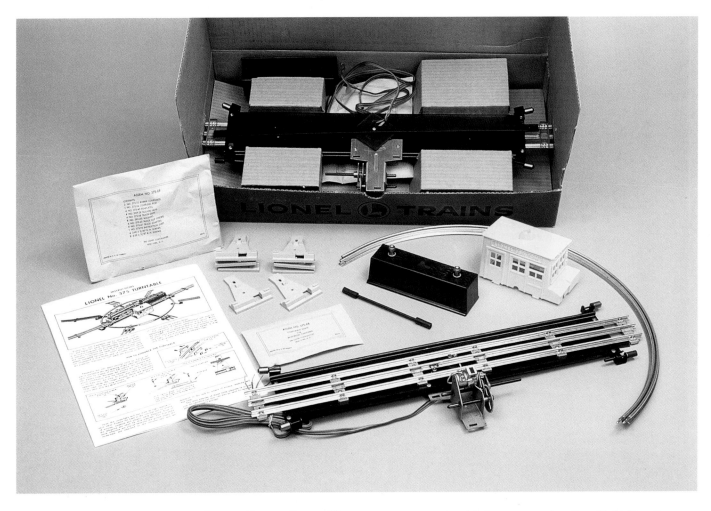

Two complete examples of the battery-powered 375 Turntable "kit." Rear: The set as it looks when first opened, with only the instruction sheet removed from the top. Front: The ingredients from a second new example. So many bits and pieces to be assembled and fine-tuned before anything that will fit on two sections of 0-27 track can be rotated!

	Gd	VG	Ex	LN

Although the 350 was cataloged for four years, no variations have been reported. In addition to the instruction sheet, new transfer tables included a number of small parts to adapt the various types of track to the table. These were contained in an envelope numbered 350-89. Although the 350 can be used without them, the small parts are handy to have for installation and are essential for an example to be considered Like New or better. Use of one or more 350-50 Transfer Table Extensions, described below, can extend the travel range of the 350 to four or more parallel tracks.

The 350-200 Controller is unique and is assumed to be present for the prices listed below. Controllers have not yet been reproduced and are essentially unavailable. A 148-100 switch is mentioned in the instructions and is used in one of the several wiring arrangements shown there. It was not included with the 350 but was available for separate sale. A single-pole double-throw (SPDT) switch can be substituted if that wiring arrangement is called for. Dimensions: 17½" x 10⅜" table, 4" high to top of lamp on house.

	Gd	VG	Ex	LN
	175	260	350	420

350-50 TRANSFER TABLE EXTENSION, 1957–60

This is a companion piece for the 350 Engine Transfer Table. Each 350-50 expands the range of the transfer table to two additional parallel tracks. It was packaged in a Classic orange and blue box with cardboard inserts. However, this was not sufficiently sturdy for the extension's size and weight. Even when an extension is found new in the original box, the box is usually in poor shape. An accompanying parts envelope, number 350-78, contained additional rail brackets and grounding strips, but not an instruction sheet. Installation instructions are contained in the 350-88 sheet mentioned in the 350 listing above. Dimensions: 17½" x 10⅜" table.

	Gd	VG	Ex	LN
	75	120	160	200

375 TURNTABLE, 1962–64

It seems odd that Lionel would introduce a turntable in 1962, considering that business had been going poorly for several years and steam had all but disappeared from American railroads. Maybe the 375 was an attempt to get back to basics when space and military items, slot cars, and science sets were not catching on. The attempt was probably helped by the availability of cheap, battery-powered motors, a relaxing of standards, and pressure to come up with something new that would make dealers happy and bring in some badly needed sales revenue. Whatever the motive, the resulting accessory was about as barebones a turntable as can be imagined and was strictly a low-budget offering.

415 Diesel Fueling Station. The tower lifts off base for shipping. J. Algozzini Collection.

Only one instruction sheet, number 375-76, dated 10/62 (with printings in both blue and black ink on white paper), is known. It recommends mounting the unit on a 24"-square piece of ¼" plywood. Shortly after production began, a supplementary sheet, "SPECIAL INSTALLATION INSTRUCTIONS," was issued requiring this mounting. This sheet was undated and did not have a part number. Other helpful hints were also included, such as using cardboard shims to raise the center of the structure from ¹⁄₁₆" to ¼" in gradual increments until maximum efficiency was achieved. It also advised filing the circular rail joints smooth and using Vaseline, never grease, on the center pivot. Operation of the turntable can be tuned for smoothness by tightening and loosening the crossbar screws, somewhat like tuning a guitar!

The Lionel Service Manual lists almost 60 different parts for the 375, not counting duplicates, and usually many of them are missing. But if you get the main pieces and mount the unit solidly to a platform, you can use substitutes for most of the hardware. One of the key pieces is the instruction sheet. Without it, and maybe even with it, the whole accessory is a mystery. Instructions at least help determine what the other main pieces

	Gd	VG	Ex	LN

are. At a minimum, the turntable, drive mechanism, and two O gauge semicircular rails are needed. Everything else can be made or faked.

The 375-3 House (simulated control cab, actually the motor cover) is a reworked 350-5 House. As with any battery-powered equipment, it is essential to check for damage from battery leakage before purchasing a 375. In this case, only the controller contains batteries. If you are a collector, nothing short of Excellent or Like New in an original box is worth having, since too much is usually missing from the lower grades. The table is 20" long, which will barely accommodate a 736 with tender and definitely will not take anything longer. The controller is a combination slide switch and battery box that turns the motor on and off. Since the motor runs in one direction only, if you overshoot alignment of the track, you have to turn the engine all the way around and try again. But the instructions say that with a little practice, you will learn to align the track accurately by moving the switch off and on rapidly. There is also an admonition to keep the circular rail clean and dry, as the table is driven by a rubber roller pressing against it. Dimensions: Requires a space 24" square.

	155	**205**	**255**	**310**

415 DIESEL FUELING STATION, 1955–57

Lionel learned that operating items with men at work were big sellers. Prime examples are the automatic milk car and the 45 and 145 operating gatemen. The many years these accessories remained in the catalog demonstrate that items stayed in production as long as they sold well. The 415 Diesel Fueling Station followed this "men at work" formula and probably represented a substantial investment by Lionel, since well over half its parts were new and unique. Yet it lasted only three years and probably was cataloged the last two years only so that dealer stocks would appear current.

In operation, the biggest shortcoming of the 415 is that the figure is hard to see. Pressing the 90 Controller button moves the man from the building (illuminated with one L53 lamp) and causes him to push the pipe into position for fueling. When the man is "fueling" a diesel locomotive, the locomotive obstructs an observer's view of the action. Placing the 415 between the observer and the locomotive does not help either, as the house then blocks the view. Operating the accessory without the presence of the locomotive makes no sense because it would mean imaginary fuel was spilling over the track! Consequently, this item did not show well on a layout or a dealer's shelf. Still, the 415 is a fairly rugged accessory and is generally available in reasonable condition.

No significant variations have been reported. One 415-124 instruction sheet, dated 9-55 (printed in black ink on white paper), is known. A 90 Controller, instruction sheet, and hookup wire were included. Dimensions: 9" x 9" base, 10" high.

	85	**110**	**130**	**200**

445 OPERATING SWITCH TOWER, 1952–57

This accessory is similar in operation to the 45 and 145 Automatic Gateman. When an approaching train activates the 145C Contactor, one figure ducks into the doorway as the other runs down the stairs. Both men return to their former positions after the train passes. This is an action accessory that should have been even more popular than the 145, since not one but two men move. Although it had a respectable run, it did not come close to matching the production volume or duration of the 145. One reason might be that the men on the 445 are always visible and merely change position, thereby lacking the element of surprise attendant to the sudden appearance of the gateman.

Whatever the reason, the 445 ran through only five holiday seasons. It was, explains the Lionel Service Manual, "first catalogued in 1952, but not built until the early part of 1953." The 1952 catalog showed what must have been the prototype. In that illustration, the tower has dark siding with white trim and the man on the stairs holds a flag instead of a lantern. The actual item produced was made with white siding and green trim.

One source of operating difficulty can be the 445-40 Tow Line that operates the man on the stairs. The tow line tends to wear a groove where it passes through a wall in the plastic house, causing sluggish movement. This can be alleviated by inserting a 259E-18 Eyelet in the wall and threading the tow tine through it.

445 Operating Switch Tower and packaging. Right: Box shows March 1953 date code. Except for OPS requirement in 1952, it was unusual for Lionel to print prices on accessory boxes.

	Gd	VG	Ex	LN

There are no significant variations known for the 445. However, there appears to be at least one way to identify very early production units. The Lionel Service Manual states, "The early production run of the 445 Switch Tower included a number of towers made with somewhat undersized plunger links which did not permit the plunger to enter far enough into the coil and thus caused the coil to overheat when used continuously for long periods of time. To prevent possible trouble the undersized link should be replaced whenever found. The old link measures approximately $^{13}\!/_{16}''$ and was generally nickel plated. The correct link is about $^{3}\!/_{32}''$ longer and is brass-colored."

Only one 445-55 instruction sheet, dated 1-53 (printed in black ink on white paper), is known. It shows various ways to electrically connect the tower to operate off any of the insulated rails on 022 switches. Normal activation is through the weight-actuated 145C Contactor included with new 445s. Dimensions: $6\frac{1}{4}''$ x $5\frac{1}{2}''$ wide, $7''$ high.

	35	50	60	90

455 OIL DERRICK, 1950–54

Back in the 1940s and '50s, bubble lights were popular items for Christmas trees. Perhaps these lights provided the inspiration for the 455 Oil Derrick. The bubbling pipe on the 455 is a glass tube partially filled with a light oil that has a relatively low boiling point. Activating the 364C Controller switch turns on the 151-51 lamp beneath the bubbling pipe, which nicely illuminates the glass pipe and supplies heat to the oil. As the oil warms, small vapor bubbles form and rise to the top, effectively creating the illusion of flowing oil. Meanwhile, driven by a solenoid and plunger mechanism controlled by a bimetallic switch, the "walking beam" on the pump starts to rock back and forth as if pumping the oil.

The operation of this accessory necessitated the change from the first 455-81 instruction sheet, dated 8-50, to the reissue dated 5-51 (both printed in black ink on white paper). Describing operation of the 455, the early version indicated that the walking beam and the simulated oil flow begin immediately after power was switched on. Probably in response to impatient customers, the second sentence was changed to read "[a] few minutes later, as soon as the heat of the lamp warms the liquid in the glass tube the liquid will start to bubble simulating the flow of oil." Not mentioned is the fact that it also takes time for the bimetallic switch to heat up and start the cycling action that makes the

Three variations of the 455 Operating Oil Derrick. The red top on right is thought to be later production, while the all-green version at left is the most common. Other paint variations, such as the pale green example in the center, are known. Note the original Sunoco signs with the legend, "OIL DERRICK No. 455." These hang on the tower (only one per tower) and are frequently missing. Sunoco billboards from 156, 157, and other platforms and reproduction billboards are often found in place of the original sign.

walking beam rock. A third instruction sheet, also printed in black ink on white paper, is dated 5-55.

Several interesting variations of the 455 appeared during the five years it was cataloged. Best known are the red-top and green-top versions. ("Top" refers to the 455-43 Platform Assembly at the top of the drilling rig.) The more colorful red top is somewhat less common and more desirable than the green. The 1950 and 1951 catalogs show a green top, which changes to a red one for the following three years. This sequence suggests that the green top was produced first, with the red introduced toward the end of production to make the accessory more appealing.

When dating a 455, look for changes that appear on the underside of the base. First, the 455-24 Lamp Housing Cover Assembly was initially produced without a reinforcing bead. Research examples have a slight bend at the outboard end of the snap clips used to keep the cover closed. It is not clear whether this bend occurred during production or resulted from the force required to open the cover. Nevertheless, Lionel did strengthen this part by adding a reinforcing bead stamped lengthwise in the lamp cover.

Check the tabs attaching the fulcrum for the walking beam at the center of the base underside. These tabs may be twisted (as are most of the other tabs that attach the tower) or bent over. Since the fulcrum is part of the 455-54 Motor and Pump Base Assembly, it may have been assembled separately. Most of the research examples have bent tabs, but more information is required before any reliable dating can be ascribed to this feature.

Note that the 455-67 Plunger Assembly has two end designs. On most, the wire passes through a hole in the plunger, which has a smooth bottom. Some, however, have an "X" slot in the bottom. The wire fits in either slot and is staked in place. This may have significance in dating the accessory or just be a modification initiated by the parts supplier. A pattern could not be discerned from the research examples. Similarly, no pattern has been observed in the color of the 455-74 Tension Nut on the speed-adjusting screw. Although most are silver, a blackened one is known to exist. The drilling rig tower is usually a glossy dark green. This tower color occurs with both red and matching green tops.

Several reported examples of the 455 have a red top and a decidedly pale, almost dull green tower. Rarer is a very pale tower with a matching top, slightly more yellowish than the shade used for the prewar Standard gauge Stephen Girard passenger cars. Recently, a 455 with a pale blue top and tower has been discovered! While quite collectible, these color variations seem to have been mid-run anomalies, probably due to paint mixing errors or batch variations. Finally, some 455s left the factory with no holes punched in the base for mounting the oil rig to a table. There are usually two holes at diagonally opposite corners of the base. Versions without holes may have been very early production.

The 455 was packaged in a box numbered 455-87. In 1950, this box had the golden anniversary year gold (actually orange) background label at each end. In 1951 and 1952, the box had only blue printing on it. Then in 1953 through 1955, "LIONEL TRAINS" appeared as unprinted cardboard through a blue background, while descriptive words are red, and there may or may not be a red border. If you are certain your 455 is in its original box, this information is useful in dating it.

Often missing is the 455-53 Billboard (Sunoco sign), which hooks onto the tower and was secured with only a piece of tape for shipping. It has been reproduced both accurately and inaccurately. In some cases, persons outside the factory have taken Sunoco billboards from the 156 and 157 Station Platforms and used them on the 455. The real sign has "OIL DERRICK No.455" on the bottom. But even this is no guarantee of authenticity. Another loose item that came with the Oil Derrick is the 455-23 Oil Drum. Four of these turned aluminum drums came with the accessory. Reproductions are available, but are not marked as such. The orange plastic 6520-17 Diesel Motor was borrowed from the 3520 Searchlight car and can be found mounted with the fuel tank on the right or left. Orange is the only correct color for the 455. Dimensions: 9⅞" x 5¾" base, 14" high.

	Gd	VG	Ex	LN

(A) Glossy dark green tower and matching top platform. The most common version and, based on catalog illustrations, likely the first production.

	Gd	VG	Ex	LN
(A)	135	160	205	265

(B) Glossy dark green tower with red top platform. Less common and more desirable than (A) but not scarce.

	Gd	VG	Ex	LN
(B)	150	175	240	295

(C) Pale, almost apple green tower, dull finish, with red top. A fairly rare item, this is probably the result of a paint error that was quickly corrected. Several examples of this and (D) are known to exist. Other variations, such as the recently discovered pale blue example, may exist and are NRS items.

	Gd	VG	Ex	LN
(C)	170	225	300	440

(D) Pale, almost Stephen Girard green, semi-gloss, with matching platform. A rare item that probably is also the result of a quickly corrected paint error or a pilot run of a rejected color.

	Gd	VG	Ex	LN
(D)	190	245	370	520

CHAPTER 3

Space and Military Accessories

Ready for Action! Here is Lionel's 347 Cannon Firing Range Set with five of the ten Multiple Products Corp. ("MPC, N.Y., N.Y.") soldiers that came with it when packaged in military sets such as the uncataloged no. 9820 set offered by Sears. Note that this is not the same MPC as Model Products Corp. of Michigan, which bought the rights to make Lionel trains in 1970.

Railroads were in a period of consolidation and decline long before October 4, 1957, when the Soviet Union launched the first of several Sputnik satellites. However, it seemed that almost overnight the focus of American youth shifted to the space age. Lionel was not oblivious to this change, and by 1958 it had military, space, and atomic energy items ready for the market.

175 ROCKET LAUNCHER, 1958–60

In terms of size and complexity, this is perhaps the most ambitious of Lionel's space and military accessories. Operating the 175 involves a combination of manual and remote control actions, all with the objective of moving a rocket from its delivery vehicle to a launch position. A manually operated boom atop the gantry can be pivoted 360 degrees to position the magnetic lifting hoist above the rocket, which is usually delivered by truck or railcar. A manual crank at the base of the boom allows for raising or lowering the boom to position the magnetic hoist closer to or farther from the launch tower. Finally, a second hand crank at the base of the boom allows for raising or lowering the magnetic hoist to a position where it sticks to the metal band on the rocket's nose. This metal band also serves to retain the rocket's foam "nose cone" that mitigates damage to the rocket, surrounding equipment, and the operator.

By manipulating the two hand cranks and manually rotating the boom, the rocket can be maneuvered from its prone position on the delivery vehicle to a vertical position on the launch pad, a task demanding patience and dexterity. Manual cocking of the spring-loaded plunger is required before transporting the rocket to the launch position. Operators quickly tire of this tedious process, so after a few attempts they are usually content to place the rocket in launch position by hand. Once the rocket is in launch position, pressing the "GANTRY" button on the 175's controller moves the gantry away from the launch platform, providing the only remote control part of launch preparation. A vibrating-armature motor supplies power to move the gantry back and forth along its rails. Since the motor runs in only one direction, the gantry must move to one end of the rails before it can start back in the opposite direction.

Before launching the rocket, the operator may set the countdown clock on the control panel. Moving the countdown lever sets the spring-operated mechanism to any desired time up to 10 seconds. This action also lights an L53 lamp, illuminating the "WARNING" message. Otherwise, the countdown timer has no connection to accessory operation. Pressing the "START" button begins the countdown. As Lionel's instructions stated, "The firing circuit is separate from the countdown circuit so that you can call for a last-second hold if the target area is not clear of personnel and equipment." The normal procedure is to fire the rocket just as the pointer reaches zero. At the operator's discretion, pressing the "FIRE" button on the control panel launches the rocket. Unfortunately, the rocket launcher was perhaps too complex and delicate for younger operators, and today this item is quite difficult to find complete and undamaged.

The tower of Lionel's 197 Rotating Radar Antenna, first released in 1957, became the basis for the 175's gantry tower. Previous use of this tower on the 197 probably contributed to Lionel's ability to quickly field as complex an accessory as the 175. Even though the 175 was discontinued after 1960, its control panel was resurrected in 1962 as the 413 Countdown Control Panel (minus illumination and the gantry button). Original foam padding in the nose of the 175-50 Rocket is prone to disintegrate over time. Be aware that excellent reproductions of the rocket are available. Interestingly, the Super-O-type rails used for the gantry are spaced 4½″ apart, just the right gauge for the 282 Gantry Crane.

197 Rotating Radar Antennas. Left: Gray platform and plated radar screen. Right: Earlier version with orange platform and later "argent" screen. M. Stephens Collection.

	Gd	VG	Ex	LN

A 6175 Flat Car with Rocket was usually pictured alongside the 175, but this car (which included a 175-50 Rocket) was not a part of the accessory package. Three instruction sheets have been reported for the 175, but only two have been confirmed. These are 175-69X (dated 10-58) and 175-69 (dated 6-59), both printed in blue ink on white paper. An "X" in a postwar instruction sheet number is unprecedented, and no explanation for it has been offered. Sheet X569-10, dated 11-60 (also printed in blue ink on white paper), has not been verified and would represent an unusual departure from Lionel's numbering system.

Excellent or Like New condition requires the presence of all pieces of this complex accessory. Gantry is often found with parts of its plastic structure cracked or missing. Dimensions: 11″ x 11″ base, 17″ high.

	Gd	VG	Ex	LN
	110	185	260	335

197 ROTATING RADAR ANTENNA, 1957–59

The 197 represented a truly new Lionel accessory, as nearly all the parts were made especially for it. In operation, the 197's radar antenna, powered by Lionel's Vibrotor, rotates at the top of the tower. This fragile item is usually missing the 197-24 Whip Antenna (which has been accurately reproduced and is unmarked as such). The rotating antenna is often broken, especially the horn. Examine the tower carefully, as the railings, latticework, and bracing are frequently cracked or broken. Lionel, always seeking to maximize use of its expensive tooling, used the 197's

base and tower in the 192 Operating Control Tower. The tower showed up in the 175 Rocket Launcher.

There are two notable variations of this accessory. In 1957, the upper platform was orange, and in 1958 it was changed to gray. Perhaps the change occurred in later 1957 production, as the orange platform is somewhat harder to find. For an item that ran for only three years, the first year usually has the largest production run. Three facts support the conjecture that orange was first: (1) orange is the predominant color for catalog illustrations of the 197, (2) only the cover of the 1958 catalog and a single appearance in the 1959 catalog show the gray variation, and (3) the window box debuted in 1958, and all examples observed new in this box are the gray-platform versions.

In addition, early versions with the orange platform usually have a chrome (actually vacuum metalized) finish, while later-production models have a painted "argent" (dull silver) color. This change provided a definite cost savings for Lionel. Since antennas can be easily changed, it is difficult to date a 197 by this part. It appears that the changes in platform color and antenna finish were not done concurrently.

Two instruction sheets are known to exist for the 197, both with part number 197-31. The first, dated 9-57, is 6¼″ by 9½″ and printed in bright blue ink on white paper. The second, dated 6-58, is 5½″ by 8½″ and printed in dark blue ink on white paper. Two changes were made in the text. First, a note about the grommets used as "feet" on the base was added to the 6-58 version. It cautioned that the groove around the circumference of the grommet was off-center, so that all four grommets should be installed with the offset in the same direction to keep the tower level. The 192, introduced this same year, forgot the grommet installation entirely and had to have a supplementary sheet that did not mention the offset. This suggests that grommet variations may exist: centered and offset grooves!

A second change relates to a note in the 9-57 instruction sheet, which says to disregard the listing of a driving slug on the small parts envelope because that part was factory-installed. This note does not appear in the 6-58 instructions. A new 1958-59 version of the 197 does not mention this slug on its accompanying 197-30 small parts envelope. Checking a new 1957 example revealed the same 197-30 envelope, but with the entry, "1 No. 197-12 DRIVING SLUG" blocked out.

Those 197s produced in 1957 came in a Classic box with part number 197-32, while 1958 production came in the first of the window boxes, part number 197-45. Dimensions: 3″ x 4¼″ base, 12″ high.

(A) 1957, orange upper platform, somewhat harder to find than gray, so this color may not have run a full model year. Usually found with a shiny chrome (actually vacuum metalized) radar antenna.

	Gd	VG	Ex	LN
	60	90	120	175

(B) 1958–59, gray upper platform. Usually found with a duller silver-painted radar antenna. Doubtful that the change in platform color coincided with the change in antenna finish (chrome finish likely went first).

	Gd	VG	Ex	LN
	50	70	90	120

199 MICROWAVE RELAY TOWER, 1958–59

This accessory is simply an adaptation of the 195 Floodlight Tower. In operation, one red lens atop the tower blinks on and off to warn approaching aircraft, while the clear lenses in the center of each of the two antennas blink to simulate microwave transmissions.

To construct the 199, the 195 tower top platform was modified to include two narrow rectangular slots so that the antenna housing could be attached. This housing contains a special L402 flashing bulb that illuminates the three lenses. The base is the same as the 195, but has "199 MICROWAVE TOWER" molded in raised letters on the underside. One 199-14 instruction sheet is known, dated 10-58 and printed in black ink on white paper. Dimensions: 3¼″ x 3¼″ base, 16″ high.

(A) Black plastic base.   **30**   **50**   **75**   **105**

(B) Tan plastic base. This base usually came with the 195, but some examples were molded in tan while the mold still had the 199 nomenclature installed. M. Rubin Collection. See entry (B) for 195 in Chapter 6.   **30**   **50**   **75**   **105**

299 CODE TRANSMITTER SET, 1961–63

The Code Transmitter set consists of a 299-25 Telegraph Key and 299-50 Beacon Tower. The key device includes a buzzer that sounds whenever the key is pressed. If the tower is connected to the key, the beacon lights and the buzzer sounds simultaneously. If the tower is connected directly to transformer power without the key, the special L402 bulb flashes. Operators complained that a slow keying rate warmed the bulb enough to cause it to flash on its own and consequently garble the coded message. (Lionel dutifully responded with a service bulletin entry telling Service Stations to substitute a steadily illuminated bulb for those customers.)

The key device has three electrical connection clips on the bottom and, on top, a silver label with the Morse Code printed in black. The 299 is the last of three accessories to share basic parts of the 195. For this adaptation, the top platform of the tower was modified to include two ears that stick up to stabilize the beacon bracket and allow it to rotate manually.

The 299 came in an orange paperboard window box that, like that for the 192, was too flimsy for the size and weight of its contents. So an original box in decent condition is scarce. Dimensions: 3¼″ x 3¼″ base, 11¾″ high.

    70   **100**   **130**   **175**

347 CANNON FIRING RANGE SET, uncataloged 1964

This is a rare and unusual accessory adapted from existing Lionel hardware and then offered exclusively as part of uncataloged department-store and other specialty sets. Each of the four cannon barrels has its own firing mechanism, which is set prior to use. After placing a shell in each cocked cannon, the operator manually rotates the firing wheel, causing the shells to fire in succession.

The 347 borrows the superstructure from the 6544 Missile Firing Trail Car, but substitutes a cannon for each missile launcher. The same launcher was used in the 448 Missile Firing Range set for three years prior to the introduction of the 347. Modifications applied to create the 347 included a plastic molded bank of cannon barrels fitted over the missile launcher, a revised storage rack to hold projectiles instead of rockets, and a change in plastic color to olive drab.

A new 199 Microwave Relay Tower showing the minimal interior packaging together with the loose packed wire and instruction sheet. J. Algozzini Collection.

299 Code Transmitter Set included a key device (right) to transmit coded messages. Special bulb in tower (left) flashes on its own if powered continuously. J. Algozzini Collection.

	Gd	VG	Ex	LN

This unique accessory needed new ammunition. Apparently, the ordnance engineer for the 347 did not communicate with his counterparts on the 6651 U.S.M.C. Cannon Car and the 3666 Minuteman Car projects, as each of the three cannons introduced in 1964-65 used a different caliber shell. While similar in appearance, they are not interchangeable, thus creating three different service parts. For the 347, the silver-painted wood shells are .175″ in diameter and 1.9″ long.

The Sears 9820 military set included a 347, as did at least one other uncataloged set. Also, 1964 may not have been the only year the 347 was available. These sets also came with 10 or 12 soft plastic soldiers and a cheap military vehicle (tank, truck, and so forth). Lionel purchased these plastic items from outside companies. Payton Plastics made the vehicles, which it also sold as bagged toys in dime stores. Although Payton also made vinyl soldiers, they were not the ones packaged in these uncataloged sets. According to Donald Simonini, those soldiers were manufactured by Multiple Products Corp. They can be identified by a tiny circular logo on the bottom of their bases. Lionel did not use the readily available Payton soldiers probably because they looked so bad!

Only the rare instruction sheet 347-10, dated 8/64 and printed in black ink on white paper, is known. This is a small folded sheet printed on both sides, with the entire center spread of one side devoted to a picture of the 347 in action. Dimensions: 8″ x 4½″ base, 2½″ high. **150   300   450   575**

419 Heliport with correct 3419-100 all-yellow helicopter. Left: Late and most common version of the gray Navy 'copter with single rotor. Right: Non-operating 'copter had tip pods and came with 6819 flatcar. Flying overhead is the earliest 'copter with two rotors. All gray versions had separate tail rotor; yellow one was always one piece.

419 HELIPORT, 1962

The 419 Heliport Control Tower was billed in the Lionel catalog as the "dual-purpose terminal of tomorrow." Probably a coincidence, but the roof of the 419 was approximately as high as the tallest trestles in the 110 Trestle set. Lionel's marketing personnel latched on to this and quickly classified the 419 as a unique railroad and heliport terminal. A passenger train traversing the adjacent elevated portion of a pike could be halted at roof level, where imaginary passengers could walk the few steps to the waiting helicopter and be whisked off to their next destination.

For a "terminal of tomorrow," the 419's mechanical remote control was disappointing. Not since the days of manual control O42 switches had Lionel suggested using string and eyelets as a remote control mechanism. But this is what is required to remotely launch the helicopter from the roof of the control tower! Turning the winder dial on the roof tightens the spring mechanism inside the tower. Then, with the helicopter mounted on the launcher, the operator manually pulls the ring protruding from the base, which releases the spring and launches the helicopter.

Four accessories were made from the basic structure used in the 419. The first was the 465 Sound Dispatching Station of 1956-57. Then came the little-known 365 Dispatching Station in 1958-59, the 419 in 1962, and the 5160 Official Viewing Stand for the slot-car line in 1963. Lionel got some mileage out of its investment in the molds. However, judging by their short runs, none of these accessories were very popular.

No significant variations of the 419 have been reported. Only one instruction sheet, 419-24, dated 7-62, is known. Printed on both sides in black ink on white paper, it uses an 8½″ by 5½″ sheet folded in half to make a four-page instruction sheet. These instructions, along with several others, have been reproduced without being marked as such. The reproduction paper is too white, the ink too bright, and the crossbar of the "H" in "Heliport" has a break the first three times the word appears. The original 419-16 box is always solid orange with black lettering and uses a lift-up lid that opens on the long side.

Reproductions of most parts, some not properly marked, are available. Excellent or Like New condition requires all the original small parts that came with this accessory. This rare accessory came with a solid yellow 3419-100 Helicopter with an integral tail rotor, although any of Lionel's operating helicopters will work. The 3419-100 was evidently a cost-reduced version, as it lacks the heat-stamped markings and door outline found on earlier models. Instead, only the window openings and a door outline were molded in on each side. It is apparent that Lionel used a new helicopter mold or an extensive modification of the original, as there are several other differences. The rotor is a single black blade without tip pods.

The 3419-100 Helicopter is very delicate, especially its tail rotor. Since the 3419-100 is one piece, a broken tail ruins the entire helicopter from a collector's viewpoint. Examples occur where a broken tail assembly has been cut off and replaced, sometimes with a reproduction tail (usually not marked as such). Some helicopters may have a thick lower tail rotor blade. In these rare examples, the upper blade is normal, but the mold was changed to make the lower blade nearly three times normal thickness and extend it so that a small bridge of plastic connects to the outer skid. Original yellow helicopters have "BUILT BY/LIONEL" molded in raised letters on the right side of the tail skid. The earlier, separate tail design had these words on the left side. A description of Lionel's helicopters appears in the first volume of *Greenberg's Guide to Lionel Trains, 1945–1969.* Dimensions: 11″ x 5″ base, 5½″ high.

	Gd	VG	Ex	LN
	155	255	360	460

443 MISSILE LAUNCHING PLATFORM WITH EXPLODING AMMO DUMP, 1960–62

Advertised as "new" in 1960, the 443 is a combination of components introduced in 1959. It is a 470 Missile Launching Platform repackaged to include a 943 Exploding Ammunition Dump instead of a 6470 Exploding Target Car. To annihilate the spring-loaded, exploding ammo dump (or any other target), the operator cocks the firing mechanism and depresses the launch

The 443 (shown with its packaging) is identical to the 470, except for a box liner that holds the exploding ammunition dump instead of the boxcar.

arm to the down and locked position, then positions the missile on the launcher, rotates it to the desired direction, and presses the firing lever. A spring, whose quick action is damped by an air diaphragm, slowly raises the launch arm. When the arm reaches the fully elevated position, a linkage trips the launch mechanism and fires the missile. See the 470 listing below for a note about the launch mechanism.

The base used on the 443 retained the 470 designation molded in the underside. There may be several original assembly combinations of the 6650-80 Missile, which was constructed in two sections, each of which was molded in white or red. Only an all-red combination of the missile parts has never been observed as original, although it is easily made. A blue rubber "nose cone" is typical for these rockets, although a few have been observed with a red tip. There are no significant variations. Refer to the listings of the 470 and the 943 for additional comments.

Since there was really nothing new in the operation of the 443, Lionel included one of the two known instruction sheets from the 470 Missile Launching Platform, both with part number 470-5 and dated 9/59. One is printed in black ink on white paper; the other is printed in blue. The original box, part number 443-6, is orange with black and white lettering. The box interior packing varies from the 470 to accommodate the 943 rather than the 6470. Dimensions: 11″ x 12″ base, 5″ high to tip of raised empty launcher.

	Gd	VG	Ex	LN
	15	25	36	75

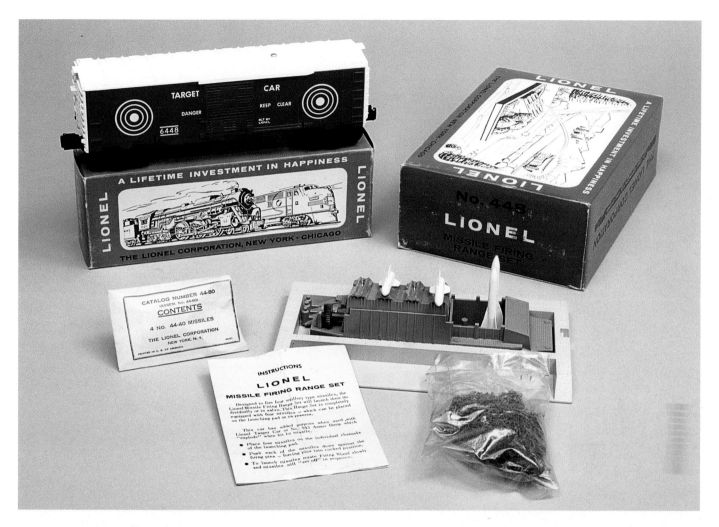

448 MISSILE FIRING RANGE SET, 1961–63

This accessory represents yet another example of Lionel's ability to combine existing items to create new offerings. Aside from the box and instruction sheet, the 448 required only one new part, the 448-3 Base. Each missile cradle has its own firing mechanism. After cocking each launcher and placing a missile in each cradle, the operator turns the firing wheel, causing the missiles to launch in succession. With a good hit or two, the missiles cause the spring-loaded Target Range Boxcar to "explode."

The 448 launcher was borrowed from the 6544 Missile Firing Trail Car, which in turn borrowed the firing mechanism and rockets from the 44 Mobile Missile Launcher. Although Lionel never produced a 448 with a figure, both catalog and instruction sheet illustrations display a man at the control panel. In the Lionel Service Manual, the control panel is shown with dials and gauges identical to those on the 6544. However, no such example has been reported. Eliminating the heat stamping of control panel graphics was likely done to minimize expenses, though this creates an opportunity to concoct a variation that is probably not a factory original. The 6544 is known with black and white heat-stamped graphics on the console. Since the whole launcher assembly just snaps in place, it is a simple matter to create a no-graphics version of the 6544 and a white or black version of the 448, none of which has been observed as original.

The 448 is not common, especially in an original 448-7 Orange Picture box. One 448-6 instruction sheet is known, dated

A brand-new 448 Missile Firing Range Set with all the trimmings! Note the blank control panel on the launcher, unmarked bag of lichen, and sealed bag of four rockets. Extra rockets were used to pose the picture. The 6448 Exploding Box Car came in at least two color schemes and was packed in its own box inside the 448 box.

	Gd	VG	Ex	LN

8-61 and printed in dark brown ink on blue-green paper. This sheet measures 5½" by 8½" and is folded to a four-page, 5½" by 4¼" size. The centerfold is an illustration of the 448 in action. A complete set has an unmarked, plastic 448-5 Bag of Shrubbery (lichen) to camouflage the platform and a 6448 Exploding Target Range Car packed in its own Orange Picture box inside the set box. Dimensions: 5½" x 9⅛" base, 2⅛" high without missiles.

	75	105	135	175

470 MISSILE LAUNCHING PLATFORM, 1959–62

The predecessor of the 443, this is the fixed-base version of the 6650 IRBM Launcher, also introduced in 1959. The launching mechanism and missiles used on the fixed and mobile launchers are identical. Only the box number, the 6470 Exploding Box Car instead of a 943 Exploding Ammunition Dump, and the single interior packing strip distinguish the 443 from the 470. For a description of this accessory's operation and variations in the 6650-80 Missile, see the 443 listing.

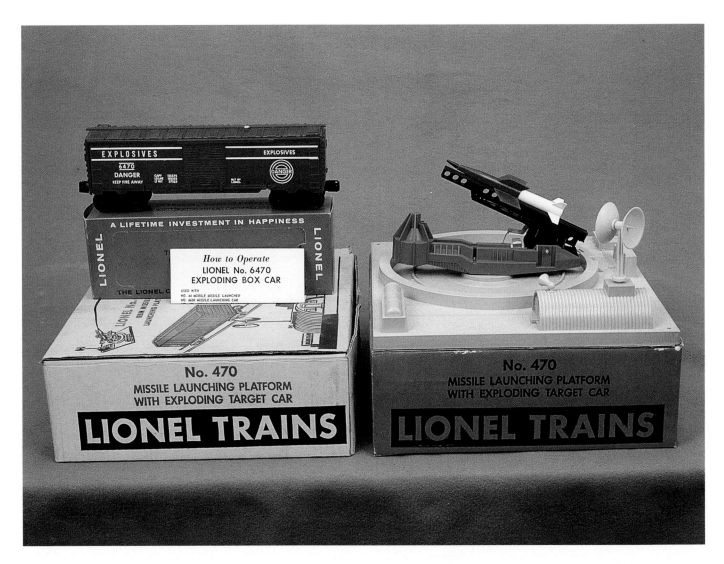

	Gd	VG	Ex	LN

There is one note of particular interest concerning all of Lionel's IRBM launchers. As a result of a hardened rubber diaphragm, which was designed to slow the movement of the launcher from the stowed to the firing position, these launchers do not always operate as they should. The diaphragm, along with the spring used to raise the mechanism, is housed in the counterweight detail on the end opposite the firing button. The diaphragm is a bellows that traps air and slowly releases it so the spring does not pop the launcher into firing position too quickly. As the rubber hardens and the spring weakens with age, many launchers fail to rise far enough to trip the firing mechanism.

There are two known 470-5 instruction sheets, both dated 9-59 and printed on white paper. One uses black ink, and the other uses blue ink. The 470 came in a yellow box in 1959 and an orange box in 1960-62. A complete set included a 6650-80 Missile and 6470 Exploding Box Car packed in its own box inside the 470 box. Dimensions: 11″ x 12″ base, 5″ high to tip of raised empty launcher. **105   130   155   180**

910 ATOMIC SUBMARINE BASE, uncataloged 1961

When found new, the pieces are packaged in a large, lightweight paper bag with faint stripes in the paper. Printed on one observed example of this bag are: "Ignore the layout shown on the enclosed instruction sheet." In this example, the set contained a second layout instruction sheet (mentioned below). Like the 908 Railroad Station with Ramp and Underpass described in Chapter 4, the 910 was also packaged in a heavy Kraft paper bag meant to be included with sets packaged in small cardboard boxes that would not accommodate the large bag.

The stamped and scored pieces of the 910 require assembly into a large cardboard structure that simulates a submarine base. Its ramp elevates a train as it runs through a cardboard "bridge," around the rear of a simulated lagoon with three cardboard submarines, back through the tall base structure, and off the ramp to floor level. Shown in the undated 10″ by 10″ instruction sheet (black ink on white paper), "HOW TO SET UP YOUR LIONEL ATOMIC SUBMARINE BASE," is a suggested layout with a 45-degree crossing at floor level in front of the ramp. A floor-level continuation of the track makes a loop around the back of the base. The 910 is the same size and construction as the 908.

At least two uncataloged sets included the gigantic submarine base: X-625 with a 228 Canadian National locomotive and

	Gd	VG	Ex	LN

X-714 with a 45 U.S. Marines Mobile Missile Launcher. A "SPECIAL LAYOUT INSTRUCTIONS" sheet 1802H, dated 5-59, shows how to assemble the track, but the other maintenance and layout instructions included are dated 1961. This and the existence of a newspaper ad for set X-714 from November 1961 date the set. Dimensions: 27¾″ x 30″ base, 17½″ high.

NRS

943 AMMO DUMP, 1959–61

Resembling a glorified mousetrap in a box, this accessory almost surely lost money for Lionel. Every part of the 943 Ammo Dump was new and unique. With the cost of tooling for injection-molded parts and unique stamped-metal pieces, the volume, just to break even, would have been far greater than the 943 seems to have achieved.

Besides the base and mousetrap mechanism, there are four olive drab plastic pieces to this accessory. The largest piece, forming one side and the roof, is labeled "A", while the other side is labeled "B." The two end pieces are identical, except that one has white heat-stamped lettering identifying the accessory. These ends are not labeled. A hit on either side or the roof deflects the assembly enough to spring the trap and scatter the pieces about.

The uncataloged 910 Submarine Base. This all-cardboard item is one of the rarest accessories included in a Lionel set.

	Gd	VG	Ex	LN

This accessory is fairly scarce, partly because the four parts are easily separated, lost, or discarded. It was always packaged in a picture box common to that era, even when included in the set box with the 443 Missile Launching Platform. This was necessary to keep all the pieces together, since it was packaged disassembled. There is no safety pin arrangement to hold it in the assembled position, as there is with the exploding boxcars. However, there is a safety pin to secure the spring mechanism while cocking it to prevent the operator's fingers from being accidentally pinched.

The 943 has two instruction sheets, both with part number 943-11 and dated 9/59. The first uses blue ink on white paper, and the second uses black ink on white paper. They measure 5½″ by 8½″ and are folded to make four pages. Dimensions: 3″ x 4″ base, 4″ high when assembled.

	25	35	45	60

CHAPTER 4

Stations

Perhaps the most magnificent of Lionel's postwar stations was the 115 Lionel City Station, whose roots go back to the prewar era. This accessory did not have any major postwar variations. F. Merriman Collection.

In railroading today, a train often appears only as a bright, oncoming headlight in the distance or as a blur as we watch it from the railroad crossing. Of the few conventional places to witness the full power, size, sounds, and operations of the railroad, perhaps there is none better than from a station platform.

Like those of yesteryear, Lionel's stations represent the confluence of numerous railroad activities. An approaching train slows to a stop in front of a 132 Automatic Station, just long enough for imaginary passengers and freight to load and unload. Farther along the platform, a 356 Operating Freight Station seemingly transfers baggage and freight between trackside and the station. The warning voice of the station dispatcher bellows from a 465 Sound Dispatching Station as the train prepares for departure. Preceded by a short blast of the horn, the train slowly pulls past a 114 Newsstand With Horn, on its way to the next stop at a distant 157 Station Platform.

In this chapter, collectors and operators alike will find plenty of intriguing variations among Lionel's wide variety of stations and trackside accessories.

114 Newsstand With Horn (left) and 118 Newsstand With Whistle, each with its original box. J. Algozzini Collection.

	Gd	VG	Ex	LN

114 NEWSSTAND WITH HORN, 1957–59

Following typical Lionel practice, the 114 and 118 make use of the same basic parts to create two different accessories. Although the 114-55 horn is the same Delta bicycle horn used in Lionel's diesel locomotives, it was given a unique part number as a result of its mounting design. Like the diesel locomotive horn, the 114-55 requires a 1.5-volt D battery to operate. As with any device that uses a battery, there is potential for leakage and battery acid damage. Transformer power is required for only the L53 interior illumination lamp. Each 114 included a 90 Controller for pushbutton operation of the horn, but the instructions explain how to use a 145C Contactor under the track for activation as a train passes.

This accessory is somewhat hard to find complete and in good condition. The poster signs, simulated hedge, window glass, and even the removable roof are often missing. Excellent or Like New requires all original parts, many of which have been expertly reproduced and, being small, not marked as such. One version of the 114-32 instruction sheet is known, dated 8-57 and printed in brown ink on yellow paper. Dimensions: 8″ x 7″ base, 3¼″ high.

	50	85	120	160

115 LIONEL CITY STATION, 1935–42 and 1946–49

Made almost entirely of stamped and formed sheet metal, this is a large accessory, but it is not to scale by any means. It is just too small for the grandeur it tries to depict. Yet this colorful station is popular among collectors and operators alike. Chronologically, the 115 began in 1931 as the 112 Station, which was available in three color combinations during its five catalog appearances (ending in 1935). The 112 had no front "porch" lights, but from 1931 to 1934 a version (the 113) was offered with two gold lighting brackets. In 1935, the 115 with silver porch lights and the new automatic train-control feature replaced the 113. An economy version without the porch lights and train-control device (the 117 replacing the 112) was cataloged between 1936 and 1942. All of these stations were marked by a black rubber-stamping on the bottom giving the Lionel nomenclature and the item's catalog number. Only the 115 was cataloged after the war.

Lionel's train-control feature is a device concealed in the interior of a 115 to automatically stop passing trains, detain them for an adjustable period, and send them on their way. It uses an inexpensive and reliable heated bimetallic strip to accomplish this control. A length of track next to the station, usually three or four sections long, must have its center rail electrically insulated by use of fiber pins at each end. When a train enters this section of track, the center rail is "dead" and the train coasts to a stop. But station wiring is such that a small current (not enough to move the locomotive) can now flow through the high-resistance heater wire (wound around the bimetallic strip) and through the locomotive motor to the outside rails.

The strip is composed of two dissimilar metals with different coefficients of expansion, so heating causes it to bend. With the small current flow through the heater winding and the locomotive motor, heating takes a little time. As a result, the train remains stopped until the strip bends sufficiently to close an electrical contact, energizing the center rail and allowing the train to proceed. By moving the lever atop the station (underneath the removable skylight), an operator can adjust the distance the bimetallic strip must bend before restarting the train. Decreasing this distance to zero allows for continuous operation.

So the length of time the train remains in the station can be adjusted from nothing to about a minute. Of course the locomotive's E-unit must be disconnected with the engine running in the forward direction for this to work.

The station's interior is illuminated by one L432 interior light. Two specially shaped 1442(W) white, frosted bulbs thread into silver-painted die-cast housings on either side of the main entryway. This is the only known Lionel item with silver-painted parts where the silver (which used aluminum diverted to wartime aircraft production) was not changed to gray for 1942. Since it had already been in production for seven years, the 115 probably was not produced in 1942. Electrical connections to the station are provided through three binding posts.

Often missing from 115s offered for sale is the original stamped-metal skylight. Reproductions, usually unmarked, are available. Original stations have Lionel Corp. nomenclature and station number rubber-stamped in black on the underside of the base. Instruction sheets start with 115-116 (dated 6-35), which the 115 shared with the 116. There followed a series of 115-2 sheets dated 5-36, 3-37, 3-39, 10-40, 4-41, and 3-46 on light blue paper with dark blue ink. Issues of 8-48, 3-49, and 3-50 are on white paper with black ink. The latter two also covered the 132 Station (new in 1949 and identical in operation to the 115). Dimensions: 13⅝″ x 9¼″ base, 8½″ high.

	170	240	310	475

118 NEWSSTAND WITH WHISTLE, 1957–58

The 118 is almost identical to the 114 and shares all the basic parts, including an L53 lamp for interior illumination. Instead of the 114's horn, the 118 contains a conventional Lionel WS-250 Whistle. Except for the relay and mounting, the whistle is identical to those usually found in steam locomotive tenders. A 90 Controller was originally supplied to complete the whistle circuit, but a 145C or 153C Contactor can be substituted to automatically sound the whistle as the train passes. Many of the 118's parts, like those of the 114, have been reproduced and usually are not marked as such. Two 118-14 instruction sheets are known, each dated 8-57. One is printed in brown ink on yellow paper, and the other is printed on dark blue ink on white paper. Dimensions: 8″ x 7″ base, 3¼″ high.

	45	75	100	125

125 WHISTLE SHACK, 1950–55

The 125 shares its house, roof, and toolbox cover with the 145 Automatic Gateman. Since it is not illuminated, only two fahnestock clips, located under the lift-off roof, are required for electrical connections. Examples have surfaced with three electrical connections and an interior lamp, but these were undoubtedly meant as 145s that somehow were mistakenly assembled as 125s. It was not like Lionel to give away a feature they didn't advertise! In any case, it would be easy to make an illuminated 125 by simply adding the necessary standard parts.

Whistles for the 125s are identical to those used in tenders with the horizontal version of the whistle, such as the 2046W. Missing is the relay, since a 96C Controller (later replaced by the 90 Controller) was furnished to activate the whistle directly. As with the 114 and 118, a 145C or 153C Contactor can be used to activate the whistle as the train passes by. Instead of using threaded studs and nuts, as was done on the tenders, Lionel

Two different base colors, roof colors, and boxes for the 125 Whistle Shack. Other base variations include a darker, duller green and a light gray.

mounted the whistle to the 125 using double-sided tape. Since the tape is constantly supporting the fairly hefty weight of the whistle, some 125s are found with the motor loose, attached only by the wires! If you have a 125 in long-term storage, it might be best to store it upside down.

Roofs are known in red and maroon molded plastic, both unpainted. Red roofs are somewhat difficult to find. For unknown reasons, the toolbox cover is always red and did not follow the roof's change to maroon. Bases for the 125 are known in four distinct molded plastic colors: dark gray, light gray, bright green, and a darker, grass green.

The boxes Lionel used for this accessory changed over the years, which aids in dating particular color combinations. According to Thomas Rollo, dark gray bases were first and are most common. Then came the bright green base, the dark green, and, starting about 1953, the light gray, which continued until the end of production. As with many items, the last catalog year was not necessarily a production year. Items that dealers had in good supply were commonly cataloged to keep them "current" while stock was being depleted.

Instruction sheets also help in dating 125 variations. Three are known, all printed in black ink on white paper. For dates of 8-50 and 4-53, the instruction sheet part number is 125-12. For the issue of 4-55, the sheet number changed to 125-23 and a 90 Controller is shown in place of a 96C. Dimensions: 6″ x 6″ base, 5″ high.

(A) 1950. Dark gray base, red or maroon roof. Box with blue lettering on orange background, instruction sheet dated 8-50.

	17	25	42	55

(B) 1951. Bright green translucent base, maroon roof. Box with only blue printing that may have an OPS (Office of Price Stabilization) price on a white sticker; instruction sheet dated 8-50. Note that the stick-on OPS prices were applied to existing stock, no matter how old, on hand at the dealer when the Fair Trade regulations became effective in 1951.

	20	30	50	65

132 and 133 Passenger Stations. Note the different colors of the chimneys. The LIONELVILLE sign is missing from the 132 shown. J. Algozzini Collection.

(C) 1952. Dark green opaque base, maroon roof. Box with blue printing and OPS pricing printed directly onto box, instruction sheet dated 8-50. T. Rollo reports an example with factory-installed light bulb and third fahnestock clip.

	Gd	VG	Ex	LN
	20	30	50	65

(D) 1953–55. Light gray base, maroon roof. Box with red and blue printing, instruction sheet dated 4-53 or 4-55.

	17	25	42	55

132 PASSENGER STATION, 1949–55

This all-plastic structure's interior is illuminated by an L431 lamp. All are equipped with an automatic train stop feature, the operation of which is described in the 115 listing above. Access to the adjustment lever for the stop feature is gained by lifting off the dark green molded roof. Of interest is the fact that a dark green molded chimney painted reddish-brown adorns the roof of all original 132s. Although interchangeable with the roof from the 133 (described below), that accessory was always supplied with a molded green unpainted chimney, matching the roof color. Electrical connections to the 132 are by means of three fahnestock clips on the underside of the base.

Since the train control mechanisms in the 115 and 132 are identical, these stations shared the 115-2 instruction sheets dated 3-49 and 3-50. Perhaps Lionel intended to carry the 115 into 1950, but it did not appear in the catalog. After that, 132 had its own 132-55 sheets dated 1-51 and 3-54. Of interest is that the 115-2 sheet of 3-46 covered the 115, 132, and 137 stations, three years before 132 was introduced! In 1949 and 1950, 115 and 132 shared a parts envelope. Dimensions: 12⅛" x 8¼" base, 6½" high.

	45	75	105	140

133 PASSENGER STATION 1957, 1961–62, 1966

Identical to 132, except as noted. The same L431 lamp illuminates the interior, but the train stop feature was removed. Only two fahnestock clips on the underside of the base are required for electrical connections. The version produced in 1966 has a smaller LIONELVILLE sign (part 145-25) than that used on previous versions (part 132-31). The older sign, framed in gold, fills the space provided, while the smaller sign used in 1966 is identical to that used on the 125 Whistle Shack and 145 Automatic Gateman.

The 1966 version came in an all-white box lettered in orange. Four 133-7 instruction sheets are known. The first two are dated 5-57: one printed in blue ink on white paper, the other in brown ink on yellow paper. The last two sheets, dated 5-61, and 5/66, are printed in black ink on white paper. Dimensions: 12⅛" x 8¼" base, 6½" high.

	Gd	VG	Ex	LN
	30	55	80	110

137 PASSENGER STATION, 1937–42 and 1946

Although pictured in the 1946 catalog, this lithographed metal station was not manufactured after World War II. The price list accompanying the 1946 consumer catalog verifies this. For a description of this item, see the third volume of *Greenberg's Guide to Lionel Trains, 1901–1942*.

These prewar and postwar 156 Station Platforms show base and roof color variations and some of the different signs. Upper left: 1942 version with gray-painted posts and blackened roof finials (note paint flaking on lighter green base). Below: Postwar versions with silver-painted posts and nickel-plated finials. The fence connecting them came in the envelope shown. All signs were identical on both sides except for the innermost one advertising Lionel Construction Sets.

	Gd	VG	Ex	LN

156 STATION PLATFORM, 1939–42 and 1946-49

This station, with its rigid Bakelite roof and base, was designed for rural station stops and for use in conjunction with regular stations, such as the 115 and 132. Includes four, two-image lithographed metal billboard-type signs that fold over and hook to the plastic fence sections between the uprights. All signs, except the one on the prewar version advertising Lionel Construction Sets, are identical on both sides. Two L50 screw-base 6- to 8-volt lamps connected in series illuminate the platform.

Besides the gray-painted uprights for 1942, the base for that year only is painted a decidedly more yellow shade of green than normal. This paint did not adhere well, so most examples of the 1942 version are flaked. Blackened finials, rather than the usual nickel-plated ones, attach the roof to this one-year version on most examples observed. For all versions of 156, the tops of the fence pickets are often found broken. Included with new 156s was a manila envelope containing an additional 156-5 fence section used to bridge the gap when two platforms are used side by side. Values shown are for stations with more common billboards. Less common billboards can easily double the value. Dimensions: 12″ x 3¼″ base, 5⅛″ high.

	Gd	VG	Ex	LN
	35	55	75	110

157 STATION PLATFORM, 1952–55 and 1958–59

Like the 156, this platform was designed for intermediate station stops and as an adjunct to larger stations. Instead of Bakelite, the 157 used less expensive and more flexible injection-molded plastic. Posts are still die-cast, but are chemically blackened rather than painted. Two L51 bulbs (6 to 8 volts) wired in series provide platform illumination.

As with the 156, four miniature billboards adorn the two fence sections and an additional 156-5 fence section was furnished for use with adjoining platforms. At least 11 different billboards exist for this particular platform, but none is as scarce as some found on the 156. Dimensions: 12″ x 3¼″ base, 5⅛″ high.

(A) Maroon base, somewhat more common than red base. Usually found without a black fiberboard mask under the roof, but examples have been noted with the mask, although they may not be original.

	Gd	VG	Ex	LN
	20	30	42	55

(B) Red base, darker green roof. Thought to be 1958-59 production. Roof of more translucent plastic requires thin black fiberboard mask underneath so it doesn't "glow" during night viewing. Some have been noted without mask, but it may have been omitted when the roof was removed during post-factory maintenance.

	Gd	VG	Ex	LN
	25	40	60	75

256 FREIGHT STATION, 1950–53

Designed as a wayside freight/passenger facility, the 256 includes one 256-10 picket fence section, identical in construction to the 156-5 used on the 156 but longer. Three lithographed billboards (Baby Ruth, Rival Dog Food, and Sunoco) from the 156 adorn this fence. Illumination is provided by two L363 bulbs, which receive power through two fahnestock clips on the underside of the base.

157 Station Platforms with different bases and boxes. In place of the Bakelite base and roof on the 156, the 157 used more flexible injection-molded plastic. Platforms with red bases usually have a fiberboard light shield under the roof. Fence in envelope can be used to connect 157s placed side by side.

The 256 Freight Station offered color and interest to operators, though it did not have any animated features.

An unusual 257 with light green roof and brown base instead of the usual dark green and maroon. Examples are known with these odd colors separately. P. Ambrose Collection.

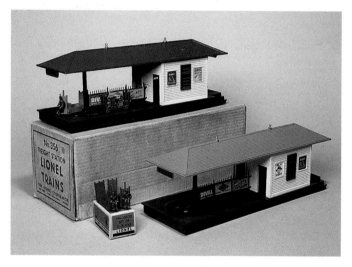

Variations of the 356 Operating Freight Station. Note unusual light green roof on lower station and lithographed baggage load on upper green cart. Bulletin board posters came in envelope and were applied by operator. J. Algozzini Collection.

	Gd	VG	Ex	LN

The 1950 and 1951 catalogs imply that this accessory did not come with adhesive posters for the station house since they state, "Inset bulletin boards where you can post your own schedules." Also, no posters are shown in the catalog illustrations. However, 1952-53 versions did include adhesive posters for the bulletin boards: 256-35 Airex, 256-36 U.S. Savings Bonds, 256-37 Airex, 256-38 Red Cross, 256-39 Be a Scout, and 256-40 Community Chest. These posters and two 81-32 Connecting Wires were furnished in a 256-42 manila envelope. Input from owners of new, original 256s from 1950-51 is solicited. Dimensions: 15" x 5" base, 5½" high.

(A) Common dark green molded roof.

	25	35	50	65

(B) Rare lighter, "Kelly green" roof. Roofs of 256, 257, and 356 are identical and can be interchanged.

	35	70	125	175

	Gd	VG	Ex	LN

257 FREIGHT STATION WITH DIESEL HORN, 1956–57

Similar to the 256 but includes a battery-powered horn. Complete unit must include a full set of six adhesive posters for the bulletin boards, the same as with 256. Be sure correct station number is molded into the underside of the base, as it can otherwise be made interchangeable with the base of the more common 256. As with any battery-powered unit, avoid those with battery damage.

New stations included a 90 Controller, connecting wires, "leak proof" 1.5-volt D battery, and instruction sheet. Three versions of this instruction sheet have been reported. First is 257-16, dated 4-56 and done in blue ink on white paper. Next are two versions of 257-20 with 6-56 and 8-56 dates. The first is done in black ink on yellow paper, and the second is dark blue on white paper. Dimensions: 15" x 5" base, 5½" high.

(A) Molded maroon base.   **35**   **55**   **80**   **100**

(B) Molded brown base. F. S. Davis Collection.

	40	60	90	110

(C) Decidedly lighter green roof, like mid-production roof on 497. This roof variation has been observed on both maroon and brown base units but is easily switched. Roofs of 256, 257, and 356 are identical and can be interchanged.

	50	70	110	150

356 OPERATING FREIGHT STATION, 1952–57

Similar in appearance to the 256, this accessory has a picket fence with billboards, and is illuminated by two L431 bulbs. The 356 also includes two moveable baggage carts and six adhesive signs or posters (see 256 for description) that can be mounted on bulletin boards molded into its walls.

Attached beneath the metal track mounted in the station base is an electrical coil that activates the track. The 60-cycle vibration of the coil causes the baggage carts to run counterclockwise (in the direction of the white arrow printed on the track) around the platform and back into the station. There, a trip mechanism holds one cart until the other enters and releases it. Similar to the cattle included with 3656 Operating Cattle Car, tiny fingers molded into two rubber pads pressed into the base of each cart provide movement along the vibrating track. Carts will run either way around the track, but the release mechanism works only when carts run counterclockwise. They jam in the station when run clockwise.

Usually, one cart is dark or medium green and the other is orange, but original (and much less common) red carts and much lighter green carts have been observed. The figure mounted on all the carts is dark blue. There were evidently two molds for the baggage carts. One of these molds made a T-shaped hole (with a broad stem) in the forward part of the baggage bay, behind the vertical front wall. Seldom is a cart found with this hole open. It was probably made to help secure the baggage load, but this is only speculation, since the known loads do not seem to make use of it. At any rate, this hole was soon plugged, but the outline of the T can still be seen on carts from this mold. Presence of the T-outline guarantees an original cart, since the reproductions do not include it. Carts from the other mold did not include this feature and are more difficult to distinguish from reproductions.

Watch also for both the long upward projection above the baggage cart driver and the small projection jutting downward from the bottom of the platform on which the driver stands. These projections are easily broken and affect the operation of

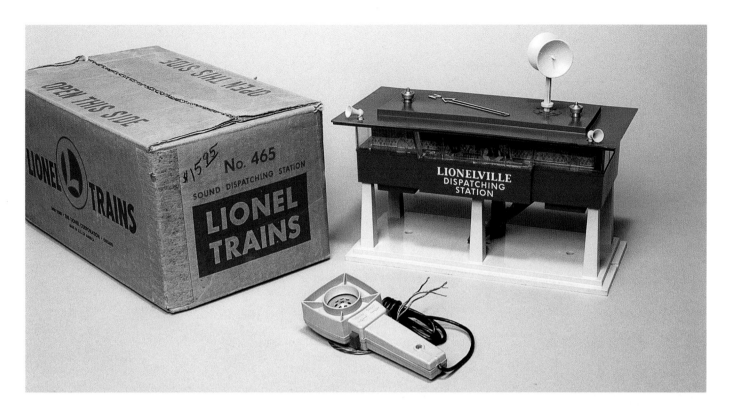

The 465 Sound Dispatching Station, its box, and microphone. The 365 Dispatching Station was identical in appearance, but lacked the sound and train control features. J. Algozzini Collection.

the accessory. The top projection is necessary for the cart hold-and-release feature inside the station. The bottom projection helps guide the cart around the curves in the track.

Illustrated in Lionel's 1952 catalog is a 356 with baggage loads on both carts and no posters on the bulletin boards. However, all observed examples have the posters. The Lionel Service Manual reports that early production had one cart with baggage and the other without. It also notes that the baggage load was discontinued because the unloaded cart would run faster than the loaded one. Original lithographed metal baggage loads have been available for many years as a repair part. Unmarked reproductions of this baggage load and the carts are also available.

Lionel issued several instruction sheets for the 356. The first, part number 356-40, was printed in blue on white paper and dated 10-52. It showed the baggage cart with baggage and explained that the trip mechanism together with one loaded and one empty cart created the illusion that the cart was being alternately loaded and unloaded inside the station. Since all examples observed have the carts in two different colors, the illusion would certainly be diminished! The sheet was revised in 11-52, given part number 356-42, and printed in black on white paper. It did not show baggage on the cart and omitted any reference to the load. All subsequent instruction sheets kept the 356-42 part number and went back to blue printing. Unfortunately, the issues of 6-53 and 8-53 retained the artwork from the original issue, which showed the baggage load. The text was also apparently copied from the original issue, which referred to the load. Final issues of 3-54 and 4-56 corrected the artwork and wording. All issues show the adhesive posters and explain their installation. Dimensions: 15″ x 5″ base, 5½″ high.

(A) Early 1952. One cart with lithographed metal baggage load. These original metal loads were available as service parts for a few years and have been added to some stations that did not come factory equipped with them. **NRS**

	Gd	VG	Ex	LN

(B) 1952–57. Carts have no loads and are usually orange and dark green. Carts may be found in less common red and lighter green colors.

	40	60	90	130

(C) Same as (B) except light green plastic roof, like mid-production roof on 497. Probably 1957 production. Roofs of 256, 257, and 356 are identical and can be interchanged.

	50	70	115	150

365 DISPATCHING STATION, 1958–59

Identical to the 456 station (described below) without the sound and train control mechanisms, this accessory shows dispatchers at work and uses the same L53 lamp for interior illumination. It is more difficult to find than the 465. As with the 465, the 365 has two simulated loudspeakers, one on either side of the front roof overhang, and a simulated radio tower with two dish antennas attached to the roof. These fragile parts are often missing. They have been reproduced and usually are unmarked. When collecting this item, make sure it has the "365" molded in the underside of the base. Sometimes a 465, stripped of its incomplete or malfunctioning speaker system, is sold as a 365. Only one 365-10 instruction sheet is known. Dated 3-58, it is printed in blue ink on white paper. Dimensions: 11″ x 5″ base, 6½″ high plus an additional 2¾″ antenna.

	Gd	VG	Ex	LN
(A) Black building painted red.	65	85	120	150
(B) Red unpainted building.	65	85	120	150

465 SOUND DISPATCHING STATION, 1956–57

The 465 features a handheld microphone connected by a long wire to a battery-powered 4″ loudspeaker. The batteries and speaker are concealed in the red molded, unpainted house with

| | Gd | VG | Ex | LN |

"LIONELVILLE / DISPATCHING / STATION" heat-stamped in white on the front. As with any battery-powered item, inspect the station for battery damage prior to purchase. Instructions include details for wiring two stations together for use as an intercom.

The transformer may be connected to the track through the station wiring so the direction control button, included in the microphone, can function. The gray microphone provides a left red button for train direction control and a right red button to activate the microphone. Decorative trim on the 465 includes two simulated loudspeakers, one on either side of the front roof overhang, and a simulated radio tower with two dish antennas attached to the roof. These parts are fragile and are often missing. Reproductions usually are unmarked.

The 465 uses one L53 lamp for interior illumination. It came with a lockon, track insulating pins, wires, and four 1.5-volt D "leak proof" batteries. Two versions of the 465-19 instruction sheet are known, both dated 11-56 and printed in blue ink on white paper. The first has no warranty on page 3, the second adds the warranty. Dimensions: 11″ x 5″ base, 6½″ high plus an additional 2¾″ antenna.

| | Gd | VG | Ex | LN |
| | 60 | 90 | 125 | 160 |

908 RAILROAD STATION WITH RAMP AND UNDERPASS, 1964 (uncataloged)

An enormous cardboard station with a ramp meant to be used with a figure-eight or similar track layout incorporating a 45-degree crossing. Half of the figure-eight is on the ramp portion that elevates the train as it runs though one portal to the interior of the station, then out the other portal, returning to floor level and completing the figure-eight outside the station. Same con-

The 908 Railroad Station With Ramp and Underpass was included in some uncataloged outfits, including X-810NA. This all-cardboard accessory could support a 246 plastic locomotive and a few light freight cars.

| | Gd | VG | Ex | LN |

struction and nearly the same size as the 910 described in Chapter 3.

A 908 was included with uncataloged sets X-810NA, 19394, 19395, and probably others. It was packaged in a large Kraft paper bag stamped on the outside in black letters, "TO BE INCLUDED WITH / OUTFIT NO. 19394" for this particular set. The small, two-tier, plain cardboard set box is stamped in black, "NO. 19394 / INCLUDE 908 WITH THIS SET." Set 19395 is identical except for the number and set content.

Included in the box with the train components for set 19394 is "SPECIAL LAYOUT INSTRUCTIONS" sheet 19394-10, dated 8/64, illustrating a track layout that goes through and around the station. This and the listing of service stations included with the set, date production to 1964. An 8″ by 10⅜″ white sheet of paper printed in black and titled "HOW TO SET UP YOUR LIONEL RAILROAD TERMINAL," but without the usual Lionel part number or date, was enclosed in the bag with the station pieces. Several examples of this station, all in unmarked Kraft paper bags, have been observed. Moreover, at least one set is known to come in a large, shallow, rectangular box with the station (in its unmarked bag) included inside the set box! Dimensions: when fully assembled, 30½″ x 28″ base, 14″ high. **NRS**

CHAPTER 5

Non-Operating Structures and Scenery

Among the most colorful and collectible of Lionel's non-operating structures are the plastic building sets containing components manufactured by Bachmann Bros. for its Plasticville line. Here are the assembled contents of a 960 Barnyard Set with original box.

Postwar collectors will find it quite a challenge to acquire many of the accessories in this chapter. Much of the scenery included here was packaged landscaping material and other items used to apply the finishing touches to a layout. Unlike engines or rolling stock, there was no need to retain the box for storing the contents. Consequently, the contents are often available, but the Lionel packaging is not.

During the later postwar years, to maintain a complete product line and no doubt to secure some extra profit, Lionel increased its offerings in the peripheral area of scenic and landscape materials. This market was dominated by smaller manufacturers whose products were often used for several different scales. Lionel made arrangements with Bachmann Bros. to supply

Plasticville items and with Life-Like to supply scenic structures and materials. Both manufacturers offered their products in Lionel packaging for sale using Lionel's distribution channels.

Aside from the distinctive Lionel name and color scheme, the packaging for Life-Like products issued under the Lionel brand was nearly identical to the packaging used for Life-Like products. Regarding the arrangement with Bachmann, the first volume of *Greenberg's Guide to Lionel Trains, 1945–1969* (1991 edition), cites a Bachmann vice president as the source for a report that Lionel shipped printed boxes to Bachmann, where they were filled with appropriate assortments of standard Plasticville items and returned to Lionel for distribution.

	Gd	VG	Ex	LN

Stitched border 89 Flagpole and two color shades for its box. The 48W Whistling Station is a prewar item not produced after the war.

Because collectors have concentrated on locomotives, rolling stock, and accessories, there are few collections of scenery materials. In some instances, it was not possible to locate a single one of the items to photograph in any condition!

89 FLAGPOLE, 1956–58

The base for this white plastic flagpole originally came with four green corner plots made of sponge, which are often badly deteriorated or missing. To fit into a smaller box, the pole came disassembled from the base. An original box with the inner liner brings a premium. The flagpole came with a fabric, 48-star American flag and a purple or blue Lionel pennant with white lettering.

Two versions of the flag are known: an early version with a stitched border and a late version with a plain border. Few appreciate this difference, but a premium would be warranted for the stitched border, as it is somewhat harder to find. Pennant color is easier to see at a glance, but the mix of pennant color and flag border has not been sufficiently researched to date. There is also the question of whether the purple pennant is just a blue pennant that has changed color with age. Dimensions: 3¾″ x 3¾″ base, 11⅛″ high.

(A) Flag with stitched border, blue or purple pennant.

	18	30	50	70

(B) Flag with plain border, blue or purple pennant.

	16	28	46	65

150 TELEGRAPH POLE SET, 1947–50

This is a set of six brown plastic poles with metal base clips that attach to the track ties and secure the poles in position beside the track. The poles have a circle-L molded in near the bottom and two ribs 180 degrees apart to align them in the clips. Track clips are usually rusted, broken, or missing from sets offered for sale, and they have not been reproduced to date.

	Gd	VG	Ex	LN

Original sets came in a cardboard box with a lift-off lid. Both the box and lid are covered with orange paper on the outside, and the box is lined with dark blue paper (hidden by the yellow liner). A drawing inside the lid, printed in black or brown on a yellow background, illustrates how to install the poles along a track section. With the lid removed and placed upright behind the box, dealers could use the drawing as a promotional display.

Two slightly different box sizes are known. Both have liners that use cardboard loops to hold the poles in place and a trough to contain the clips. These liners are yellow on the exposed side. The smaller box, probably the later version, has the clip trough in the center with the poles spanning it. The larger box has the trough located along the bottom, below the poles. These variations do not seem to affect the value, but the box condition and presence or absence of track clips does. Like New requires the complete box, liner, and all six clips. Dimensions: 6⅞″ high installed in track clip.

	25	40	55	70

310 SET OF FIVE BILLBOARD FRAMES, 1950–68

A sheet of paperboard ads in billboard format was included with this set, just as they were included with Lionel's train sets and catalog offers. These sheets of billboard ads are collectible apart from the frames. The value of the billboard frames is influenced by the ads included and their condition, particularly if the billboards are still joined together along their perforated borders. Some operators use the billboards without the plastic frames, as each ad has a simulated frame printed around it.

The plastic frames are found in two distinct shades of green. Darker green is the most common. Much less common is green that is distinctly lighter, although not as light as the light green

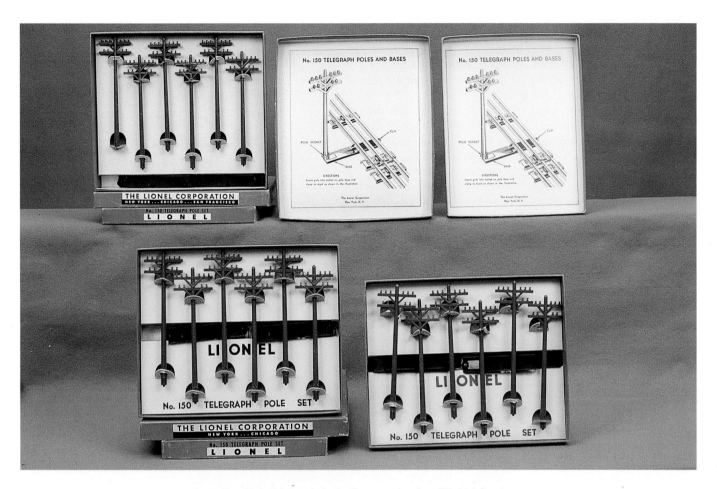

The earliest 150s had their track clips in a lower trough and used black ink for printing the instructions inside the lid. Later packaging was slightly smaller and simpler
with dark or light blue ink for printing the inner liner and brown for the instructions.

Billboards and 410 Blinkers made to snap onto them with some of the 310 box variations. Although not apparent in this picture, some billboard frames were more a
blue-green than the usual dark green.

roof of a 497. Successors to the Lionel Corp. have continued producing these frames in various colors. Originals have Lionel nomenclature molded into the rear side.

The 310 was usually packaged in a Classic orange, white, and blue box that is difficult to repack. Later box styles, such as the Hagerstown Checkerboard, are harder to find and command a premium. The blister pack of 1966 and 1968 is rare, as are the billboards included with that set. Like New must include the box and unseparated set of billboards. Top price requires a complete set of frames and an "uncut" sheet of billboards in a complete, original box. Dimensions: 5⅛" x ⅞" base, 3¼" high.

(A) Common dark green frame. Frames tend to be either broken or perfect and rarely between. Thus, only Excellent and Like New are shown. — — **10** **45**

(B) Much less common lighter green frames.
— — **20** **55**

B310 SET OF 5 BILLBOARD FRAMES, 1966 and 1968

Included with this set are rare billboards of the period, printed only in a shade of purple. The frames are molded in the usual dark green. Value shown is for Like New only, since the packaging is all that distinguishes the B310. It must be intact and include the uncut set of five billboards.
— — — **125**

410 BILLBOARD BLINKER, 1956–58

Meant for attachment to a 310 Billboard, this accessory can be adjusted to provide blinking or continuous illumination. Its metal construction combines unique pieces with a lamp housing and bracket from a 70 Yard Light, the bimetallic element from a 193, and adjusting parts from a 455. The lamp and heater element are connected in series, which accounts for the 12- to 16-volt operating requirement for the 6- to 8-volt L51 bayonet-base bulb. Two printings of the 410-19 instruction sheet are known, both dated 6-56. One is printed in black ink on yellow paper and has an ad for the 110 Trestle Set on the back. The other has brighter dark blue ink on white paper with an ad for the *Model Railroading* paperback book on the back. Only known packaging is the Classic orange, white, and blue box. Dimensions: 4⅝" x 1½" base, 5" high. **25** **35** **45** **55**

919 ARTIFICIAL GRASS, 1932–42 and 1946–64

While the content is eight ounces of green-dyed sawdust, the white cloth bag with a red-dyed cotton drawstring has some collectible variations. At least some prewar production used black, predominantly serif lettering, and this may have carried over into the first year of postwar production. Then the lettering changed to red but remained serif. This must have lasted only a short time, as examples are rare. Finally, the red lettering changed to the common, predominantly block style. There is not much excitement among collectors regarding the 919, but few have bothered to note these variations. The bag is the important factor. You can make green sawdust. — — **6** **15**

Lionel's 919 Artificial Grass amounted to nothing more than eight ounces of green sawdust. So collectors focus on the bags, which varied in color and printing.

920 SCENIC DISPLAY SET, 1957–58

Contents of this scenery set include a 36" by 48" piece of special felt for building mountains; two gray molded plastic 920-2 Tunnel Portals; clear plastic bags (one of each) of 920-6 Dry Glue, 920-3 Green Grass, 920-4 Yellow Grass, 920-5 Artificial Rock (an expanded mica used for insulation), and 920-8 Dyed Lichen; a package of a dozen 920-11 steel clips for fastening the edges of the felt to the tunnel portals; and a tray of water colors. These and the 920-22 instruction sheet dated 11-57 (blue ink on white paper) came in a unique display box.

The 920-5 Artificial Rock and 920-8 Dyed Lichen were also offered for separate sale in 1958. The 920-2 Tunnel Portals were offered for separate sale too, but were packaged in their own Classic box. Otherwise, they are identical to those included in the 920. The 920 is another case where the packaging was usually discarded, so it is relatively hard to find in good, let alone complete, condition. To be considered a collectible piece, this item must be at least Like New. It may be difficult to gather the necessary pieces to complete a set with missing components.
— — **95** **150**

920-2 TUNNEL PORTALS, 1958–59

These two simulated cut-stone tunnel portals are realistically molded in gray plastic. Originally made for the 920 Scenic Display Set of 1957, they later were packaged in their own Classic orange, white, and blue box for separate sale. An original portal has "1957" molded in raised numerals on one cornerstone and "HILLSIDE" molded above the arch. Portals tend to be either broken or perfect. Thus, only Excellent and Like New are shown, with not much room for conditions in between. A complete box in good condition is required for top price. Dimensions: 2⅜" x 8" base, 7" high, 4⅞"-wide portal.
— — **36** **55**

| | Gd | VG | Ex | LN |

920-3 GREEN GRASS, 1957–58

The 11″ x 5″ clear plastic bag is printed "GREEN GRASS / FOR / MODEL TRAIN LAYOUTS / L / THE LIONEL CORPORATION / NEW YORK / N. Y. / Made In U. S. of America / 920-17." This item was part of the 920 Scenic Display Set and not cataloged for separate sale. The value listed is for an intact bag with legible printing. — — 10 35

920-4 YELLOW GRASS, 1957–58

The 7″ x 7″ clear plastic bag is printed "YELLOW GRASS / FOR / MODEL TRAIN LAYOUTS / L / THE LIONEL CORPORATION / NEW YORK / N. Y. / Made In U. S. of America / 920-18." This item was part of the 920 Scenic Display Set and not cataloged for separate sale. The value listed is for an intact bag with legible printing. — — 10 35

The 920 Scenic Set contained several separately cataloged items, including 920-2 Tunnel Portals, 920-5 Artificial Rock, and 920-8 Dyed Lichen. Other items, such as 920-6 Dry Glue, were not sold separately.

| | Gd | VG | Ex | LN |

920-5 ARTIFICIAL ROCK, 1957–58

This bag contained "vermiculite," an expanded mica sold as attic insulation. The bag is similar to those described above for yellow or green grass. This item was also part of the 920 Scenic Display Set and was cataloged for separate sale only in 1958. The value is for an intact bag with legible printing.

 — — 20 50

| | Gd | VG | Ex | LN |

920-8 DYED LICHEN, 1957–58

Lionel used an imported lichen which, when dyed various colors, is ideal for simulating shrubbery, hedges, and so on. The bag is similar to those described above. This item was part of the 920 Scenic Display Set and was cataloged for separate sale only in 1958. It should not be confused with the 971 Lichen, which is the same lichen in a different package. The value listed is for an intact bag with legible printing.   —   —   **20**   **50**

All the following items (951-969 and 980-988) are Plasticville structures packaged in Lionel boxes. For the most part, the contents of the boxes are unimportant to Lionel collectors, except perhaps for the few cases where parts of an item may vary from the standard Plasticville colors. It is the original boxes and their instruction sheets that are the most significant items to a collector. Instruction sheets evidently were not included in the first year of production (1958), as none of the items that were cataloged only in 1958 are known to have one. All items after 1958 have an instruction sheet whose part number consists of the item number followed by -10 (for example, 963-10). All known examples are printed in black ink on white paper and may or may not include a date.

Thanks to Don Corrigan, the Lionel boxes for Plasticville have been categorized as shown below. The "Hat Logo" refers to the inverted top hat full of toys that was the logo of the American Toy Manufacturers Association, an organization to which Lionel belonged for many years. During these years, the group's logo appeared on Lionel's boxes.

Type I.   1958; orange, white, and blue box with a flat (matte) finish and hat logo.

Type II.   1959–60; similar to above, only a more glossy finish. Has the words "For Use With Super 'O'" below name and number on box ends, hat logo.

Type III.   1961; same as Type II but no hat logo.

Type IV.   1962 and later; Orange Picture box with graphics showing a train and a view of how the contents should look when fully assembled.

Part of the complete set of Lionel-Plasticville kits. Pictured are sets 951 through 969. On top is a side view of set 963-100, the only set with a picture of its contents on the box. Known only as part of the Gifts Galore "Halloween" train outfit, this item may have accompanied other uncataloged train outfits as well. J. Lampert Collection.

| | Gd | VG | Ex | LN |

Several Plasticville items may also appear in plain cardboard or white-paper-covered boxes with only Lionel's part number stamped on one or both ends. Due to the low volume involved and the effort to minimize cost, Lionel apparently elected not to use the usual colorful boxes. It appears that these items were packaged in this manner to increase the piece count for the low-budget uncataloged sets Lionel aggressively merchandised in the 1960s. Such plain-boxed items appeared with these sets later (sometimes several years) after the items disappeared from the consumer catalog.

When found new, these items (except for those cataloged only in 1958) include the Lionel instruction sheet. Values shown reflect the quality of the box rather than the contents. Since the contents can usually be replaced from the more-common Plasticville pieces, even an empty box in nice condition (with instruction sheet if applicable) will command a price approaching that of a box with complete contents. If originally furnished, the instruction sheet must be included for Excellent or Like New. In general, the smaller and earlier Lionel/Plasticville items are easiest to find; those of later years and those packaged in larger boxes are more difficult.

Each entry starts with a piece count (i.e., came with 13 pieces). These are Lionel's counts, taken from the consumer catalog entries. An actual count of all the bits and pieces in each set usually finds more actual parts. Especially in later years when larger structures were offered, a multi-piece house, for example, would be listed as one piece, and an individual animal figure would be another piece. By actual count, the house itself may well have more individual parts than claimed for the whole set.

951 FARM SET, 1958

Came with 13 pieces, including a truck, tractor, jeep, horses, cows, harrow, plow, wagon, and footbridge, in Type I box without an instruction sheet.

| | — | 135 | 200 | 400 |

952 FIGURE SET, 1958

Came with 30 pieces, including people, fire hydrant, fire alarm box, and mailboxes, in Type I box with no instructions.

| | — | 135 | 200 | 400 |

953 FIGURE SET, 1959–62

Came with 32 pieces, most of which are human figures, but also includes fire hydrants, traffic light, benches, palette of paint colors, bottle of thinner, and paintbrush, in Type II or Type III box. It is the only Lionel Plasticville item known to have more than one box type (not counting the uncataloged white boxes). This set ran four years in the Lionel catalog and has the distinction of including two instruction sheets. The Lionel instruction sheet is 953-10, dated 3-59. The Bachmann instruction sheet, which was included along with the Lionel sheet in every new example observed, contains instructions on how to use the paints to decorate the figures. Same price for either box type.

| | — | 135 | 200 | 400 |

954 SWIMMING POOL AND PLAYGROUND SET, 1959

Came with 30 pieces, including 12 fence sections, six trees, slide, swing, teeter-totter, merry-go-round, bench and table with umbrella, two chairs, two chaise lounges, and pool, in Type II box with a 954-10 instruction sheet, dated 3-59.

| | — | 135 | 200 | 400 |

The rest of the family of Lionel-Plasticville kits. There are 29 different set numbers in Lionel's offerings over the years. Pictured are sets 980 through 988. Note the box design change from Classic to Orange Picture. The three sets in the Orange Picture boxes are among the most difficult to find in the entire series. J. Lampert Collection.

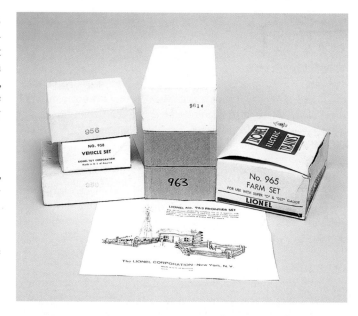

Uncataloged Lionel-Plasticville known to have been included in uncataloged Lionel sets, some furnished well after Lionel discontinued the particular item in its regular line. On the right is a Classic boxed 965 Farm Set where the orange printing is missing on the box. Two examples of this are known. In the center are two 963 Frontier Sets, with the center box unmarked. In front is a typical instruction sheet that was included in all sets, cataloged or not, after 1958. J. Lampert Collection.

| | Gd | VG | Ex | LN |

955 HIGHWAY SET, 1958

Catalog describes set as having 22 pieces, but it illustrates 27, including two buses, automobile, seven telegraph poles, 10 traffic signs, and seven street signs. Came in Type I box without an instruction sheet.

| | — | 135 | 200 | 400 |

	Gd	VG	Ex	LN

956 STOCKYARD SET, 1959

Came with 18 pieces, including a corral made up of several fence sections and other parts, cows, and trackside railroad signs, in Type II box with a 956-10 instruction sheet, dated 3-59. This set has also been observed in a rare cardboard box with a lift-off lid covered with white paper. The box is unmarked except for "956" stamped in black ink on each end of the lid. Price is for a Type II box.   — **135 200 400**

957 FARM BUILDING AND ANIMAL SET, 1958

Came with 35 pieces, including four multi-piece farm structures, several fence sections, gate, pump, horse, fowl, and many domestic animals, in Type I box without an instruction sheet.
— **135 200 400**

958 VEHICLE SET, 1958

Came with 24 pieces, including three automobiles, two fire trucks, ambulance, bus, several street signs, fire alarm box, mailbox, fire hydrant, and traffic light, in Type I box with no instruction sheet. This set has also been observed in a rare white paperboard box rubber-stamped in blue ink on each end with the words "Vehicle Set" and the number. Price is for the Type I box
— **150 230 440**

959 BARN SET, 1958

Came with 23 pieces, including a multi-piece barn, two horses, fowl, and domestic animals, in Type I box with no instruction sheet. This set has also been observed in a rare white box with a lift-off top marked only with a rubber-stamped "959" on two sides. Price is for the Type I box. — **150 230 440**

960 BARNYARD SET, 1959–61

Came with 29 pieces, including three multi-piece farm buildings, doghouse, tractor, truck, wagon, hoe, fowl, and domestic and farm animals, in Type II box with a 960-10 instruction sheet, dated 3-59.   — **135 200 400**

961 SCHOOL SET, 1959

Came with 36 pieces, including a multi-piece school building, flagpole, two yellow school buses, street signs, several fence sections, shrubs, and benches, in Type II box with a 961-10 instruction sheet, dated 3-59. This set has also been observed in a rare white box with lift-off lid and only "961" rubber-stamped on each end. Price is for the Type II box.
— **135 200 400**

962 TURNPIKE SET, 1958

Came with 24 pieces, including a multi-piece tollbooth structure (Lionel referred to this item as an "interchange"), stanchions (traffic lane dividers), five telegraph poles, four automobiles, ambulance, bus, and numerous street signs, in Type I box without an instruction sheet.   — **160 250 470**

963 FRONTIER SET, 1959–60

Came with 18 pieces, including a multi-piece cabin and windmill, fence sections, cows, horses, and pump, in Type II box with a 963-10 instruction sheet, dated 3-59. This set has also been observed in a rare plain, medium gray paperboard box with a lift-off lid with no markings that appears to have been designed

The 963 and 963-100 Frontier Sets had the same contents and instruction sheet. Although the windmill counted as only one piece, every fence and cabin section was used to get the "18 Pieces" advertised on the 963-100 cover.

	Gd	VG	Ex	LN

solely for the Frontier Set, as it is sized perfectly to fit the contents and instruction sheet. Another observed rare example is in a cardboard color box that appears to be otherwise identical to the medium gray box. This variation, which came from Madison Hardware Co., has "963" written in marker on one end only. Price is for the Type II box   — **150 230 440**

963-100 FRONTIER SET, 1960

The contents and instruction sheet are identical to those included in the 963. The 963-100 came in a unique box that is difficult to date precisely. First of the Orange Picture boxes, it is different from the style that appeared in 1962, the last year Lionel/Plasticville was cataloged. It appears to be a combination of 1961 and 1962 styles. Yet this box came with the 1882 Halloween General Set, so named because of its orange and black color scheme. A brand-new example of that set, packaged for Gifts Galore (which is not the same as the set shown in the Christmas 1959 Sears catalog), contains two instruction sheets dated 1959. Apparently the 1882 Halloween General Set, which included the 963-100, was available in 1960. It is possible that the 963-100 also came with other uncataloged sets, but none has been reported.   — **260 400 600**

Lionel's 971 Lichen (right) was supplied by Life-Like, which sold the same product in a nearly identical box (left). Lionel's spelling of lichen is correct.

	Gd	VG	Ex	LN

964 FACTORY SITE SET, 1959

Came with 18 pieces, including a multi-piece factory building with roof-mounted water tower, automobile, four telegraph poles, and numerous railroad signs, in Type II box with a 964-10 instruction sheet, dated 3-59.   — 150 230 440

965 FARM SET, 1959

Came with 36 pieces, including a multi-piece barn and three smaller buildings, farm equipment, numerous fowl, and domestic and farm animals, in Type II box with a 965-10 instruction sheet, dated 3-59.   — 135 200 400

966 FIRE HOUSE SET, 1958

Came with 45 pieces, including a multi-piece firehouse, fire engines, alarm box, hydrant, ambulance, bus, automobiles, traffic light, street signs, streetlight, bench, mailbox, people, telegraph poles, and pine trees, in Type I box without an instruction sheet.   — 135 200 400

967 POST OFFICE SET, 1958

Came with 25 pieces, including a multi-piece post office, mailbox, streetlight, traffic light, two benches, three vehicles, numerous people, and traffic signs, in Type I box without an instruction sheet.   — 135 200 400

968 TV TRANSMITTER SET, 1958

Came with 28 pieces, including a multi-piece TV station and antenna, mailbox, fire hydrant, jeep, two automobiles, fence sections and gate, people, and pine trees, in Type I box without an instruction sheet. Two variations of the station have been

observed: red roof with white walls and white roof with red walls.   — 135 200 400

969 CONSTRUCTION SET, 1960

Came with 23 pieces, including a multi-piece partially constructed house, construction materials, and several workers and automobiles, in Type II box with a 969-10 instruction sheet, which is undated.   — 150 230 440

971 LICHEN, 1960–64

The lichen included in this accessory's "window" box is dyed green, yellow, and brown. It is usually dried out or missing. This was a Life-Like product made for Lionel and packaged in a box almost identical to the Life-Like window box, but with Lionel graphics. An empty box in nice condition is worth as much as a full one because the box is what makes the readily available lichen a Lionel product. Don Corrigan has identified four versions of this collectible box. In uncertain order, there is a version with no weight printed on the front or ends of the box, a weight of 4¼ oz., and finally, a weight of 4½ oz., which appears to be the last and most common version. But there is one more! The box with 4½ oz. markings comes with and without, "MADE IN U.S. of AMERICA" at the bottom of the back panel. Most collectors, if they bother to collect this item at all, are not aware of the variations, so no premium is indicated. However, those with no weight and 4¼ oz. are much harder to find.

  — — 190 340

Two large and rare items made by Life-Like for Lionel. In foreground are the contents of the 974. The 973 had a long grass mat and three short mats simulating earth, ballast, and road.

Among the rarest of Lionel's accessories, the 972 was made by Life-Like. The box and not the contents make it collectible. Note the bag of lichen to the right of the divider.

	Gd	VG	Ex	LN

972 LANDSCAPE TREE ASSORTMENT, 1961–64

Another Life-Like product packaged for Lionel in which the window box and its liner represent the collectible elements. Even when the box is located in nice condition, it is usually missing the unmarked plastic bag of lichen and the white paperboard liner (with a Lionel part number) that separates it from the four evergreens and three flowering shrubs. According to Don Corrigan, this box is available with and without, "MADE IN U.S. of AMERICA" on the bottom of the back panel.

	—	—	300	500

	Gd	VG	Ex	LN

973 COMPLETE LANDSCAPING SET, 1960–64

Yet another case were the box is the collectible element. Unfortunately, this box is difficult to find in decent shape because it is made of thin paperboard and is slightly over 4 feet long. It was packaged by Life-Like for Lionel, and its contents included a 4- by 8-foot roll of grass mat, plus a 16″ by 48″ roll (one of each) of earth, ballast, and road material.

	—	—	400	550

974 SCENERY SET, 1962–63

This is an enormous, colorfully printed cardboard box packaged for Lionel by Life-Like. It's a fairly substantial box with the number "974" printed on the side in one of the two known sizes. However, this box is difficult to find in any condition because of its size and the fact that it had no purpose once its contents were used. The contents are a 4- by 8-foot grass mat, two molded and painted Styrofoam background mountains, unmarked bag of lichen, and nine assorted trees. **NRS**

	Gd	VG	Ex	LN

980 RANCH SET, 1960
Came with 14 pieces, including a loading pen, cattle, pigs, sheep, two vehicles, and farm implements, in Type II box with a 980-10 instruction sheet, which is undated. This set has also been observed in a rare plain white box with lift-off cover and "980" rubber-stamped on each end. Price is for the Type II box.

— 135 200 400

981 FREIGHT YARD SET, 1960
Came with 10 pieces, including a multi-piece loading platform and switch tower, baggage carts, telephone poles, and railroad men, in Type II box with a 981-10 instruction sheet, which is undated.

— 135 200 400

982 SUBURBAN SPLIT LEVEL SET, 1960
Came with 18 pieces, including a multi-piece house, sections of ranch fence, automobile, people, and several pine trees, in Type II box with a 982-10 instruction sheet, which is undated.

— 135 200 400

983 FARM SET, 1960–61
Came with 7 pieces, including a multi-piece barn, windmill, colonial-style house, horse, cows, and automobile, in Type II box with a 983-10 instruction sheet, which is undated.

— 135 200 400

984 RAILROAD SET, 1961–62
Came with 22 pieces, including a multi-piece switch tower and loading platform, railroad signs, and accessories, in Type III box with an undated 984-10 instruction sheet.

— 135 200 400

985 FREIGHT AREA SET, 1961
Came with 32 pieces, including a multi-piece water tower, loading platform, switch tower, watchman's shanty, work car, telegraph poles, automobiles, railroad signs, and accessories, in Type II box with an undated 985-10 instruction sheet.

— 135 200 400

986 FARM SET, 1962
Came with 20 pieces, including a multi-piece New England–style farmhouse and barn with silo and 18 farm animals (horses, cows, sheep, and pigs), in Type IV Orange Picture box with a 986-10 instruction sheet, dated 3-62.

— 135 200 400

987 TOWN SET, 1962
Came with 24 pieces, including a multi-piece church, gas station with pumps, combination bank and store, automobile, 12 street signs, and five telephone poles, in Type IV Orange Picture box with a 987-10 instruction sheet, dated 3-62.

— 500 800 1000

988 RAILROAD STRUCTURE SET, 1962
Came with 16 pieces, including a multi-piece railroad station with freight platform, water tank, hobo shacks, work car, bench, figures, crossing gate, and shanty, in Type IV Orange Picture box with a 988-10 instruction sheet, dated 3-62.

— 160 300 500

CHAPTER 6

Signals, Signs, and Lights

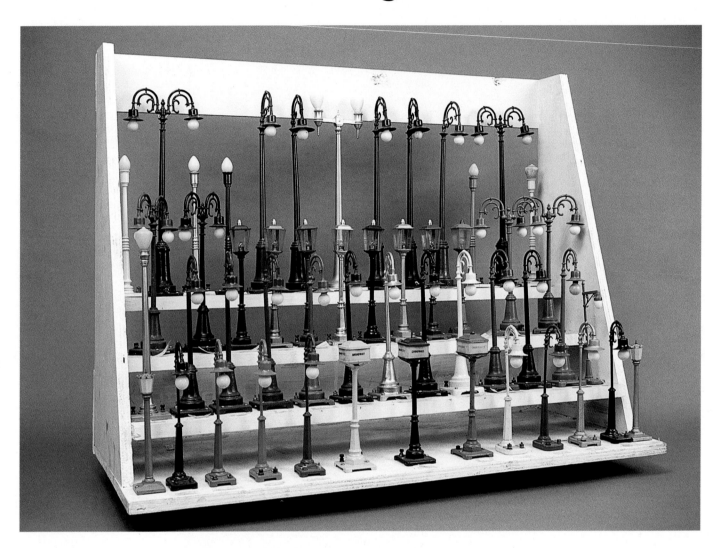

This assortment of lampposts spans more than half a century of Lionel production.
E. Barbret Collection.

While the action of freight-handling accessories adds a new dimension to daytime operations, lamps and signals help extend this activity into the night. Over the years, operators, young and old, have turned off the room lights to observe their miniature rail-road empires in a different mood and setting. This is where lamps and signals literally shine. Advanced Lionel railroaders even use additional colored lights and dimmer switches in the room lighting to provide a real-istic transition from daylight to nighttime effects.

Packaging of lamps and signals

A number of the accessories described in this chapter were packaged in blister packs. First issued in 1966, blister packs are known to exist in two different forms: the card type and the frame type. In both forms, the accessory was securely encased in a vacuum-formed bubble of clear plastic that held the item against a thin paperboard card printed with background scenery, advertising, instructions, or all of the above.

The frame type further enclosed the blister card in a four-sided box-like structure, also made of paperboard, resulting in a picture-frame appearance. There often was room in the box section to house other necessary items, such as a lockon, contactor, wiring, and instructions, although sometimes one or more of these items was packaged elsewhere. Instruction sheets have been found behind the card (sandwiched between it and the back surface of the frame), with the more bulky contactor included in the bubble, along with the accessory in one example. Generally, the frame treatment was reserved for larger accessories, such as the semaphore and crossing signal, while smaller items, such as smoke pellet bottles and tubes of lubricant, warranted only a card. Some larger, non-operating items, such as the B310 Billboard Set and B214 Plate Girder Bridge, were packaged only within an unframed card.

Two kinds of frame-type packaging construction have been observed: easy-open and lock-tab. Two examples of the B262 Highway Crossing Gate covered in this report have the easy-open box. These frames are fairly easy to open and close since the tabs do not lock into the side rails. The color of the easy-open frames is red-orange on all the examples observed. The top and bottom portions of these frames are cut straight across where they overlap the side frames. Lock-tab frames have tabs that are smaller than those on the easy-open frame, and they do lock into the side rails. All examples observed so far are close to a true orange.

The easy-open box was probably made first and may have proved troublesome due to premature opening and loss of contents from inside the frame rails. It is much less common than the lock-tab design. The top and bottom portions of these frames are cut at a 45-degree angle where they overlap the side frames.

35 BOULEVARD LAMP, 1940–42 and 1945–49

Both the 35 Boulevard Lamp and the 64 Lamp Post, introduced in 1940 as "New Scale Models," were replicas of prototype designs that can still be seen. The base and post of the 35 lamp constitute a single die-cast part with "NO. 35" and Lionel's nomenclature molded into the underside in raised letters. The bottom insulator has two spring clips to hold the electrical wires, eliminating the need for traditional binding posts. A nickel-plated bracket is clipped at the top of the post on each side to provide a fastener for the top finial. A cap shaped like a crown of thorns topped the opalescent, octagonal lampshade. This cap was usually molded of ivory-colored plastic and painted on the outside to match the lamppost. Four tiny holes at the top of the cap allow heat to dissipate.

Today, the lamp is often found with one or more of the thorn projections broken off. Reproductions have been made of both the lampshade and cap. As is the case with most other accessories normally painted silver, the 35 was painted a semi-gloss medium gray during the 1941–42 period. The silver color was restored after World War II. Along with most other lampposts, the 35 was apparently assembled first and painted last. Evidence of this is the paint-covered solder on underside connections,

making it easier for a collector to tell if a lamp has been rewired or repaired. Solid-core wire with woven cloth insulation was typically used in Lionel's earlier miniature lampposts.

The top finial, which unscrews to provide access to the bulb, is usually nickel-plated, but can be found in unplated brass, typically as part of the gray wartime version. For some reason, the 35 was omitted from most bulb-replacement charts. However, the bulb chart in the back of the 1950 catalog lists L1447 as the proper bulb. Each 35 came in a separate box. All research examples of these boxes include the names of the three cities where Lionel had sales offices. This suggests that no new boxes were produced for 1949, the year "San Francisco" disappeared from the Lionel label. Dimensions: 6⅛" high.

(A) 1940–41 and 1945–49. Silver-painted post and top. Finial is usually nickel-plated.   **15**   **20**   **32**   **50**

(B) 1941–42. Semi-gloss medium-gray painted post and top. Finial of this lamp is usually unplated brass.

    15   **25**   **35**   **60**

045/45/45N AUTOMATIC GATEMAN, 1935–42 and 1945–49

Perhaps Lionel's most popular accessory, this small metal gatehouse (and its plastic successor, the 145, last cataloged in 1966) spanned 30 years of catalog appearances. As a train approaches, the gatehouse door swings open and the gateman pops out with his lantern (illuminated by a light in the accessory base) to warn motorists. Abrupt movement of the gateman in exiting the house causes his pivoted right arm to swing. Once the main line is clear, he steps back inside the house and the door closes.

Number 45 was originally intended for Standard gauge and 045 for O gauge, although the accessories are identical. The difference was in the method of activation. Prior to the introduction of the 41 Accessory Contactor in 1936 and its use with the 45 in 1937, the gateman was supplied with a section of straight track, either Standard or O gauge, with one outside rail insulated. Since the track section was included inside the box, the different track necessitated different size boxes and different item numbers. When the 41 replaced the insulated track sections in 1937, Lionel changed the accessory's number to 45N, indicating suitability for either track. After World War II, the "N" appeared only in 1945 before being dropped from the catalog listing. Apparently, the bottom stamp did not change, as "45N" stamps are reported through 1949.

Catalog pictures from 1935 through 1947 show the gateman's stamped-metal diamond-shaped sign oriented 90 degrees to the door, which is the correct orientation for layout use so that oncoming drivers can see the sign. After 1947, the catalog illustration was changed to show a crossbuck oriented parallel to the door side of the shanty. The actual product always had the sign or crossbuck facing toward the front, parallel to the door side of the shanty, probably for sales appeal on the dealer's shelf. However, the sign can be repositioned on the post by removing the cap, lifting off the sign, and reassembling in the desired position.

Instruction sheets for the 45 and 045 are numbered 45-50 and dated 11-35, 1-36, and 10-36, all printed in dark blue ink on light blue paper. When the accessory number changed to 45N in 1937, the instruction sheet part number changed to 45N-1 for the 3-37 and 7-38 issues, then to 45N-2 for issues of 1-42 and 10-45. One reason for the change from 45N-1 to 45N-2 may have been a switch from the 41 contactor to the 153C Track Contactor.

	Gd	VG	Ex	LN

versions of the 56 are always green, either the lighter shade used on the base of the 45N, or a darker green. A clear lens, which usually yellows with age, surrounds the L432 screw-base bulb. The nickel-plated finial has the same design as the finial used on the prewar 57 Lamp Post. Traditional terminal posts and nuts are used to attach the wiring. Unlike its long-time production partner, the 58 Lamp Post, the base of the 56 retained its open design with corner legs throughout its production. The values listed are only for postwar versions. Dimensions: 7¾" high.

	21	32	43	55

58 LAMP POST, 1922–42 and 1946–50

Described by Lionel in the 1947 consumer catalog as having "a graceful, ornamental design," the 58 is popularly referred to as a "gooseneck lamp." During its 21-year prewar run, this lamp came in ten colors or shades, but only the ivory, or cream, was produced in the postwar era. Ed Barbret notes that the key feature distinguishing postwar production from prewar was the mold change made to eliminate the "feet" on the lamp's base.

Besides this lamp's susceptibility to paint chipping, the brass "bell" surrounding the teardrop-shaped L1441(W) bulb sometimes cracks from the rim to the base of the bulb. These lamps typically were sold with the bulb packed in a separate box, marked 39-3, placed inside the main accessory box. Examples observed with the separately packaged bulb include a new prewar post and a new, late production post (identified by the box having only New York and Chicago, a style that debuted in 1948). Two solid, single-conductor coiled wires with brown insulation accompanied these two examples. There were probably at least two mold cavities used in the manufacture of this lamp, because slight casting variations have been observed. Dimensions: 7½" high.

	20	33	46	60

64 HIGHWAY LAMP POST, 1940–42 and 1945–49

The last page of the 1940 consumer catalog announced two new scale models: the 35 and 64 lampposts. At $1.50, the 64 cost only 25 cents more than the 35, but it appears to have been considerably more expensive to produce. Instead of using the one-piece casting of the 35, the 64 used two castings: a base and a

70 Lamp Posts showing two- and three-city boxes, terminal nuts, and base detail. Center left: Underside has swivel stop not soldered to center post. Center middle: Solder has been applied to underside to improve electrical contact. Center right: No swivel stop or flair on central tube (held by a spring washer).

	Gd	VG	Ex	LN

combination arm/socket/support. A brass tube, topped with a brass finial, holds the arm. A brass channel caps the wire trough in the arm. Like the 35, the entire 64 was apparently painted after it was assembled, including the soldered wire under the base. Number 64 is known only in 45N green.

A unique 64-15 light bulb (later renumbered L452W) was created for this delicate accessory and never used elsewhere. As a result, the bulb is scarce today. It has not yet been reproduced in the same form as the original. (A replacement bulb has been made, but it does not have the same shape.) The 64 should be operated, if at all, at considerably less than 12 volts to preserve the life of its all-but-irreplaceable bulb. Several mint-in-box examples examined came with a red circular tag warning against operation at over 12 volts.

The base of the 64 has the same spring-clip electrical connections as the 35 Boulevard Lamp as well as similar "feet" along the two long edges. The feet of the 64 (unlike those of the 58) remained unchanged for postwar production. Prewar versions included two coiled wires, but postwar examples have the brown insulated wires already stripped and inserted in the clips. The remaining wire is either loosely wrapped around the pole or left hanging beside it.

Although replacement bulbs were available individually boxed for separate sale, all new 64s observed had the bulb installed. New lampposts were wrapped in plain or Lionel-imprinted paper, with a separate small wrap of paper around the arm and bulb. Earlier, probably prewar, examples had a U-shaped cardboard liner over the arm pointing downward. No boxes with only New York and Chicago have been reported for the 64, which indicates that it was probably not produced after 1948. Excellent or Like New requires a working original bulb. Dimensions: 6¾" high.

	30	45	60	75

70 YARD LIGHT, 1948–50

This interesting accessory first appeared as a component of the 397 Operating Diesel-Type Coal Loader in the 1948 catalog. Apparently, the 397 barely made it into production in 1948, as the earliest known instruction sheet is dated 12-48. Nevertheless, there is evidence that the 70 Yard Light was also sold separately in that year, possibly well before the 397 was actually produced. Boxes with New York, Chicago, and San Francisco (last made in 1948) are fairly common for the 70. Later examples are in boxes without San Francisco, while no 397 has been reported with the earlier box with three cities. Black molded Bakelite was used for the base of the 70. It is prone to cracking at the top due to the brittle nature of this material and the design of the base. A 70 with a red base is shown on the early prototype coal loader in the 1948 catalog, but only black is known for actual production lampposts.

The method used to attach the pole to its base is useful in tracking production changes and dating lamps. Looking at the underside, note that the base is molded with two stops that project inward from the skirt ringing the base. Early versions have a small metal finger tab attached just under the rolled end of the post. The bottom end of the post is rolled like an ordinary rivet. Since the post does not grip the base tightly, the lamp and post can be swiveled with respect to the base. The finger tab contacts the molded-in stops to limit movement. This is necessary because the power wire runs up the center of the post and can be twisted and eventually broken by unrestricted swiveling. The stops are recessed on one edge to accommodate the thickness of the finger tab and to provide about 180 degrees of swivel. One example was observed with the finger tab installed on the wrong side of the stops, thereby greatly restricting swivel.

Electrical "ground" for the lamp is provided by the nickel-plated brass post, so it is necessary to have good electrical contact from the post, through the swivel joint, to the stationary ground terminal post on the base. Evidently, the weak link was the non-moving joint between the metal finger tab and the rolled edge of the pole, so a drop of solder was added to later lamps to improve contact. This remedy can still be applied to the early lamp if the bulb burns dimly or not at all.

Riveting the center post to the Bakelite base was probably a tricky operation and may have resulted in many cracked bases, especially at the thin top section where the pole exits. The design was finally changed to eliminate the rolled post and the finger tab. The pole remained straight, and a four-finger spring washer was pressed down around it to contact the ground pad extending from one of the terminal posts. This change simplified production and probably greatly reduced the incidence of cracked bases.

However, it also resulted in three distinct disadvantages. It forced the center wire to cross the sharp bottom edge of the pole, it permitted unrestricted swiveling of the lamp and post (making it possible to twist the center wire too much), and it prevented the lamp from sitting flat. This last problem occurred because the pole length was not properly adjusted when the rolled post was eliminated. The extra material for the roll was left pointing down, where it exceeded the depth of the skirt on the base when the thickness of the wire exiting the pole is considered. Further, the sharp edge of the pole can cut through the insulation of the center wire and cause a short circuit.

An L363 bulb came installed in the 70. There was no inner packing or wrapping for 70 as there had been for earlier lamp-

Rare dealer master cartons for a dozen 70 and a dozen 71 Lamp Posts. J. Lampert Collection.

	Gd	VG	Ex	LN

posts. Boxes with three and two cities are known. A mint-in-box example with the earlier box has taller terminal nuts with only the top half of the nuts knurled (raised ridges for easier gripping). Later examples seem to have used a nut about half the standard height with the entire outer surface knurled. Two coiled wires and an inspection slip accompanied each boxed 70. The 70 lasted only three years, but its top lamp bracket and housing were subsequently used on the 395 Floodlight Tower through 1956. Dimensions: 4½″ high.

	Gd	VG	Ex	LN
	23	35	50	70

71 LAMP POST, 1949–59

Referring to the introduction of the 71, the 1949 catalog stated, "simplified construction is (the) reason for low cost of this die cast, enameled Lamp." Although similar to the 35 Boulevard Lamp, the 85-cent price of the 71 (compared to $2.25 for a 35 in 1949) indicates the extent of the simplification. Eliminated were the electrical spring-clips, finial, separate top, and inner top-retaining bracket. All that was left (beside the lamp contact, bulb, and spring) was a one-piece base and post casting, press-on globe, and ground eyelet staked to a stud cast in the base. Stripped and tinned wires dangle from beneath the base, eliminating the need for terminals. A notch in the base allows these wires to exit to the side when the lamp is mounted to a tabletop.

Bayonet-base bulbs were still relatively new, and their use on the 71 introduced a necessary part, the R-91 Lamp Spring. This spring was not needed on the 35's screw-base bulb. Offsetting the cost of the spring was the benefit of slightly faster assembly and the fact the L53 bulb would not shake loose in shipping or service. Dimensions: 6″ high.

	Gd	VG	Ex	LN
	12	16	22	30

75 GOOSE NECK LAMPS, 1961–63

Displayed in a cream color in the 1961 catalog, production versions of the 75 Lamp Post are known only in unpainted black plastic. Two thin, stranded wires with clear plastic coating extend from the bottom of each lamp to provide electrical connections. A notch in the base allows the wires to exit when the lamp is fastened to a tabletop. An L19W two-pin, 14-volt bulb came installed in each lamppost. This is the only Lionel application of the frosted (W) version of the L19 bulb. Two lampposts were packaged in a part number 75-17 Window Box and were held in place by an inner liner cut out to receive the outline of the lamp's base and bell-shaped reflector.

Despite its single-structure appearance, the lamp can be disassembled for repair. The bell-shaped reflector can be gently twisted from side to side, although not far in either direction, and pulled off. The small piece that contains the pin receptacles also can be pulled off the curved portion of the post with a gentle twisting motion. Then the wires can be pulled through and repaired or replaced.

No significant variations have been reported. Prices shown are for a pair of the 75s, because that is how they were sold and are usually found today. There is only one known instruction sheet, part number 75-15, dated 11-61, printed in black ink on pale green paper. Dimensions: 1¾″ x 1½″ base, 6½″ high.

	12	17	25	45

76 BOULEVARD STREET LAMP, 1959–66 and 1968–69

Although shown as silver in the 1959 catalog, the 76 has appeared only in green. It is a plastic replica of the 71, which was cataloged for the last time in 1959. The 76 came packaged in a set of three at an introductory price of $2.95, or just under $1.00 each. This compares to $1.25 for the die-cast 71 in its last year. A two-pin, clear L19 bulb was installed in each new 76, and the ordinary black insulated connecting wires were left dangling from the bottom. A notch in the base allows the wire to exit when the lamp is attached to a tabletop. Four different packages for the three-lamp set are known: B76 blister pack, window box, Hagerstown box and Orange Picture box.

Like the 75, the 76 looks as though it cannot be disassembled, but the piece that houses the pin receptacle terminals does separate from the top of the column with a gentle side-to-side twisting motion. Then the wires and terminals can be reached for repair or replacement. The lamp globe is interchangeable with a 71-8, but the design of the top on the globe is slightly different, indicating a new die or a rework of the original. Prices shown are for a set of three lamps, since that is how they were sold and are usually found today. Instruction sheets have part number 76-10, dated 2-60 or 9-65. Earlier sheets are printed on pale green paper in dark green or black ink, while the later ones are printed in black ink on white paper. Also available as B76, an NRS blister pack. Dimensions: 6″ high.

	10	17	24	40

140 AUTOMATIC BANJO SIGNAL, 1954–66

This is a warning sign with a moving arm that passes in front of a steadily illuminated red light and creates the illusion of flashing. Like many other accessories, the 140 uses Lionel's Vibrotor motor with a vibrating coil mechanism like the one used in the 3520 Searchlight Car or the 494 Rotating Beacon. Attached to the coil, a neoprene washer with tiny molded fingers causes an adjacent metal driving cup to rotate when 12 to 16 volts of alternating current (AC) are applied. The AC causes the coil to vibrate. Use of a separate variable voltage supply is recommended to obtain the precise voltage required for best operation.

It is important to keep the inside of the driving cup and the surface of the driving washer free from oil or grease. Once free of grease, a light dusting of talcum powder inside the cup helps prevent sticking. If required, the bearing and mating cup shaft should be thoroughly cleaned and lubricated with Molykote, using care not to get any on the cup or washer. (Molykote is the brand name of a powdered molybdenum disulfide lubricant.) Inspect the driving washer to insure that all the tiny fingers are intact.

Thomas Rollo suggests that radial scratches made on the inside of the cup may improve operation. They allow the fingers to get a better bite, which drives the cup faster and more forcefully. Unfortunately, this procedure also tends to wear out the fingers faster. Therefore, if you intend to operate a 140 regularly, you should clean and lubricate it before resorting to the radial scratches.

Although the 140 came in several different packages over the 13 years it was offered, only one minor variation has been found. This is the paint finish on the base, which occasionally appears in a crackle black, instead of the usual smooth finish. An L53R red bulb is used for the signal light. The illustration on the instruction sheet says, in bold letters, to pull out the stop sign to access the bulb. This can be confusing, since there are two stop signs on the signal. To change the bulb, move the stop sign on the wig-wag carefully to one side. Then the front of the lamp housing behind the wig-wag, which includes the stop sign on the signal post, can be pulled out.

Each 140 came with a 145C Track Contactor and instruction sheet. Two versions of the sheet are known, both dated 8-54 with part number 140-59. One is printed in black ink, the other in bright blue ink, both on white paper. Starting in 1955, a 145C instruction sheet (covering all accessories using this contactor) was included. Dimensions: 1¾″ x 3″ base, 7⅜″ high.

(A) 1954–65, as described, in a box appropriate to the year. Examples with a crackle finish on the black base are rare and should command a premium, but usually the variation is not even noticed!

	22	30	38	50

(B) 1966. Same as (A) except packaged in a blister pack as B140. The packaging is everything, since the signal itself is identical to other years' production. Removal from the packaging destroys the unique character of this collectible. Like New indicates an intact but shopworn package. A perfect blister pack can bring a substantially higher price than shown.

	50	75	100	225

Left to right: B163 Block Signal, B151 Semaphore, B262 Crossing Gate, and B140 Banjo Signal, all in blister pack form of packaging used in 1966. ("B" prefix indicates a blister pack.) The 262 in the foreground is in an earlier window box. Note the variation in corner construction of the box "frames."

145 AUTOMATIC GATEMAN, 1950–66

A redesigned version of the 45 (described above), this popular accessory retained the same basic operation. Instead of a stamped-metal construction, however, injection-molded plastic was used to create a more realistic and detailed house. Stamped steel remained for construction of the somewhat redesigned base. Instead of the robust steel post and die-cast crossbuck of the 45, the "RAILROAD/CROSSING" sign from the 309 Sign Set was used. Perhaps more to scale in appearance, this plastic sign with metal base is not nearly as sturdy as its predecessor and is prone to breaking.

Surprisingly few changes were made in 145's design over its 17 years of catalog appearances. Most noticeable is the change in roof color from the initial red to the much more common maroon. Red remained as the toolbox cover color throughout.

Less obvious is the change to the base. While the 45 had a bottom plate painted to match the rest of the base, the 145 used a galvanized metal plate, obviously added after the rest of the base was painted. This plate initially had the usual Lionel nomenclature stamped into it. As the years passed, however, this die was evidently not maintained and the nomenclature became less distinct and was finally removed. Later examples show no evidence of this nomenclature, leaving nothing but the "LIONELVILLE" sign above the house door to identify the accessory as a Lionel product.

Two methods were provided for wiring the 145. For a realistic appearance, the required three wires could be brought in overhead, from a nearby pole perhaps, and run through three holes provided in the rear of the house near the roof peak. For those desiring underground wiring, holes were provided in the base and the ceiling. This permits wiring to enter from under the layout and go unseen to the top of the house. Lifting off the roof allows wiring entering either way to be connected to the three fahnestock clips provided. There is one common wire and a power wire for the lamp and for the activating solenoid.

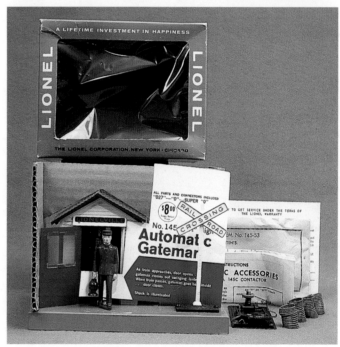

Later – and flimsier – packing for 145. J. Algozzini Collection.

The 145 dispensed with the glowing lantern of the 45 (illuminated only when the gateman was activated) and illuminated the shanty with an L363 or L431 bayonet base 14-volt lamp whenever power was applied to the lighting circuit. This required three circuits for 145 (the 45 needed only two).

Only two other changes were noted in the 145. While the figure usually has painted hands and face, this decoration was eliminated toward the end of production, leaving a completely unpainted blue figure. Sometime during the first year or two of production, an eyelet was substituted for a washer in the bottom door hinge, perhaps to provide better clearance between the door and base. Also noted in the Lionel Service Manual is the recommended addition of an RCS-40 washer to the stud below the figure to elevate it slightly to prevent it from rubbing on the base.

148 Dwarf Trackside Light with original box.

A window-boxed 151 Semaphore with an array of four other variations. Note the single unused hole in the upper post of the red blade example and green base example on the ends. Two unused holes are in the left center example and three in the right center example. A typical parts envelope, instruction sheet, and 145C Contactor are in the foreground. Often the more versatile 153C Contactor was included with 151s instead of a 145C. The rare red blade example has the flat lenses and raised V in the blade typical of early 151s; the others have the more common domed lenses and recessed V.

	Gd	VG	Ex	LN

So far, 26 different printings of the 145 Track Contactor instruction sheet that accompanied each 145 have been observed. These include three different part numbers (145-40, -51, and -56) and 23 different dates, beginning with the issue of 6-50 and concluding with the issue of 4/65. Dimensions: 7″ x 5¼″ base, 4½″ high.

(A) 1950. Galvanized steel underside on base with the usual Lionel nomenclature stamped into the metal; red molded, unpainted roof; blue-suited figure with painted face and hands.

	26	33	45	60

(B) 1951. Same as (A) except maroon molded, unpainted roof. Probably during this year, an eyelet replaced the washer in the bottom door hinge.

	26	33	45	60

	Gd	VG	Ex	LN

(C) 1952–57. Same as (B) except during this period the Lionel nomenclature stamped into the base bottom wore out and disappeared.

	26	33	45	60

(D) 1957–66. Same as (C) except figure is entirely blue with unpainted hands and face. Lionel nomenclature is gone from the underside of the base.

	26	33	45	60

148 DWARF TRACKSIDE LIGHT, 1957–60

Instructions for the 148 state, "Lionel No. 148 Dwarf Signal is sold with a No. 148-100 manual controller which, electrically, is a single-pole, double-throw switch, and which can be used to control the signal by itself, or to interlock it with an insulated track block or siding so that the operator can control both simultaneously." The accessory itself is nothing more than L19(R) and L19(G) two-pin light bulbs in a plastic housing.

The switch does the controlling. It can be connected to turn on the red or green light or also to turn current on and off in an insulated track section. Electrically, it does with manual control what the 153C Controller does using the weight of a passing train. In fact, the instructions mention that a 148 can be used with a 153C.

Many 148s sold today, even those in original boxes, are missing the switch, perhaps because it looks like a 364C switch, leading people to believe that it was placed in the box by mistake. The switch number (148-100) is printed on the bottom. Having it with the 148 should add at least $10 to the prices shown. Only one instruction sheet is known, part number 148-13, printed in blue on white paper and dated 10-57. Dimensions: 1⅝″ x 1⅞″ base, 2″ high.

	18	35	45	80

151 SEMAPHORE, 1947–66 and 1968–69

Considering that the 151 was Lionel's first new signal in postwar production, it received only a minimal amount of promotion in the 1947 catalog, not even the customary "NEW" banners to herald its debut. Instead, the catalog description explains that with an empty block, the semaphore blade points upward and the bull's-eye glows green. As a train passes, the blade drops to a horizontal position and the bull's-eye glows red. A green base was shown in the 1947 catalog illustration. Similar artwork was used the next year, but the base was changed to black, the usual color found on this accessory.

A unique instruction sheet was never issued for 151. Instead, it was covered in 153C instruction sheets, starting with 153C-22, dated 8-47. A 153C Contactor was included with each new semaphore for at least the first two years of production. The 145C instruction sheet also showed connections for the 151, beginning with its initial issue, dated 6-50. These were simplified because the 145C offers no train-control function, as is possible with the 153C. One mint-in-box 151 has envelope 151-39 containing a 145C and 145-40 instruction sheet, dated 5-52. Further research is required to determine when the 145C replaced the 153C as the 151's controller and whether the 153C was later restored.

Interesting changes occurred in the 151 Semaphore over the years. Since its base is borrowed from the 153 Block Signal, these changes are common to both accessories. When introduced, the 151 used the 153 base with no change except color, although several 151 examples have been found with a green base as used on the 153. Earliest of the 151 research examples has a black base with "NO. 153" located just above "MADE IN U.S. OF AMERICA." Both these nomenclatures are located on the underside of the base oriented lengthwise. "PART NO. 153-3" also appears on the base underside, oriented crossways between the terminals and ladder tabs.

There are two curious features to look for in examining the underside of these early bases. First, even though the raised printing is uppercase sans serif, all the "I"s are dotted! Second, "NO. 153" is found in two different positions with respect to the words below it, and the roughness of the casting in only one indicates that there were at least two mold cavities, or maybe separate molds, for 153-3 (the part number of the base).

To avoid having the wrong accessory number on the 151 base yet continue to use a common part, Lionel first removed "NO. 153." The base part number (153-3) remained, but the area where the accessory number appeared was modified to a blank, raised plaque. At the same time, the type was revised to eliminate the dots above the "I"s. Probably not too long afterward, the part number 153-3 was removed by thickening the entire end of the mold so that it appears to have a step beginning just past the ladder tabs. The method of clinching the terminals also changed, most likely because of the slightly thicker base. Early bases have rolled crimps on the terminals, while the thickened bases use a star crimp.

Toward the end of production, the painting process for the base may have been simplified, since the underside of the base, usually well coated with black paint, exhibits only some overspray. Generous amounts of bare metal appear on these late examples.

Apparently, Lionel engineers were not content to change the base and leave the rest of the accessory alone. Very early examples were fitted with red and green lenses that are flat on the front, more like those in the early catalog pictures, and are "heat-staked" in back. That is, the lens is inserted through the hole in the arm and the rear of the lens is heated to melt it and make it flow outward to form a ridge that holds it in place. That was soon changed to the familiar rubbery domed design that is pressed into place. These lenses go in best by twisting them slightly. The radial ridges around the edges were probably as much to assist in assembly as for appearance.

A close examination of several arms reveals that at least two different molds were used. Note particularly the hub on the front side and the depressions and ejector pin mark on the rear. The yellow or red paint on the arm appears to be done by hand on earlier models. Later models were roller-painted yellow. To facilitate these two operations, the black "V" shape in the blade was raised above the surface in early, hand-painted production. By recessing the "V" in later production (this is the common version), Lionel simplified the decorating operation to one sweep of a paint roller.

Although the lamp socket almost always houses a bayonet-base bulb, Lionel apparently experienced problems casting the socket. This socket is the part that attaches with a small screw and can be removed to gain access to the bulb. Early examples use a casting about .49″ in diameter near the wire entry end. The top of this early base, where it mates with the upper housing surrounding the globe of the bulb, has a small band that brings its diameter flush with the upper housing. On the bottom there is a round hole where the wire enters. There are differences in forming the edge of this hole, suggesting that two mold cavities were used. This type of housing has been observed both with and without two tiny holes on the side, one in front and one in back, 180 degrees apart. Looking into these holes, you can see the pins on the bulb base used to retain it in the socket.

Lionel probably had the same problem molding the slots for the bayonet-base bulb here as it did with the 71 Lamp Post. Certainly by 1949, and sometime after the base changed to the final configuration without any numbering, the bulb socket casting changed to a larger diameter, about .53″ near the wire entry end. This larger diameter fits flush with the upper housing without the need for a larger-diameter top ring. Where the wire enters the bottom, a rectangular slot replaced the round hole of the earlier design. If you look at the flats on each side of this slot on several 151s, you will discover a slight difference, reinforcing the conclusion there were probably two mold cavities for this part.

Not even the pole escaped variation. Besides the aluminum temporarily substituted for steel in 1957, there are differences in the hole pattern on the top front of the pole. For some reason, all 151s have at least one unused round hole in this area. On all examples observed that had either the first or second version of the base, there is only one unused hole. Semaphores with the third version of the base (no numbers at all) are found with two or three unused holes. Later versions, dated by their boxes, have three holes. The purpose of these holes, and why the number varied, is unknown, but they likely aided assembly.

The cap on top of the pole is nickel-plated on all examples observed. The 151-11 Semaphore Arms are frequently found broken. Excellent reproductions are available, although they are not marked as such. The rubbery red and green lenses have not been as successfully reproduced. Other variations of interest are noted in the following listings.

Either L363 or L53 bayonet-base bulbs can be used for the 151. They draw .20 and .10 amps, respectively. The Lionel Service Manual calls for a 151-51 bulb, which translates to L363 in Lionel's revised numbering system. However, the Lionel Replacement Lamp charts in the same manual show L53 as the correct bulb for the 151. Both bulbs appeared in original 151s. Due to heat from the closely cased bulb, operators are advised to use the lower-power L53 bulb to avoid heat damage to the green lens.

Two bulb housings for 151 have been found tooled for a screw-base rather than a bayonet bulb, as seems to be found in production examples of the 151. These housings were found at Madison Hardware Co., suggesting that a screw-base bulb was planned but abandoned after the housing had been tooled. No bulb listing yet found lists anything but a bayonet base for this application. Dimensions: 4″ x 1¼″ base, 9¾″ high to tip of raised arm.

(A) 1947. Earliest version with a green base. Base underside has two numbers ("NO. 153" and "153-3") and dots above both uppercase "I"s in MADE IN U.S. OF AMERICA. One unused hole in the pole, below the lamp housing. Yellow hand-painted blade with raised black "V." Red and green lenses are flat, heat-staked on the rear of the blade. Several examples of this variation have been reported.   25   40   80   100

(B) 1947. Same as (A) except with the usual black base.
                                              15   20   25   35

(C) Same as (B) except red-painted semaphore blade instead of yellow. A rare variation, but enough have been found to authenticate it. Reproductions not reported, but caution in buying is advised, as a yellow blade with a raised "V" could be repainted red.   NRS

Left to right: 152 Automatic Crossing Gate, 252 Crossing Gate, and 155 Ringing Signal (early version). Operation of the 252 surpassed that of 152.

	Gd	VG	Ex	LN

(D) Common version with black-painted base, silver-painted steel pole, and yellow arm paint with recessed black "V." Dome-shaped press-in lenses. Pole may have two or three unused holes in front, below lamp housing. Base may have "153-3" or no number. Dots removed above "I"s in MADE IN U.S. OF AMERICA.

	22	35	46	50

(E) 1957. Same as (D) except unpainted aluminum pole with three unused holes. This version came in an orange-red box known to have been produced only in late 1956 and 1957. Its instruction sheet is dated 1957. T. Rollo comment.

	25	40	50	60

(F) 1966. Same as (D) except came in a blister pack as B151 Automatic Semaphore. Several accessories were packaged this way in 1966; it is the packaging that makes this variation collectible.

	—	—	—	125

(G) Same as (D) except no ladder and no holes in the base where the bottom of the ladder can be inserted. M. Goldey Collection. Reader input requested.

				NRS

152 AUTOMATIC CROSSING GATE, 1940–42 and 1945–49

The prewar versions of this accessory are known with gates painted silver, white, and, in 1941–42, gray. Postwar production has been reported with only silver-painted gates. Hash marks on each side of the gate are provided by punch-outs that expose the black color of construction paper strips inside. They also serve to lighten the arm. A single L431(R) red bayonet-base bulb hangs on the larger gate to warn approaching motorists.

Of interest is the fact that the 152 may have represented Lionel's first use of a bayonet-base bulb. In 1950, several accessories, such as the 154 Automatic Highway Signal and O22 switches (but not the O22C Controller) were converted to bayonet-base bulbs. But the 152 evidently had one from its beginning a decade before!

Unlike the more detailed 252, which replaced it in 1950, the all-metal 152 includes a pedestrian gate (a small arm meant to block passage on the adjacent sidewalk). Many examples are

found without it, leading some collectors to speculate that some 152s were produced that way. However, research indicates that all production 152s included a pedestrian gate. Supporting evidence for this conclusion comes from the original boxes used for prewar and postwar examples, which are long enough to accommodate this gate. Also, examples of the 152 without a pedestrian gate typically have missing paint on its two pivot studs, which usually indicates wear from the action of the gate. All known Lionel illustrations and photographs in catalogs and instruction booklets show the second gate.

The pedestrian gate can be temperamental and difficult to adjust. A spring in the base returns the main gate to its upright position, whereas the later 252 uses a counterweight for this purpose. The 152's return spring is adjusted by means of a screw in the base. If the spring tension is too light, the main gate will not rise all the way. If the tension is too great, the solenoid may not be strong enough to lower the gate.

Operation of the pedestrian gate depends on a small tab on one side that fits under a mating tab on the main gate. When the main gate rises, its tab presses down on the smaller gate's tab and forces it to rise. When the main gate lowers, the smaller gate falls by gravity. Unfortunately, this mechanism can malfunction if either tab is slightly bent or the spring tension for the main gate is not adjusted correctly. Many frustrated owners removed their pedestrian gates to avoid this problem. Some pedestrian gates were lost, which is probably why examples turn up without them. However, Lionel undoubtedly equipped all 152s with a pedestrian gate at the factory. Thomas Rollo and Charles Weber comments.

Number 152-40 instruction sheets, all with dark blue ink on blue paper, are dated 9-40, 2-41, and 10-45. They were superseded by the 153C-18, dated 3-46. An undated note, part number 152-54, explaining how to adjust the gate elevating spring, was also included with new 152s. Dimensions: 3⅞" x 1⅝" base, 13¼" from tip of main gate to tip of pedestrian gate in the lowered position, raises to 9⅝" high.

	16	20	38	45

153 AUTOMATIC BLOCK SIGNAL, 1940–42 and 1945–59

Lionel's advertising copy might lead you to believe that this signal had train-control powers and was able to prevent collisions when two trains operated simultaneously on the same track. In truth, the 153 is nothing more than two light bulbs in an attractive housing. Train control is provided by a 153C, the special single-pole double-throw (SPDT), weight-operated switch designed for this accessory and used for several others. SPDT simply means one terminal of the switch (number 3 on the 153C) is connected to either of two other terminals, depending on which of the two possible switch positions is selected.

Two main events account for most of the variations in the 153: the 1947 introduction of the 151 Semaphore, which shared the same base casting, and the switch from a 6- to 8-volt screw-base bulb to a 12- to 16-volt bayonet-base type in 1950. Neither change results in much difference in value, but most operators prefer the later version. Details of the base changes, described in the listing for the 151, apply to the 153, whose base was always painted green. Although the 151 is known to have been made with a 153 green base, the 153 with a black base has never been reliably authenticated.

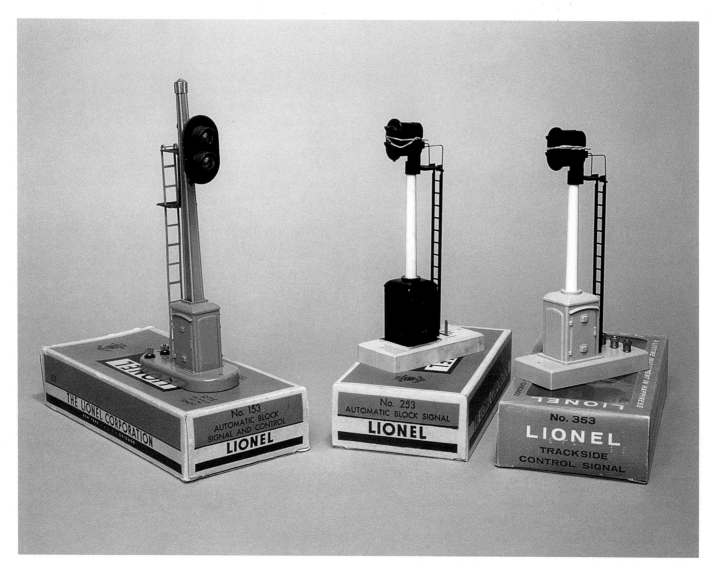

Prior to 1950, all 153s have a resistor in the common wire (shared by both bulbs) leading to the center terminal. Its purpose is to allow use of 6- to 8-volt L50(R) and L50(G) bulbs with the normal 12- to 16-volt operating range for running the train. In those days, 6 to 8 volts was the standard for automotive use, so the bulbs were most likely off-the-shelf for that industry's suppliers. Fortunately, the volume of bulb usage in the toy train market eventually made it attractive for manufacturers to produce bulbs in the higher voltage and special shape that this application required. For 1950, the target (lamp housing) was redesigned for 12- to 16-volt L53(R) and L53(G) bayonet-base bulbs. This eliminated the resistor on the bottom, which probably reduced production costs. The catalog price remained $4.25, as it was in 1949.

Chronologically, the 153 started in 1940 with both part number "153-3" and "NO. 153" in raised letters molded in the underside of its base. A resistor was included (different configurations are known), and the steel pole was painted silver. Screw-base 6- to 8- volt bulbs were used, and the pole cap was nickel-plated. In late 1941 and possibly into 1942, the pole color changed to semi-gloss medium gray, and the cap was plated or painted gray. After the war, just in time for the 1945 holiday season, the signal returned to its 1940 configuration. Probably not long after the introduction of the 151 in 1947, the base began to change, first with the removal of "NO. 153" and then, somewhat later, of the 153-3 base part number. Silver-painted pole caps,

instead of the usual nickel, have been observed on what otherwise appear to be 153s of this vintage. In 1950, the 153 was modified to use bayonet-base bulbs. In 1957, aluminum briefly replaced steel for the pole.

For each of the 18 years the 153 was cataloged, it was supplied with a 153C Contactor. Instruction sheets for the 153 begin with part number 153-30, dated 8-40. This sheet, known in two variations, has dark blue ink on lighter blue paper. In addition to the initial printing, there was a reprint with corrections in red ink on page 5. A second printing incorporating the changes was dated 9-40. One more issue, 11-41, was printed before the war interrupted production. After the war, the part number changed to 153-45 for issues of 10-45, 4-46, and 12-46. Then the 153C-18 instruction sheet took over, with issues dated 3-46 and 11-46. Note that the only two issues of 153C-18 (the part number changed to 153C-22 with the 8-47 issue) overlap with the last two issues of 153-45. It was unusual for Lionel to concurrently have two instruction sheets covering the same accessory. Dimensions: 4″ x 1¾″ base, 8¾″ high.

(A) 1940–41 and 1945–49. Base with one, two, or no numbers, steel pole painted silver, nickel cap, screw-base bulbs, and resistor

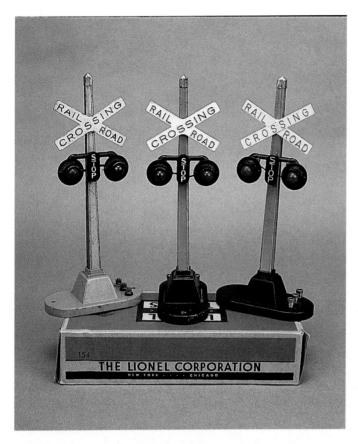

Variations of the 154 Highway Crossing Signal. Left to right: Prewar version with *Hiawatha* orange base, mis-assembled version with gray post from 1942, and common post-1950 version with plastic crossbuck.

	Gd	VG	Ex	LN

mounted on bottom. Silver-painted caps observed on what appear to be postwar signals. — **17 30 40 50**

(B) 1941–42. Same as (A) except steel pole painted semi-gloss medium gray, base has two numbers and cap nickel-plated or painted to match pole. — **25 40 55 80**

(C) 1950–59. Bayonet-base bulbs, no number on base, steel pole painted silver, nickel cap. — **17 30 40 50**

(D) 1957. Same as (C) except unpainted aluminum pole lighter in weight than others, came in Late Classic box with 1957 instruction sheet. — **17 30 40 50**

154 AUTOMATIC HIGHWAY SIGNAL, 1940–42, 1945–66, and 1968–69

The color of the die-cast base is the most interesting aspect of this long-running accessory. Was it ever made in red? From the point of introduction in Lionel's 1940 catalog through 1948, the 154 appeared with a red base. In 1949 the catalog changed it to black. Then in 1950 it went back to red. Finally, all subsequent catalog illustration showed it as black. So if the base exists in red at all, as some reliable sources claim, it is certainly one of the rarest of Lionel's many variations. Unfortunately, it could be convincingly faked, so an exorbitant premium is probably not justified. Some prewar examples are found in *Hiawatha* orange, a fairly rare color.

A special contactor, 154C, was designed for the 154 and never furnished with other accessories. It is practically the same as the 1045C used for the 1045 Operating Watchman, except that the contact plate is divided into two sections. The 1045C will work

	Gd	VG	Ex	LN

for the 154, since the intermittent contact caused by a train's wheels passing over the contactor make the lights flash on and off. The split contact of the 154C provides the added touch of making the lights flash alternately. Starting in 1954, this contactor was offered for separate sale under the heading "Replacement Accessories" in the consumer catalog, but it may have been available earlier in a separate-sale package.

From 1940 to 1949, the 154-11 Targets (light sockets) were made to accept a 154-18 (new number L1449R) 14-volt screw-base bulb. In 1950 the target was redesigned to use 153-50 (new numbers L53R or L363R) bayonet-base bulbs and given a 154-36 part number. Most likely, the 154-13 Cross Arm (metal) was changed to 154-34 Cross Arm (plastic) at the same time. This is the sign that has "RAIL ROAD/ CROSSING" on it and is hereafter called a "crossbuck." Both old and new parts for the crossbuck and the target are listed in the Lionel Service Manual pages issued 10-53. Until 1950 the crossbuck was die-cast metal, enameled white, with raised letters painted black, just like the signs in the 308 Yard Set. In 1950, the sign changed to molded white plastic, but still with raised letters that were painted black, like signs in the 309 Yard Set.

The usual color for the steel post is silver, but as with almost all other accessories, those from 1942 were painted semi-gloss medium gray. The cap, usually nickel-plated brass, may be found painted to match the post. According to reliable reports, in 1957 Lionel tried a batch of posts made of unpainted aluminum.

Numerous variations of the instruction sheet were issued over the years. All are part number 154-20. The issues of 6-40, 11-41, 10-45, 3-46, 12-46, 2-48, and 2-49 used dark blue ink on lighter blue paper. White paper with black ink was used for the issues of 7-49 and 2-50. There are three known versions of the next issue, 5-53. One uses dark blue ink on white paper and specifies only an L363(R) replacement lamp. The other two specify either L53(R) or L363(R) lamps and are printed in black or dark blue ink on white paper. The issue of 2/57 is available on white paper with dark blue ink and yellow paper with black ink. Starting with the issue of 8-59, the paper is reduced from approximately 9½″ by 6¼″, to 8½″ by 5½″. This issue is known in both black and blue ink on white paper. The last two issues, 4-61 and 4/65, have black ink on white paper. Lionel's varying use of a hyphen or a slash in the date should not be overlooked. Dimensions: 2″ x 4″ base, 8¼″ high.

(A) 1940–41 and 1945–49. Steel post painted silver, screw-base bulbs in target, die-cast crossbuck, base painted black. If a red base version of 154 exists, it would be this variation. — **16 25 40 45**

(B) 1941–42. Same as (A) except steel post painted semi-gloss medium gray. Cap on top of post usually painted to match but may be nickel-plated, black, or unplated brass. — **20 35 55 75**

(C) 1940–41. Same as (A) except base painted *Hiawatha* orange. — **25 40 60 80**

(D) 1950–69. Most common version with steel post painted silver, black base, target with bayonet-base bulbs, and white plastic crossbuck with raised black letters. — **16 25 40 45**

(E) 1957. Same as (D) except unpainted aluminum post lighter in weight than other versions. T. Rollo Collection. — **20 30 40 50**

(F) Same as (D) except with a black base from 151 Semaphore. Reportedly Hagerstown production, but more likely 1970 MPC using leftover original parts. **NRS**

(G) 1966. Same as (D) except packaged in a framed blister pack as B151. **NRS**

155 RINGING SIGNAL, 1955–57

This is another clever adaptation of Lionel's versatile Vibrotor. Here the motor is used to ring the bell and flash the warning lamps. For the 155, the disk driven by the vibrating coil has three impeller vanes mounted on top. As the disk turns, the vanes trip a bell clapper. In its travel, the clapper strikes the bell and closes either of two contacts to alternately flash the lamps. A 145C Track Contactor controls the action.

Except for the target from the 154 and the crossing sign from the 140, all the major parts were new for the 155. To improve operation and minimize adjustment, the ringing mechanism was redesigned in 1956 by replacing the leaf-type contact springs with coil springs. Other changes that year included the addition of rubber mounting grommets to the mechanism and feet to the signal base. The new mechanism, Part No. 155-70, was interchangeable with the previously made Part No. 155-40. The Lionel Service Manual for 1956 suggested that repairs should not be made on the old mechanism, recommending instead that the entire mechanism be replaced. This suggests the possibility of finding a repaired 1955 model with the new mechanism in an old base without the feet. The absence of feet on the base is the easiest way to distinguish the more common 1955 model.

Another interesting aspect of the 155's base relates to the propensity of some of the white plastic Lionel used in this era to turn a cream color (and in some cases almost a caramel color). This phenomenon is well known on such items as the 57 AEC Switcher, 6014-150 Wix Boxcar, and 6376 Circus Car. Pure white examples of these three are scarce. The fact that other items molded in white, such as the 6014 Frisco Boxcar and later 3472 and 3482 Automatic Refrigerated Milk Cars, do not show such a change seems to indicate that two different kinds, or batches, of plastic were used. There seems little doubt that most if not all the cream items started out as white. Bases of 155 Ringing Signals are usually white, but an example was examined that was cream, bordering on light caramel. However, scratches in some of the black hash marks on the side reveal that the plastic underneath is white.

The 155 uses the same 3520-16 Drive Washer and 3520-42 Adhesive Washer as the searchlight car. These parts need to be replaced when the tiny driving fingers on the washer wear off or are damaged. The Lionel Service Manual recommends brushing Molykote powder (see 140 listing) or powdered graphite on the surface of the washer and inside surface of the driven cup. Never use oil or grease! Don't forget to thoroughly clean the bearing and all surfaces before applying new lubricant. If you remove the mechanism for any reason, be sure that upon reassembly the terminal lug engages the speed nut that holds the post to the base. This provides the electrical ground for the warning lamps.

Only one instruction sheet is known for this accessory; part number 155-44, dated 9-55. Two printings were made, one using light blue ink and the other black ink, both on white paper. Although these instructions specify only L53(R) replacement lamps, the L363(R), which is the replacement bulb for the 154, can be used. The only difference in these bayonet-base bulbs is their current rating: 0.10 amps. for L53 and 0.20 for L363. Dimensions: 3″ x 3⅛″ base, 8½″ high.

(A) 1955. Early mechanism with copper leaf-type contacts, small holes in metal tabs projecting from mechanism for mounting accessory, no feet on base.   **30   45   60   75**

(B) 1956–57. Improved mechanism with spring contacts, rubber grommets in metal mounting tabs, and feet on plastic base. If grommets are missing, tabs can be seen to have a larger hole that's open at the end so the grommet can slide in. Lionel recommended replacement of early mechanisms with the grommet version, so examples may be found with grommet-type tabs, but no feet on the base.   **30   45   60   75**

(C) Same as (A) except probable factory error with no black stripes on base. Stripes are molded in base but are not painted black on this one. G. Salamone Collection.   **NRS**

163 SINGLE TARGET BLOCK SIGNAL, 1961–66 and 1968–69

Except for the target, the 163 and 353 signals are identical. Their common ancestor is the 253 Automatic Block Control, which included a time-delay controller in its base. That mold was reworked to provide the base for the 163 and 353. Several other components, such as the pole, ladder, and platform, are 253 parts. The 163 is slightly more complex than the 353, since it has a three-piece target assembly consisting of a one-hole target, white translucent flat-plate lens, and socket cover or lamp housing.

Indirect illumination from L19(R) and L19(G) two-pin, 14-volt miniature lamps located in the housing caused the 163's single lens to display the appropriate red or green color. Light intensity of the 163 is greatly diminished compared to the 353 Track Side Control Signal, which has a two-hole target fitted with directly viewed red and green bulbs. Functionally, these two signals are identical to the 153 Block Signal. They have no train-control function and are simply two bulbs electrically connected to a common return. Both the 163 and 353 were supplied with a 153C Contactor. As with the 153, the contactor lights the appropriate lamp and has the capability to control a train.

The instruction sheets for these two signals underwent some interesting twists over the years. Part number 153C-23, dated 3-60, came with the 353 in 1960. This is the final known issue of 153C-23. For some reason, the instruction sheets beginning with the issue of 4-61 were assigned part number 452-15, even though the title remained "How to Install No. 153C Contactors." Two printings of this are known, one in brown ink and the other in black ink, both on white paper. They are six-page foldout sheets, unlike the four-page final edition of 153C-23. The 352 included a 452-15 in its final year of 1961, and the 163 included it every year it was produced. After the 4-61 date, the next and final issue seems to have been dated 6/65, but it is possible there was also an issue dated 3-62. None has yet been reported, but on page 4 of the 6/65 sheet appears, "452-15 3-62." It is most unusual to see two different dates on the same instruction sheet.

A few variations of the 163 and its packaging are known. It can still be found as B163, the blister pack version. The usual packaging was the all-orange or the checkerboard boxes, but for the last year (1969) only a plain white box was used with identification stamped on only one end flap.

The terminal nuts started out with the usual nickel-plating, but toward the end of production they were left unplated and so appear in their natural brass color. Knurling on all these terminal nuts has a diamond design, unlike the earlier vertical line patterns. In earlier production, the base was unpainted beige plastic. This changed to an unpainted tan in later years. Dimensions: 4″ x 1¾″ base, 7⅜″ high.

(A) 1961–66. Beige unpainted base, nickel-plated terminal nuts. Conventional box adds somewhat to values shown, depending on box condition.   **20   28   38   50**

(B) 1968–69. Buckskin tan molded base, darker than the beige used previously, terminal nuts usually unplated brass. Last year (1969) known to have been packaged in a plain white box identified only on one end flap.   **20   28   38   50**

(C) 1966. Same as (A) except packaged in blister pack as B163. Value is based only on unique packaging. Like New indicates an intact but shopworn package. A perfect blister pack can bring a substantially higher price than shown.
                          —   —   —   250

195 FLOODLIGHT TOWER, 1957–66 and 1968–69

A very useful accessory for nighttime operations, the 195 had an unusually long run, considering its relatively late introduction. Although it is a simple accessory, there are a surprising number of variations. Three accessories used the same base and tower: 195 Floodlight, 199 Microwave Relay, and 299 Code Transmitter Beacon. The 195 was first and remained in production longer than the others. Using the same mold for different products led to the variations.

The 195, cataloged first in 1957, was designed only as a floodlight tower. When the 199 was introduced the following year, the tower top (Lionel called it a "platform") had to be revised by adding two narrow rectangular slots, which were used to attach the top structure of the 199. The base was also revised to remove the 195-15 part number. This resulted in a raised, blank plaque where the part number had been. An insert for the mold was made to replace the previously molded accessory name and number with a nomenclature appropriate for the accessory in production. As a result, a slight outline around the nomenclature appears on all towers produced after 1957. As noted in variation (B) below, this led to some bases that had to be renumbered! Earlier bases were molded in a lighter tan, while later ones are a darker tan.

With the advent of the 299 Code Transmitter Set in 1961, the tower top again had to be changed. This time two ears were added that served as guides for the 299's beacon top. Since the 195 was produced concurrently with the 199 and 299, it can be found with all three tower tops, both base nomenclature variations, and both shades of tan.

Additionally, the tower changed. In the beginning it was painted silver and had the raised word "LIONEL" heat-stamped in red. Some of the last examples made have an unpainted tower, and "Lionel" is not colored, which probably was done in an effort to cut costs. While the variations are of interest in dating a 195, all variations except (B) seem to be valued equally. Dimensions: 3¼″ x 3¼″ base, 12¼″ high.

(A) As described, with any of the tower top, tower, and base variations.   **30   45   60   75**

(B) Medium tan base with "199 MICROWAVE TOWER" molded in the underside in raised capitals, but the underside is

Variations of 195 Floodlight Tower and boxes. Note base colors and absence of red heat-stamping on raised "Lionel" on right example.

	Gd	VG	Ex	LN

also rubber-stamped "195 FLOOD LIGHT" in red. J. Breslin and J. Bratspis Collections.   **60   75   90   100**

252 CROSSING GATE, 1950–63

This long-produced accessory is made mostly of plastic. It replaced the all-metal 152 and eliminated the troublesome pedestrian gate. Like most real gates, the 252 uses two reliable counterweights to balance the gate arm, instead of the finicky spring and adjusting screw of the 152. A clear plastic bar transmits light from the L363 clear bayonet-base bulb concealed in the gate base to the two scale-like lenses that adorn the gate.

Only one production variation, concerning alignment of the central pivot axle with the gate and the cam that actuates it, is mentioned in the Lionel Service Manual. The axle, which has a square cross-section, presses through the two parallel gate arms and locks their position relative to a fiber cam inside the housing. A plunger inside a solenoid is activated by the 145C Track Contactor. This plunger pops up from the solenoid and bears against the cam, overcoming the force of the sintered-metal counterweights and forcing the gate down.

Initial production in 1950 had the square holes positioned so that one side was parallel to the top and bottom edges of the gate arms. The holes look like squares when the gate is in a horizontal position. In 1951 and beyond, these holes were rotated 45 degrees, so they look diamond-shaped when the gate arm is horizontal. The cam was changed to match, and the Lionel Service Manual cautions that the cam and gate hole orientations must match. The reason given for the change is an improvement in operation.

Throughout its 14-year availability, the 252 was always supplied with a 145C Track Contactor, and the gate's operation was always a part of the contactor's instruction sheet. No special or separate instructions for the 252 were issued. The 252 continued to be covered in the final issue of 145-56 some two years after the gate disappeared from the catalog. Aside from a shade difference in the white plastic of the gate, which is possibly due to aging, no significant variations in the 252 are known. Since the 262 Highway Crossing Gate, introduced in 1962, used a modification of the 252 base mold, it is unlikely that the 252 was produced after 1961. Note that examples of this accessory with red instead of black hash marks on the gate appear regularly. These have Lionel Corp. nomenclature molded in, but are early MPC production. Dimensions: 3½" x 1⅛" base, 9⅛" overall length when lowered, raises to 9⅞" high.

(A) White plastic gate arm.   **19   23   27   35**

(B) Cream-colored gate arm (may be due to aging or different batch of plastic, as explained in listing for 155).

                                19   23   27   35

253 BLOCK CONTROL SIGNAL, 1956–59

This is simply the block signal version of the 115 and 132 Passenger Stations with Automatic Train Control. The 253 is the only postwar signal to have a train-control function built in, as opposed to depending on a 153C Contactor or 148-100 manual switch. Like the stations, the 253 requires an insulated block. Each new signal included two insulating pins for O gauge and two for O27.

The signal control uses a bimetallic strip (two dissimilar metals bonded together so that, when heated, the differing expansion rates of the metals causes the strip to bend, thus moving the electrical contact on one end). When the control lever is placed on "CONT." ("continuous"), the control contacts are held closed, which completes the circuit to the insulated block and allows the train to pass without stopping. Moving the control lever toward "SLOW" opens the contacts, which causes the train to stop when it enters the insulated block. The presence of the train completes a circuit through the locomotive motor and the heater winding around the bimetallic strip. This current causes the strip to bend and eventually close the contacts that energize the block, sending the train on its way.

The farther the control lever is positioned toward "SLOW," the farther the contact has to move, and the longer the train stays in the block. Due to the resistance of the heater coil, the current passing through the locomotive motor is not enough for it to move the train. The green signal lamp is energized while the locomotive pauses in the block, but the current is so low that the light is imperceptible.

Two instruction sheets for the 253 are known, both with part number 253-43. The first is printed in light blue ink on white paper and is dated 10-56. The second, dated 3-57, is in black ink on yellow paper and adds a note on how to make an insulated block with the new Super O track. Both instruction sheets omit some interesting details covered by the Lionel Service Manual, which was not available to the average customer:

"Operating note: Satisfactory adjustment of the system usually requires some experimentation. The frequency with which a train enters a block, the type of locomotive, the prevailing air temperature, all affect the operating cycle of the bimetal leaf and thus the delay time in the block. Normally, the locomotive reversing unit must be disconnected so that the train can resume

its forward motion after being stopped within the block. However, if it is desired to retain the reversing feature of the locomotive, current may be 'bled' from the live center rail to the insulated one through an adjustable resistor of about 7.5 ohms, 10 watts. Enough current must be passed to the insulated block to maintain the 'holding' voltage of the E-unit, (about 6 volts) but not enough to drive the engine. The insulated block may have to be lengthened because the bleed current will cause the train to coast farther. Because the resistor is in parallel with the heater wire, the operating characteristics of the circuit will be affected and more adjustments may be needed."

For 1956 production only, the 253 uses L12(R) and L12(G) two-pin lamps, which require 6 to 8 volts, and a resistor to reduce the normal 12- to 16-volt track power. Unlike other instruction sheets, neither of those for the 253 mentions replacement lamps, so Lionel must have anticipated a change. Two-pin bulbs were new in this era, and the 253 was their first Lionel application. It is probable that availability of a 14-volt version was delayed, forcing Lionel to release the 6- to 8-volt L12(R) and L12(G). These two bulbs were not used in any other Lionel application. Not until the issue of 4-57 did Lionel's Replacement Lamp chart show the 14-volt L19(R) and L19(G). These bulbs, without the resistor, were used on 1957 and later 253s. The Lionel Service Manual pages dated 3-58 state, "If 14 volt lamps are used the resistor can be by-passed or eliminated." The lamp housing for the 253 is the same 450-13 Socket Cover used on 450 and 452 Signal Bridges.

Only one significant variation in the 253 Block Control Signal has been noted. Early production, probably the first year or two, had the control-box portion of the base painted black. Later, as another cost-cutting move, this painting was eliminated, leaving the base beige. The black-painted versions are slightly harder to find than those with unpainted bases. Dimensions: 4" x 1¾" base, 7⅜" high.

(A) 1956–57. Control box portion of base painted black.

                                20   30   45   60

(B) 1958–59. Entire base left in unpainted beige plastic.

                                15   25   35   50

262 HIGHWAY CROSSING GATE, 1962–66 and 1968–69

The 262 is a modified version of the 252 Crossing Gate with the addition of a "Railroad Crossing" crossbuck and red warning lights. Because the 252 base was altered for the 262, the earlier gate, although cataloged, probably was not built after 1961. The new accessory's mechanism and all gate parts are from the 252, either exactly or with slight modification. Gone are the clear plastic bar and warning lamps, as well as the interior bulb that made them light. The slot in the base for the light to shine through remained.

Two issues of the 262-11 instruction sheet were published: the first dated 8-62, and the second dated 3/65. These small sheets measured only about 5½" by 8½" and were folded to make four pages. This was an economy measure that allowed Lionel to make two instruction folders from a single standard sheet of paper. The only difference in the two issues is the name change to Lionel Toy Corporation and the insertion of a warranty in the later version. There is no mention of the required L19(R) replacement bulbs. The sheets do state, incorrectly, "Lionel No. 262 automatically flashes the red lights." In fact, the two lamps

308 (die-cast metal) and 309 (molded plastic on sintered-metal base) Railroad Sign Sets and a variety of packaging.

are simply wired in parallel and glow steadily while the gate is lowered. Descriptions in consumer catalogs said only that the passing train turned on the warning lights.

Installation of the 262 is covered in the last two issues of 145-56, dated 2-62 and 4/65, and each 262 included a 145C Contactor. But, as far as is known, these instructions did not accompany 262s. Why Lionel decided to issue special instructions for the 262 but not for signals like the 163 is unclear. Both 145-56 instruction sheets list replacement bulbs for several of the accessories covered, including the 262. Unfortunately, the 262 entry shows an L53(R) bayonet-base bulb instead of the correct L19(R) two-pin lamp.

Although other types of packaging should and probably do exist, only two have been reported: window box and blister pack. Finding either in decent condition is a challenge. The window box has a yellow paperboard liner designed to secure the gate, but the box is relatively large and flimsy. The blister pack was sturdier but had to be destroyed to remove the accessory, so it has not survived well. A plain white box with identification on one end and a Hagerstown box may also exist, but no reliable reports are available. Original boxes can add considerably to the values indicated.

One interesting variation of the 262 exists, but there is some doubt as to whether it is original Lionel production or an early General Mills Model Products Corp. piece. This is the version with red, instead of black, hash marks on the white crossing gate. Several of these crossing gates have been examined, and all have original Lionel Corp. nomenclature on the underside of the base. However, MPC sometimes used leftover parts in its early production. No 262 with red hash marks has been observed in any but MPC original packaging. Dimensions: 3½" x 1⅝" base, 9⅞" overall length, raises to 9⅞" high.

	Gd	VG	Ex	LN

(A) 1962–69. Black hash marks on gate. Values shown are without box. Inclusion of window, Hagerstown, or plain white box packaging in decent shape adds considerably to value.

	25	45	70	100

(B) 1966. Same as (A) except packaged in blister pack as B262. Value is based only on unique packaging. Like New indicates an intact but shopworn package. A perfect blister pack can bring a substantially higher price than shown.

	—	—	—	125

308 RAILROAD SIGN SET, 1940–42 and 1945–49

Five-piece set of die-cast metal signs: "W" (whistle), "Yard Limit," "Danger Do Not Trespass," "RR" (round), and "Railroad Crossing" (crossbuck). Each item is painted in white enamel with raised lettering painted black. Packaging for the 308 is a box with lift-off lid. The box bottom is dark blue with a matching die-cut liner to hold the signs so they can be displayed with the lid removed. Lettering on the liner is silver. The lid is covered with paper printed in the classic orange, blue, and white design. Presence of the original box is imperative for collectors. Excellent or Like New requires an original box in comparable condition to the complete set of signs.

	25	40	55	70

309 YARD SIGN SET, 1950–59

Eight-piece set of plastic signs with metal bases packaged in an orange box with blue lettering on the lift-off lid. Each sign has raised lettering painted black. Included are "W" (whistle), "RR

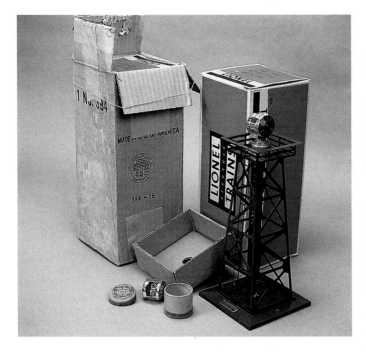

New dark green 394 and packaging, with rare one-unit shipping box. Beacon cap usually came packaged as shown, though later units had plain brown box. M. Stephens Collection.

	Gd	VG	Ex	LN

Property Keep Out," "Resume Speed," "Yard Limit," "Stop," "Danger Do Not Trespass," "RR" (round), and "Railroad Crossing" (crossbuck).

The box liner is blue cardboard die-cut to hold the signs in place and has silver lettering so it makes a nice display with the lid removed. Orange paper printed with blue lettering covers the box lid. Both the orange covering and the blue lettering vary in shade. Some of the orange covers are almost red. Whatever the outer color, it is prone to fading. A few examples have been found with the printer's name on the portion of the paper that folds up inside the box lid. Presence of the original box easily doubles the value of a complete set. Excellent or Like New requires a complete set with the original box and liner in comparable condition. **12   20   28   40**

353 TRACK SIDE CONTROL SIGNAL, 1960–61

Except for its conventional two-light target (lamp housing), this accessory is identical to the 163 and uses the same bulbs (see the 163 listing above). Each signal included an instruction sheet, either part number 153C-23 (1960) or 452-15 (1961). Normally came packaged in an Orange Picture box and included a 153C Contactor. Dimensions: 4″ x 1¼″ base, 7⅜″ high.

14   25   35   50

394 ROTARY BEACON, 1949–53

Lionel referred to this as a Rotating Beacon on the box, but as a Rotary Beacon in the catalogs and instruction sheets. Heat generated by its special 394-10 dimple bulb rotates the 394's delicately balanced lens housing. The dimple in the top of the special bulb provides a bearing cup for the needlepoint that supports the lens housing. Air heated by the bulb creates an updraft through the housing that exits through canted vanes in the housing top, causing the top to rotate. So sensitive is this arrangement

that the Lionel Service Manual mentions that drafts and slight air movements may affect lens rotation.

Of special interest to the collector are the several colors given the 394 over the years. A similar accessory, the 395 Floodlight Tower, appears almost identical, except for the lights on top. The 395 also came in several colors, some of which differed from those used for the 394. Towers of the two can be switched to create more variations.

The Lionel Service Manual section covering the 394 (dated 11-51) states, "Tower Assembly 394-5 and Tower Assembly 395-5 are identical with the exception of the fingers which are lanced at the diamond-shaped holes in the 394-6 Platform in order to retain the Light Base casting. While the 394 Tower and Platform can be used for 395 Floodlight Tower, the reverse is not true. The tower structure and its component parts have been made in various colors. The available color will be shipped."

This serves as a check on the authenticity of a given tower. Since the tower and top platform were assembled before they were painted, it is usually obvious if they have later been separated. Lionel may have used 394 towers for the 395, but this has not been verified.

Charles Weber reports a variation with a stick-on nameplate on the tower base. (The usual plate is attached with tabs at each end.) This is a metal plate similar to that used for the Fruehauf labels on the green vans and later forklifts that were part of the 460 Piggyback Transportation Set. Since it is fairly rare, it can be assumed that Lionel did only a brief trial run on these plates and found them unsatisfactory. Although a stick-on nameplate was used, the slots for attaching the usual nameplate were not eliminated. Because the two nameplates look similar, it takes a sharp eye to spot one.

Seven instruction sheets for the 394 are known, all part number 394-30. Dates are 8-49, 5-50, 9-50, 2-52, 2-53, 6-53, and 8-53. The first and last are printed black on white while all others are blue on white. Dimensions: 5″ x 5″ base, 11¾″ high.

(A) 1949. Stamped-steel tower and platform painted red. Silver lamp base casting. Serif lettering on nameplate. Late 1949 box (no San Francisco markings or box part number), instruction sheet dated 8-49. T. Rollo Collection.

25   35   50   60

(B) Same as (A) except sans-serif lettering on the nameplate. Most nameplates secured with flexible tabs; they are so easily changed that no significance is given to nameplate type on a particular beacon. **25   35   50   60**

(C) 1949–50. Same as (B) except stamped-steel tower and platform painted dark green (like 455 tower).

35   50   70   90

(D) 1950–53. Stamped-aluminum tower, platform, and base completely unpainted. Much lighter than steel tower versions, should not be confused with the steel tower painted silver found only with 395. **22   28   35   45**

(E) Same as (B) except aluminized stick-on nameplate (with sans-serif lettering) instead of aluminum nameplate attached with tabs **25   35   50   60**

(F) Same as (D) except red-painted stamped-steel base with unpainted aluminum tower and platform. Although this version could easily be made, enough have been observed over the years to authenticate them as factory production. H. Powell and M. Rini Collections. **25   35   50   60**

395 Floodlight Towers in assorted colors. Box part number typically on only one end flap (left). Silver tower on left is unpainted aluminum; one on right is silver-painted steel. J. Algozzini Collection.

395 FLOODLIGHT TOWER 1949–50 and 1952–56

Although the 395 shares most of its parts with the 394, typical 395 top platforms do not have lanced tabs to hold the 394 lamp base casting. A 394 tower with tabs could, however, be used for the 395. Each 395 has four floodlights that use the lamp housing and bracket from the 70 Yard Light. These floodlights use 6- to 8-volt L51 bulbs and are wired so that there are two pairs of bulbs, with each pair wired in series. Consequently, if one bulb of a pair burns out, the other will not illuminate either.

The catalog years for the 395 are easily established, but the sequence of color changes is still uncertain. The Lionel Service Manual states that "the color available at the time will be shipped" whenever a replacement tower is ordered. However, reliable information about the relative scarcity of the various colors is available. The yellow tower seems to be hardest to find, especially in collectible condition. Next in scarcity is the steel tower painted silver, followed closely by the red tower. The unpainted aluminum tower appears to be a common version, while green may be the most common variety of all. There are also reports of factory conglomerations of parts of different colors in the same 395, although these factory "errors" are quite uncommon. We welcome reader comments regarding the dates and scarcity of each version.

Five instruction sheets for the 395 are known, all part number 395-37, but there are only three issue dates. First is 8-49 with and without "-NDEX" after the date, both black ink on white paper. Next, the issue of 7-53 uses black or dark blue ink on white paper; the final issue of 12-55 is black on white. Dimensions: 5" x 5" base, 11½" high.

	Gd	VG	Ex	LN

(A) 1949–50. Stamped-steel tower, platform and base painted yellow. Not really rare, but the hardest 395 version to find in collectible condition.

	50	90	120	190

(B) 1952. Same as (A) except painted silver. Not to be confused with the unpainted aluminum version, which is noticeably lighter. One observed example has a box with a printed OPS price, which dates this example to 1952 only. T. Rollo Collection.

	25	35	55	70

(C) 1953–54. Same as (A) except painted all red.

	25	35	55	70

(D) 1954–55. Stamped-aluminum base, tower, and top platform, all unpainted. Lighter weight distinguishes this version from the stamped-steel version painted silver. A magnet will not stick to it either!

	22	35	50	65

(E) Same as (A) except painted a green similar to 3656 Operating Stockyard. A common variety previously dated as 1955-56. However, a photo developed in January 1951 shows a 1950 Christmas layout with the green tower. Therefore the color may have run much longer or may have been discontinued and revived. Michael Ocilka and Roland LaVoie report examples rubber-stamped "APR 20, 1955" on the underside of the base.

	22	35	50	65

450 Signal Bridge with box. This accessory came with a 153C Contactor, envelope, and instruction sheet. Separate 450L light heads could be added. J. Algozzini Collection.

452 Gantry Signal Bridge and packaging. The "window" weakened an already fragile box, which is why examples in collectible condition are scarce.

450 SIGNAL BRIDGE, 1952–58

Like most of Lionel's signals, the 450 has no train-control capability. It included a 153C Contactor, which can be used to control a train, the signal lights, or both at once. The functioning features of the 450 (the two 450L light heads) are lamp housings, each containing an L53(R) and an L53(G) bayonet-base lamp wired with a common return so they can be lit independently. Brighter L363(R) and (G) lamps can be substituted if desired, although they produce more heat.

The bridge has two identical plastic bases with identical black-painted stamped-steel towers. The towers are connected by a stamped-steel bridge that spans two tracks and supports the two 450L light heads furnished with new 450s. Additional heads could be purchased separately, and there is room on the bridge to add several. If you want to control trains on both tracks, it is nec-

essary to buy an additional 153C Contactor or use a manual control switch or an insulated track section. The instruction sheet tells how to do this. Electrical connections are via three spring-clip fahnestock terminals on the underside of each base. One 450L light head was originally connected to each base, but the electrical connections can be altered as desired. No significant variations of the 450 have been reported.

Six printings of the 450-42 instruction sheet were made. All use dark blue ink on white paper and are dated 10-52, 4-53, 3-54, 4-55, 12-55, and 2-57. After the first edition, a paragraph was added covering lamp replacement. Other than that, the only changes came as new transformers were added and the address of the Lionel Service Department changed. Probably due to its simplicity, the 450 never had a Lionel Service Manual illustration. Yet the 452 Overhead Gantry Signal, which was really half a 450, did rate an illustration! It debuted three years after the 450 had been discontinued. Dimensions: 1 1⁄16" x 3 1⁄4" bases, 7 3⁄4" high, 7 1⁄2" inside clearance width.

Gd	VG	Ex	LN
26	45	58	75

452 OVERHEAD GANTRY SIGNAL, 1961–63

This accessory is essentially half a 450 Signal Bridge. The 452 does add a "foot" to the base that extends back toward the track to keep the signal from falling over when it is not screwed down. Otherwise, it is identical to one side of a 450, both in appearance and electrical connection.

The 452-15 instruction sheet included with this accessory is not specific to the 452. Instead, it takes over where 153C-23 (the instructions for the 53C Contactor) left off and includes all the relevant accessories of the era. These instructions are six-page

Unusual mixed colors for 394 Rotary Beacons. Other mixed-color examples have been reported. Identification tags usually attached with tabs, but the separate piece in the foreground is a stick-on tag Lionel apparently tried for a very brief time. T. Olexsy and C. Weber Collections.

	Gd	VG	Ex	LN

foldout sheets measuring 8½" by 17" when fully opened and carry dates of 4-61, 3-62, and 6/65. All are printed in black ink on white paper, except for one printing of 4-61, which has been reported in brown ink. It is interesting that page 4 of the 6/65 sheet still has 452-15 3-62 at the bottom. Two different dates on the same instruction sheet! Packaged in an orange paperboard window box. Dimensions: 1⅟₁₆" x 3¼" base, 7¾" high, 5" overall length.

	65	90	115	150

494 ROTARY BEACON, 1954–66

The 494 Rotary Beacon was the successor to the 394. The parts used in the 394 were reworked to accept a Vibrotor-driven beacon with a mechanism similar to the 3520 Searchlight Car. This change resulted in improved operation with immediate, more rapid, and consistent rotation of the beacon. Of the two beacons, operators prefer this version. So far, 10 printings of the 494-35 instruction sheet have been reported. Dimensions: 5" x 5" base, 11¾" high.

(A) Stamped-steel base, tower, and platform, all painted red. Blackened metal nameplate with silver lettering attached to base with tabs.

	25	35	45	60

(B) Unpainted, stamped-aluminum base, tower and platform. Nameplate same as (A).

	25	35	45	60

(C) Same as (A) except painted silver. This version weighs more than (B).

	25	35	45	60

1045 OPERATING WATCHMAN, 1938–42 and 1945–50

When introduced in 1938, the 1045 Operating Watchman was priced at $1.95 and was the lowest priced action accessory in the Lionel line. By comparison, a 52 Lamp Post was $2.00 and the 77N Crossing Gate was $4.00. With the watchman standing 16 scale feet tall, customers certainly got their money's worth! Since Standard gauge was still being produced, you might think that the 1045 was really meant for that size. Indeed, the 1938 catalog states it is suitable for any track except OO. It says the signal is 12" high and shows the watchman waving a red flag in his left hand, carrying a lantern in his right hand, and standing on a green base. The catalog never did correctly describe this accessory for any of the ten years it appeared. But the error in the height (it is really 7" high overall) is a fairly good indication that the 1045 was originally intended for Standard gauge.

The size of the figure may have been dictated by the operating mechanism inside his body. In keeping with its low cost, the mechanism is simple. The arm is attached to a wire shaft held by a hole in the plastic in each shoulder. In the center of the shaft there is a metal piece that resembles a pick-up roller with a slot cut lengthwise to the center. The shaft is crimped in the slot so the roller is off-center. Below the roller is the iron core of a simple solenoid. The arm is positioned so when it is at rest, it hangs by the watchman's side and the off-center roller is raised. When a train approaches, the solenoid energizes and attracts the roller, which applies torque to the shaft due to the offset. This causes the arm to rise. When the current is interrupted, gravity restores the arm to its resting position.

Getting the arm to swing required some ingenuity. The solution was the new 1045C Track Contactor. This clever yet simple device has a connection to the center rail and a metal pad that clips over one of the outer rails but is insulated from it by a thin sheet of fiber. When a train crosses the 1045C, the wheels complete a circuit from the center rail, through the solenoid, and back through the wheels to the outer rails. The rolling train causes the current to repeatedly start and stop. The instructions caution against letting the train stand on the contactor with power applied, lest the heat generated from the solenoid give the watchman a severe case of heartburn!

Since the 1045C was made for only O and O27 track, production watchmen were obviously not intended for Standard gauge. For 1939 the catalog was corrected to state that the 1045 was suitable for any track except OO, solid rail, and Standard gauge. Of course all that remained were O and O27. But the 1939 catalog still showed the lantern and the swinging left arm. For 1940, the flag was in the right arm and the lantern was eliminated. However, for that year and every year thereafter, the flag remained red, and—except for 1950—the base remained green. All known production examples have a red base and white flag.

The figure is molded Bakelite, with painted hands and face. Some prewar versions have been observed with black and brown molded figures, but most prewar and all postwar 1045s seem to be the more common medium or dark blue. As with other Lionel items, the silver-colored paint on the crossing sign post changed to a semi-gloss medium gray toward the end of prewar production in 1941 or 1942 and then back to silver in the postwar years. The cap on top of the post is usually nickel-plated but is known to exist in brass, black, gray, and silver as well. The diamond-shaped crossing sign may be brass or silver-colored. All reported

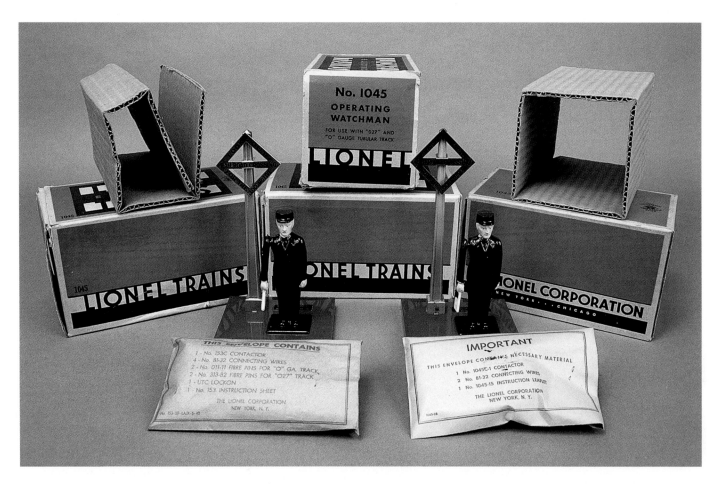

| | Gd | VG | Ex | LN |

examples have "THE" on the left lower leg and "MADE / IN / U.S.A." in small letters at the top, contrary to some catalog illustrations. A similar sign, used on the 45 Automatic Gateman, exists with and without these features.

Instruction sheets, all with part number 1045-15, are printed in dark blue ink on light blue paper for issues of 9-38, 2-39, and 1-42. The printing changed to black ink on white paper for 8-47, 1-48, and 6-49. Packaging for the 1045 is the Classic orange, blue, and white box with a cardboard liner. With few exceptions, no matter what the contents, Lionel printed its Classic boxes with "NEW YORK . . . CHICAGO . . . SAN FRANCISCO" on the dark blue band at the bottom. After 1948, the San Francisco designation was removed. For some reason, the 1045 box was an exception. Several observed examples have the bottom band blank and no reference anywhere to the cities. Yet a 1949 box with two cities listed is known to exist. It would be interesting to know if any collectors have a 1045 box with three cities listed. Dimensions: 4″ x 4″ base, 7″ high.

(A) Nickel sign with black letters. Silver-painted sign pole.

| | 15 | 27 | 41 | 55 |

(B) Probably 1942 only. Semi-gloss medium gray sign pole and brass sign with black lettering.

| | 25 | 35 | 50 | 65 |

(C) Same as (A) except brass sign with black lettering.

| | 15 | 27 | 41 | 55 |

Left to right: Silver and brass sign variations of 1045 Operating Watchman. Note differences in cardboard box liners and parts envelopes. Early postwar boxes omitted all city names on the lower dark blue band. Those from 1949 have two cities. Both types of signs are known to exist in both types of boxes.

1047 SWITCHMAN WITH FLAG, 1959–61

In operation, the 1047 Switchman with Flag is similar to the 45 and 145 Automatic Gateman. When a train approaches, the switchman waves his flag. Unlike the 45 and 145, the switchman on the 1047 has no shack and always remains in view. Besides the absence of shelter for its figure, the 1047 lacks the element of surprise provided by a gateman popping out of his shack. The 1045 Operating Watchman also lacked a shack but apparently was more successful than the 1047.

Although cataloged for three years, the 1047 probably had only one run. It is mostly a conglomeration of existing parts from other items, with the flagman's arm being the only unique part. The 1047 Switchman carries a flag instead of the lantern held by the 145's figure. While the figure itself is identical to that used on the 145, it is interesting to note that the 1047's figure has painted hands and face in 1959 and the 145's dropped the paint, beginning in 1957. The 1047-2 Base Assembly is just a slight modification of the 145 base. All reported authentic examples of the 1047 have a blue fuel tank, which was borrowed from the 3530 Operating Generator Car of 1956-58. The fact that black and blue fuel tanks were made for this car, suggests that blue is the later color and was still around for the 1047.

| | Gd | VG | Ex | LN |

No significant variations of the 1047 have been reported. A 1047-10 parts envelope came with new 1047s and contained a 145C Contactor, three green connecting wires, six pieces of 264-11 Timber, and a 145-56 instruction sheet dated 7-59 in bright blue ink on white paper. The 1047 came in an orange paperboard window box (part number 1047-1), one of the flimsiest Lionel made and a rare item today. Dimensions: 7″ x 5¾″ base, 4½″ high to top of crossbuck. **50   100   160   120**

The 1047 Switchman With Flag used parts from 145 Automatic Gateman, 264 Operating Fork Lift Platform, and 3530 Operating Generator Car. The box was too light for its contents, making examples in collectible condition quite scarce.

CHAPTER 7

Bridges, Trestles, and Tunnels

The 313 Bascule Bridge provides incredible action and excitement on any layout and has been a favorite of collectors and operators since its introduction more than 60 years ago. Here are silver (foreground) and gray versions, each with the floor frame that is necessary when bridge was not attached to a permanent layout. The gray version dates to 1942 and is shown with the prewar-style of coiled wire packed with it.

Even on a layout without scenery, an operator will find that adding trestles to create grades, a steel bridge that stretches across the main line, or a darkened tunnel that engulfs a speeding freight enhances a relatively simple track plan. Amid many common throwaway items, collectors will find some of the scarcest collectibles in the realm of Lionel products. Just when all 50,000 trestle piers in a junk box start to look alike, collectors with an eye for detail will notice a tall pier that does not have a tie strap molded across the base. Reading this chapter, they will discover that the pier is a rare and special variation made only for the 2555W Father and Son set in 1960!

The large "shipping box" (rear) contained 16 108 Trestle Sets packed in overstamped boxes (foreground). An uncataloged item, this partial trestle set was included with outfit X-870 and probably other uncataloged sets. J. Algozzini Collection.

	Gd	VG	Ex	LN

108 TRESTLE SET, 1959 (uncataloged)

Virtually unknown, several examples of this uncataloged accessory have recently been found in 1044 transformer boxes overstamped "NO. 108." Most are plain cardboard boxes printed in blue, but a few yellow 1044 overstamped boxes from 1959 (the only year Lionel supplied the yellow boxes) have been observed. All observed sets contain 12 black trestle piers with two of each A-F size. Some contain no hardware, but most have a 108-10 envelope containing 12 of the 110-29 Tie Channels, 24 sheet-metal screws, and a 110-30 instruction sheet with blue printing on white paper, dated 5-59.

This accessory was included with uncataloged outfit X-870 and probably others. Set X-870 also contained a 111 Trestle Set, "SPECIAL LAYOUT INSTRUCTIONS" sheet 1802N (dated 6-59), and a 45-degree crossing. The instruction sheet showed how to assemble all this into an entirely elevated layout!

— — — 75

109 TRESTLE SET, 1961

A partial trestle set whose only catalog appearance is as part of the 2574 Super O five-car Defender Diesel Freight set in 1961. In another of the exciting "finds" since the publication of the first edition of this guide, a brand-new 2574 outfit has been observed and complete documentation for the 109 can now be provided. As packaged in set 2574, the trestles are strung together with two dark, waxy cardboard strips identical to those used in some packages of the 110 Trestle Set. The trestles are placed as a unit (with no additional packaging) into the set box, along with the other set components, which are individually boxed.

Differing slightly in content from the 108, set 109 contains 12

gray trestles, whereas there are 24 (later 22) trestles in a standard 110 set. These 12 trestles elevate a train only a few inches rather than the full height of a 110 set. Also packed separately in the set box is "Assem. No. 109-2," an envelope containing two black 110-13 "L" (the smallest) trestle piers (or "bents," as Lionel called them), ten 110-29 Tie Channels, 20 sheet-metal screws no. 4 by ½", and a standard 110-30 instruction sheet, dated 1-60, with black printing on white paper. A 2574-10 "Special Track Layout Instructions" sheet, printed in black on blue-green paper and dated 8-61, shows how to assemble the track and 109 trestle set.

NRS

110 TRESTLE SET, 1955–66 and 1968–69

Set of 24 (later 22) "simulated steel" molded plastic piers of graduated height. Piers are gray or, in part of 1959, black. Early versions came with two sets of track clamps, one for O gauge and the other for O27. Later, probably for 1957 when Super O was introduced, 110s included one set, which could accommodate all three types of track. Screws for attaching the clamps to the trestles were always furnished. These small parts came in manila envelopes that varied in size and part number, with its content list printed in black. Packing boxes varied in size and color. To date, 15 instruction sheet variations with seven dates have been found.

(A) 1955. Plain cardboard box 23″ long, 5⅛″ wide, and 4⅛″ high, labeled "110-23" (Lionel's part number for the box) in

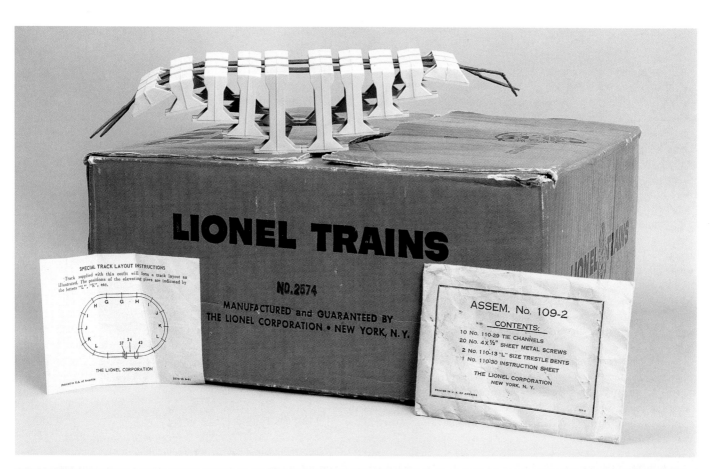

Top: Critical packaging elements for the 109 Trestle Set are the set box for the 2574 Super O freight outfit, 109-2 manila envelope, 2574-10 "Special Track Layout Instructions," and the two long, waxy cardboard strips that tie the piers together.

Above: During the many years Lionel cataloged the 110 Trestle Set, this accessory came in a number of different packages. The plain cardboard box in the lower center came first, followed by yellow (not shown) and then orange boxes (the white circled "L" appeared in 1960, the black in 1961-63). Next came the orange and blue picture boxes in two variations (upper left and upper right). Not shown is the last version, a white cardboard box with black lettering, similar in size and lettering style to the left orange box.

Gd VG Ex LN

black on one of the long sides. The box, made by Densen Banner, opens on both ends. Interior packaging consists of a white paperboard liner with yellow, red, and black graphics that holds the gray trestles so they can interleave when the liner is folded and serve as a display when opened. Includes 110-22 parts envelope. Usually found with 110-21 instruction sheet printed black on white with a 9-55 date. Mo Rose reports finding this set with a yellow instruction sheet dated 1-56. Like New requires complete packaging. **10 20 35 70**

(B) 1956–58. Plain cardboard box 15″ long, 5⅛″ high, 3¾″ high, labeled "110-35" in black or red on bottom. Red and blue lettering for balance of box decoration. The box, made by Express Container Corp., has one lid along the wide part of the long side; the bottom is not made to open. Includes 110-25 manila parts envelope that contains the hardware and a 110-30 instruction sheet dated 1-58, printed in blue on white paper. Twenty-two gray piers (the smallest "L" piers are in the parts envelope) are strung together in two rows with dark, waxy cardboard strips. **10 20 30 40**

(C) 1959. Most have black trestles, but some examples observed with gray trestles. All have a yellow box labeled "110-35," manufactured by Star Corrugated Box Company, Inc. Two known variations of this box: blue or black background rectangles on "LIONEL/TRAINS" label; rectangles differ in size as well as color. Came with a 110-26 parts envelope.
10 20 30 40

(D) 1960. Orange box 14¾″ long, 5¼″ wide, and 3⅞″ high, with black and white lettering. Has part number 110-35 and manufacturer's label (Kraft Corrugated Containers, Inc., Bayonne, New Jersey) on bottom. Came with 24 gray trestle piers and 110-31 manila parts envelope (measuring 6½″ by 4½″) containing 22 of the 110-29 Tie Channels, 44 No. 4 by ½″ sheet-metal screws, a 110-30 instruction sheet printed black on white and dated 1-60, and two 110-13 "L" piers. For comparison with later orange 110 boxes, note that the black rectangle on each end that serves as background for "LIONEL / TRAINS" is 2¾″ by 1½″. The circled "L" on each side is much larger than the adjacent black lettering and is printed in white. New examples have been observed with the piers strung together by two long, thin strips of dark, waxy cardboard threaded in parallel through the tie channels in the pier tops.
10 20 30 40

(E) 1961–63. Same as (D) except circled "L" on box sides is printed in black, like the other lettering, and is about the same size as that lettering. On the ends, the 3¾″ by 1⅞″ rectangular background for "LIONEL TRAINS" is larger than the 1960 box printing. Came with a 110-31 envelope (now 10″ by 2⅞″) containing a 110-30 instruction sheet dated 3-61.
10 20 30 40

(F) 1964. Orange and dark blue picture box 11″ long, 8″ wide, and 4″ high, labeled "Lionel No. 110 22-piece Graduated Trestle Set." The box, part number 110-38, was made by United Container Co. Came with gray trestles. Lionel address is Hillside N. J., and the box date code is "64." Around four sides of the box is a "rails and ties" track design printed in red. The 110-32 manila parts envelope measures 9½″ by 4″ and contains a 110-30 instruction sheet dated 3-61. A difficult box to find.
10 20 30 40

(G) 1965. Same as (F) except the blue is lighter and the track design is on only two sides of the box. The box date code is Oct. '65. Example observed has a 10″ by 2⅞″ 110-31 parts envelope.
10 20 30 40

(H) 1966 and later. White cardboard box with black lettering, same size as (D), with "No. 110 / TRESTLE SET / LIONEL TRAINS" in a black, 1⅞″ by 3⅝″ rectangular background on each end. Manufactured by Mead Containers with box part number 110-35 and no date code on box maker's label. Two versions of box reported: one has "6 895 G" on a bottom end flap, other has "6 895." 110-31 manila parts envelope measures 9½″ by 4″ and printed "LIONEL TOY CORPORATION." Usual 3-61 instruction sheet date, but with "LIONEL TOY CORPORATION."
10 20 30 40

Note: It appears that for the first few years, all 110 sets included 24 piers. Sometime around 1960 or 1961, the count was reduced to 22, but the instruction sheets, last published 3-61, always stated that 12 pairs were included. Only the boxes for variations (F) and (G) state on the box that 22 piers are included. Of course, it was the two smallest "L" piers (always included in the parts envelope) that disappeared.

111 TRESTLE SET, 1956–66 and 1968–69

Set of ten "A" piers (the largest size). Available in gray or black and in several different packages, reflecting Lionel's changing styles. **— — 22 30**

111-50 TRESTLE SET, 1960

Available only in an orange box with black and white lettering (characteristic of 1960), the 111-50 came only with outfit 2555W. Known as the "Over and Under" or "Father and Son" set, it came with a complete Super O train set with one operating accessory and a complete HO set with a whistling engine house. Observed trestle box examples are all part number 111-19 with a May date code from the St. Joe Paper Co. All examples appear similar to 110(D) but are larger, measuring 15¼″ long, 5½″ wide, and 5″ high. One box reported with a paste-on 110 Trestle Set label that contained only a standard trestle set! Evidently Lionel had a few of the rare 111-50 boxes left over and didn't want to waste them.

All the 22 piers are gray "A" size and lack the tie bar across the base that "A" trestles typically have. Lionel changed the mold to eliminate the tie bar, so originals are easily distinguished from a normal "A" trestle with the tie bar cut off. Also included in the 111-50 set are 44 spacers, each about ⅜″ high, used to raise the piers even higher. When installed below the special piers, these spacers provide enough clearance for the HO train to travel under them. Each spacer also includes a small "wing" protruding from one side of the base. When properly assembled, these wings serve to center the HO track beneath each trestle pier.

Two piers support the corral for the 3366 Operating Circus Car included with the train set. Packed in this otherwise common Circus Car set box is a 111-20 sheet, with "Supplementary Instructions / LIONEL CIRCUS CAR CORRAL" printed in black on orange-yellow paper and dated 8-60. These instructions describe the installation of the piers to support the corral. Also

A 119 Tunnel, cataloged in 1957 and 1958. Unlike the later 121 Straight Tunnel, which was made of Styrofoam, the 119 is vacuum-formed plastic. Note the lip around the bottom edges, which is necessary to hold the plastic sheet during forming.

	Gd	VG	Ex	LN

included in the 111-50 box is "ASSEMBLY NO. 111-16," a 111-17 manila envelope containing miscellaneous hardware for installing the Circus Car corral. A complete train set instruction sheet, 111-18 printed black on white paper and dated 6/60, came in the 2555W set box (see page 121 of the third volume of *Greenberg's Guide to Lionel Trains, 1945–1969*). **NRS**

111-100 TRESTLE PIERS, 1960–63

A set of two normal 111-10 gray "A" piers came packaged in a 111-10 manila envelope similar to those used to package small accessory parts but larger in size. Also included were two 110-29 Tie Channels and four No. 4 x ½ screws. The envelope is the whole story in this hard-to-find collectible. The piers are common.

NRS

119 LANDSCAPED TUNNEL, 1957–58

In another of the exciting "finds" since publication of the first edition of this guide, three examples of what is believed to be a genuine Lionel postwar 119 have surfaced, thanks to Robert Pasztor. Unlike any other tunnel Lionel has ever been known to supply, the 119 is vacuum-formed plastic! Visible in the photograph, but not shown in the catalog, is the "lip" around the base of the tunnel, necessary for clamping the plastic sheet in position as it is formed. Otherwise the examples found are identical to the catalog picture and description, including dimensions.

	Gd	VG	Ex	LN

A 1959 advertisement for a Colgate-Palmolive-Wildroot Toiletries contest, featuring Lionel trains as prizes, has recently appeared. One thousand tunnels were promised as sixth prizes, and the picture in the ad clearly shows the lip around the base.

Unfortunately, these tunnels have no identifying marks, so only an original box can conclusively connect them to Lionel. According to the 1957 Lionel order sheet, 119s were packed six to a carton. They lend themselves to stacking and were probably shipped that way. However, there may be a prize winner from the 1959 contest who still has the individual shipping carton! It is unlikely that Lionel made these tunnels, but the actual manufacturer is unknown. Only one other vacuum-formed straight tunnel, also of unknown origin, has been observed, but it has a flocked coating as part of its decoration and is quite different from the 119.

Of all the postwar Lionel cataloged items, the 119, 121, and 131 tunnels remain among the most elusive to collect. Reader input is sought regarding any of them. Note that Lionel also cataloged a 119 stamped steel tunnel (12″ x 9″ base, 8½″ high) between 1920 and 1942. Dimensions: 14″ x 10″ base, 8″ high.

NRS

| | Gd | VG | Ex | LN |

121 LANDSCAPED TUNNEL, 1959–66

Although cataloged for eight years, not a single authenticated example has been discovered. The 121 was wider and taller than the 119, and its catalog picture is different too, especially the portals. Judging by these catalog pictures over the years, this item was most likely a Life-Like product made for Lionel. Life-Like marketed a similar tunnel, and an original box for it has been found, a window box that would have lent itself to Lionel graphics. As noted with the 131 Tunnel, Lionel may have never boxed the 121 Tunnels individually, opting instead to ship them stacked in larger shipping boxes. Lionel's 1966 order sheet shows the 121 sold six to a package. In any case, the 121 probably was completely unmarked, which makes it impossible to identify as a Lionel supplied accessory without the box. Dimensions: according to the catalog, 14″ x 12″ base, 12″ high.
NRS

131 CURVED TUNNEL, 1957–66

The only one of the three postwar tunnels cataloged by Lionel to have so far been conclusively linked to Lionel by its discovery in an original shipping carton. Four were packed in a plain cardboard Lionel shipping carton with black printing, and the example discovered still had one tunnel remaining. These Styrofoam tunnels have been confirmed as Life-Like products and are completely unmarked. Dimensions: 28″ x 14″ base, 12″ high.
NRS

An authenticated example of the 131 Curved Tunnel, cataloged from 1959 to 1966 and manufactured for Lionel by Life-Like.

| | Gd | VG | Ex | LN |

213 RAILROAD LIFT BRIDGE, 1950

The predecessor to the Lionel Trains, Inc. (LTI) 12782 Lift Bridge. Unfortunately, the original Lionel Corp. could not get the bridge to operate without binding, so it was never produced. Two examples known: an engineering mock-up in the Lionel Archives and a preproduction sample in a private collection. In the 1950 advance catalog, what appears to be the center section of this bridge is shown as a 317 Trestle Bridge (see 317 listing below). **Not Manufactured**

214 PLATE GIRDER BRIDGE, 1953–66 and 1968–69

This traditional bridge has a thinner sheet-metal base than that of the much heavier 314. Instead of die-cast girders, as on 314, the girder sides of 214 are molded in black plastic. The bridge number and Lionel nomenclature were always stamped into the metal on the underside of the bridge base prior to painting. Cataloged for 17 years, this readily collectible bridge is found in several variations. Dimensions: 10″ x 4½″ base.

(A) "LIONEL" on outside of black molded girders (some of which appear to be painted black over the black mold) in raised outline letters with crosshatching, heat-stamped in white. "BUILT BY / LIONEL" in small raised letters in rectangular box in second panel from left. This rectangle is the same height above the girder's bottom as "LIONEL," but is not stamped.
8   14   20   28

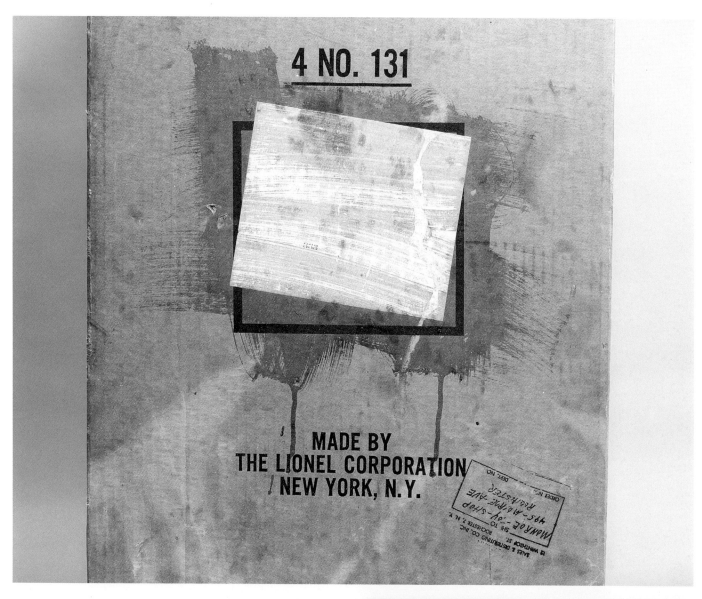

Among the rarest Lionel boxes is this shipping carton for four 131 Curved Tunnels. It serves to authenticate this Life-Like-manufactured item that cannot otherwise be associated with Lionel.

	Gd	VG	Ex	LN

(B) Same as (A) except no white heat-stamping on bridge side. Molded-in lettering still raised with crosshatching but no further decoration. **8 14 20 28**

(C) Same as (A) except "U S STEEL" on outside of girders in outline style with crosshatching in the letters. Also has "U S S" within circle to left of U S STEEL on each girder. All lettering is raised and white heat-stamped, including the circle. "BUILT BY / LIONEL" in small raised letters in rectangular box has been moved to the lower part of first panel on the left and is not stamped. **10 17 25 35**

(D) Same as (C) except with the addition of "6418" in the far right-hand panel of the bridge girders just below the level of the bottom of the main lettering. The raised 6418 lettering is also heat-stamped in white. This variation dates from 1956, when "6418" was added to the girder mold. This addition was made necessary because the 6518 Transformer Car, introduced in

Left: Common 214 Bridge with three box variations. Right: U.S. Steel bridge shared sides with the load for the 6418 Machinery Car. If the rivet holes on that load have been "used," the load is coming from and not going to a bridge construction site.

1956, shared the frame of the 6418. To use a common frame for these two cars without having an incorrect number on the bottom of the 6518, the "6418" was removed from the frame underside and the appropriate car number was added to the load of each car. Since the girders were common, the 214 received the same

| Gd | VG | Ex | LN |

A 313 Bascule Bridge in its original packaging.

change. Many 214s of this vintage have become loads for the flatcar. Original loads have unmarked mounting holes where the bridge base attaches. **10** **17** **25** **35**

(E) Same as (D) except that the raised 6418 has no white heat-stamping. D. Corrigan Collection. **10** **17** **25** **35**

(F) 1966. Same as (E) except in a B214 blister pack. Only the packaging makes this item unique and accounts for the premium price. **—** **—** **—** **275**

313 BASCULE BRIDGE, 1940–42 and 1946–49

Both prewar and postwar versions have a silver-painted, stamped-steel superstructure, except for 1942 production, which is the usual semi-gloss medium gray. Lionel's engineers made some major redesigns during World War II, so it is fairly easy to date a particular example. Prewar 313s have a square gearbox, which can be seen inside the base of the tower next to the house. The gearbox base is part of the die-cast bridge base (313-50). For postwar production, the drive mechanism was extensively redesigned, requiring an L-shaped gearbox and a new base casting (313-46).

The bridge tender's house was also revised, mostly to accommodate the new drive mechanism. Prewar houses have a slot about ³⁄₁₆" wide cut from the bottom edge to a window cutout. This is where the drive shaft goes to the gearbox, so there is no decorative lattice insert in this window. Postwar houses have lattice inserts in both windows facing the bridge. The shaft cutout is between the windows and consists of a narrow vertical slot with a rounded top.

There are two versions of the prewar house, one with a door and one without. Two narrow horizontal slots appear above and to either side of the door version. These could have been used to mount a porch enclosure, as was done on Lionel's prewar 184 and 185 Bungalows, but nothing was ever supplied for this purpose. Note that the postwar version of the bridge tender's house never had a door.

The light on the bridge was redesigned in 1949, replacing the R-68 Red Jeweled Cap, borrowed from transformers of the period, with the larger RW-27 Red Jeweled Cap that is most commonly seen as the short circuit lamp cover on ZW transformers.

The 314 Scale Model Girder Bridge with die-cast metal girders. Left: Gray example with packing inserts came in box with two cities listed in 1949 and later. Right: Silver one is from 1948 or earlier.

	Gd	VG	Ex	LN

The cross-bracing along the top of the bridge superstructure is made of thin stamped-steel pieces with tiny open triangles to simulate truss work. Comparing the pattern of the triangles on the bridges with small and large red lenses shows that the pattern is reversed. This cannot be accomplished by turning the braces around. They are stamped in mirror image. The patterns are usually not mixed on a given example, but extensive research has turned up a few samples where both patterns are used on the same bridge.

All 313s were originally supplied with a black-painted, stamped-steel aligning frame. This frame engages two posts on the underside of the bridge base and allows operation on floor layouts when it is not fastened down. Although not essential, a missing aligning frame detracts from the value of a 313. Also, watch for chunks of metal missing from the bridge base casting. This zinc die-casting, especially on prewar models, sometimes crystallizes and disintegrates, rendering the bridge good only for parts. Like New requires the special short O27 track section and all the small parts that were originally included. Dimensions: 10¼″ x 22¾″ base (not counting floor frame), 9½″ high in closed position.

(A) 1940–41. Square gearbox, drive shaft goes through window in house, house has no door. Silver-painted bridge structure. Red lens cap for light atop bridge is R-68 press-in design identical to those used on R, V, and Z transformers.

	240	375	550	700

(B) 1940–41. Same as (A) except house has door.

	240	375	550	700

(C) 1942. Same as (A) except bridge structure painted semi-gloss gray.

	340	475	650	800

(D) 1946–47. Same as (A) except L-shaped gearbox and no door on house. House has red lattice insert in all windows; drive shaft goes through vertical slot between window locations.

	240	375	550	700

(E) 1948–49. Same as (D) except lens cap for light on bridge is the larger threaded and ribbed RW-27, which does not interchange with earlier cap. Triangles in bridge's cross-bracing are reversed from those in earlier designs. This represents final production and is fairly hard to find.

	240	375	550	700

	Gd	VG	Ex	LN

314 SCALE MODEL GIRDER BRIDGE, 1940–42 and 1945–50

This single-span girder bridge spanned the pre- and postwar years. It featured a heavy sheet-metal plate for the base and die-cast side girders fastened to the base with rivets. Both girders have "LIONEL" rubber-stamped in black. The first full panel on the left side of each girder has "BUILT BY / LIONEL" molded in small raised letters, surrounded by a raised border with rounded corners. This sign was never decorated. Dimensions: 10″ x 4½″ base.

(A) 1940–41. Silver paint, ³⁄₃₂″-high black lettering.

	15	23	32	45

(B) 1942. Same as (A) except semi-gloss gray paint.

	15	30	45	65

(C) 1945–46. Flat gray paint with rubber-stamped black lettering, now ⁵⁄₁₆″ high, positioned with its centerline slightly above an imaginary centerline drawn along the bridge side.

	15	23	32	45

(D) 1947–50. Slightly darker shade of gray from (C), with a hint of gloss. Black rubber-stamped lettering ⅜″ high, centered on bridge side. C. Rohlfing and J. Algozzini Collections.

	15	23	32	45

315 ILLUMINATED TRESTLE BRIDGE, 1940–42 and 1946–48

A silver-painted (except in 1942, when semi-gloss gray was used) stamped sheet-metal bridge. Essentially the same as the 316, but with a special lamp housing with two binding posts serving as the center cross-brace on the top. Requires an L431 bulb. The red lens on the top of the light unit is part number R-68, also used on several transformers and the 313. Look for "315" and the Lionel nomenclature stamped only on the side of the cross-brace/lamp housing. A similar housing without the binding posts is used on the 313 and is stamped with that number. One counterfeit has been observed where the lamp housing from a 313 was used to create an example of the fairly rare 315.

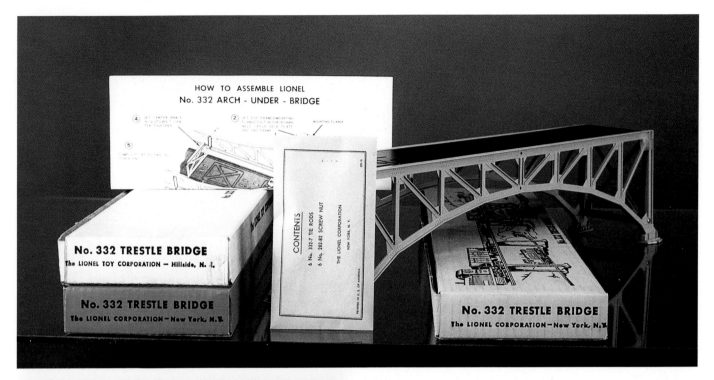

New versions of the 332 Trestle Bridge box and the instruction sheet identifying it as an Arch-Under Bridge. F. Davis Collection.

Front to rear: 317 (gray), 316 (silver), and 315 (with light) Trestle Bridges. 317 is only known in gray, while the other two were made in both gray and silver.

	Gd	VG	Ex	LN

No information is stamped on the top or bottom surface of the 315's base on the examples examined, since the required information is already on the cross-brace. The values provided below are for silver bridges. Gray examples from 1942 can be expected to have at least twice the value. Dimensions: 24″ x 6⅛″ base, 6″ high to top of lamp lens.

	50	70	90	115

316 TRESTLE BRIDGE, 1941–42 (uncataloged) and 1949

Except for the number, this stamped sheet-metal bridge is identical to the 317. As noted in the 213 listing, the 1950 advance catalog shows the separate center span of the 213 as a 317. When 213 was not produced, the 316 was restored to production with a new 317 number. Dimensions: 24″ x 6⅛″ base, 5½″ high.

	Gd	VG	Ex	LN

(A) Painted silver and rubber-stamped in black on bottom "No. 316 BRIDGE / BUILT BY / LIONEL CORPORATION / NEW YORK, N. Y. / U. S. OF AMERICA." Earliest prewar version. D. Johnson Collection.

	20	30	45	60

(B) Painted semi-gloss gray, rubber-stamped "316 TRESTLE BRIDGE" on bottom. 1942 version. C. Rohlfing Collection.

	25	35	50	65

(C) Painted silver, no rubber-stamping but bridge number and Lionel nomenclature stamped into the underside of the bridge base prior to painting. Postwar version. C. Rohlfing Collection.

	20	30	45	60

317 TRESTLE BRIDGE, 1950–56

A duller gray-painted (not semi-gloss like the 1942 version of the 316) stamped sheet-metal bridge. Bridge number and Lionel nomenclature are stamped into the underside of the base prior to painting. Except for number and paint, the 316 and 317 are identical. Dimensions: 24″ x 6⅛″ base, 5½″ high.

	15	23	32	45

321 TRESTLE BRIDGE, 1958–64

The 321 consists of a sheet-metal base with molded gray plastic sides and top. "BUILT BY LIONEL" is molded into the lower right corner of both side trestles. Observed examples of the thin cardboard box for this bridge are orange, white, or plain cardboard, each lettered in black. When new, the 321 was packaged disassembled. It is assembled using snaps and two screws. Three instruction sheets are known, all 321-8 printed on white paper: dark blue ink dated 9-58, green ink dated 2-59, and black ink dated 2-59. Dimensions: 24″ x 4½″ base, 7″ high when fully assembled.

	11	21	32	45

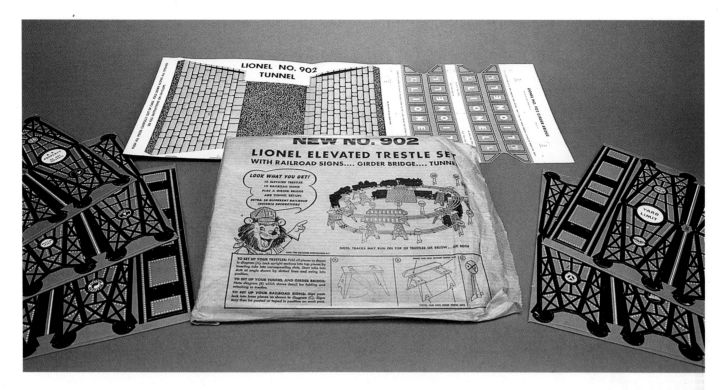

| | Gd | VG | Ex | LN |

321-100 TRESTLE BRIDGE, 1965 (uncataloged)

This trestle bridge is identical to the 321, except that it does not have a metal base. It came in a thin brown cardboard box with black lettering, similar to the one for 321 except for color and number. The 321-100 is known to be a component of the 9836 uncataloged Sears set that also included the rare 2347 Chesapeake & Ohio GP7; it may have come in other uncataloged outfits, but there are as yet no confirmed reports. This bridge included a small capsule of glue for assembling plastic bridge parts and an 8½″ x 5½″ instruction sheet (part number 321-101), undated, printed black on white paper. Dimensions: 24″ x 4½″ base, 7″ high when assembled. **NRS**

332 ARCH UNDER BRIDGE, 1959–66

This bridge is really a "kit" consisting of a flat-black painted steel baseplate and gray plastic bridge parts. There are two 332-3 main arches (one marked "4" on the side, the other marked "2"), two 332-4 bridge ends, and a 332-5 center brace. Came with a parts packet containing six 332-7 tie rods, six 282-82 screw nuts, and an instruction sheet.

(A) 1959. Yellow box with double-circled L, box part number 332-11, ends marked "NO. 332 TRESTLE BRIDGE / THE LIONEL CORPORATION New York, N. Y." Came with a stapled manila packet 332-15 and instruction sheet 322-16, dated 9-59. Note apparent error ("322" instead of "332") in instruction sheet part number. F. Davis Collection.

| | 20 | 30 | 46 | 60 |

(B) 1960–65. Same as (A) except orange box with double-circled L, corrected instruction sheet number 332-16, dated 9-59. F. Davis Collection.

| | 20 | 30 | 46 | 60 |

902 Elevated Trestle Set, including railroad signs, tunnel, and girder bridge, all made of cardboard, was a component of uncataloged outfit X-204 from 1959 and other uncataloged sets.

| | Gd | VG | Ex | LN |

(C) 1966. Same as (A) except white box without double-circled L, ends marked "NO. 332 TRESTLE BRIDGE / THE LIONEL TOY CORPORATION-Hillside, N. J.," white parts packet 332-14 sealed with glue, instruction sheet 332-16 with 5/66 date. F. Davis Collection.

| | 20 | 30 | 46 | 60 |

902 ELEVATED TRESTLE SET, 1959–60 (uncataloged)

This accessory was included with uncataloged sets X-568NA, X-204, and probably several others. Contents packed in a paper bag that is printed, "NEW NO. 902" in large black letters with pictures showing assembly. There are faint stripes imbedded in the lightweight, waxy bag, which bears a 1959 Lionel copyright. The trestles, signs, and other components must be punched out from cardboard sheets. Packed in the bag are five heavy cardboard sheets containing the 10 trestles, 10 Rail Road signs, and 10 insignia decorations from 10 different road names. A lighter white paperboard sheet contains the punch-outs for the bridge girders and tunnel. J. Algozzini reports that another version of this accessory came in a cardboard container marked, "MADE 1959 THE LIONEL CORPORATION."

NRS

6418 BRIDGE, see entry above for 214 (D)

CHAPTER 8

Track and Switches

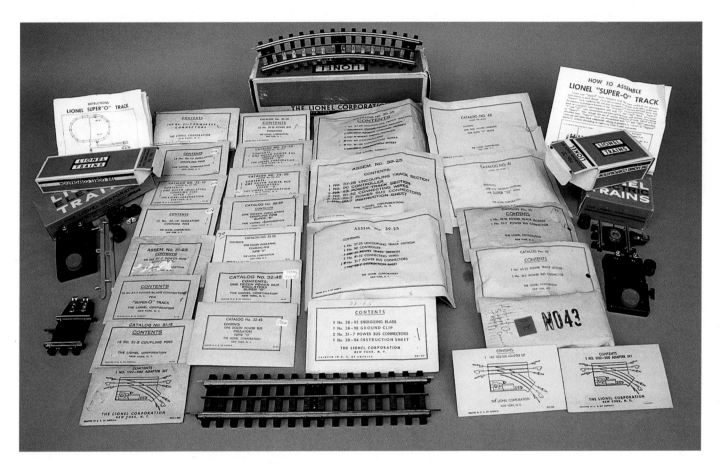

Super O track, introduced in 1957, created the need for a whole range of equipment.
Here is some of that equipment with variations of its packaging.

Track and switches are the foundation of any railroad, model or real. Since real railroads mostly run on two-rail track, Lionel always took pains to explain why three-rail track was best for model railroads. For its market segment—beginning railroaders with temporary layouts—they were right, of course. American Flyer successfully promoted the superior realism of its two-rail track in the postwar years, but Lionel stuck to its guns and prevailed in the marketplace. True, the company did try to disguise the center rail and improve realism with Super O, but it never forgot its two-rail experience

with 2⅞″ gauge and OO gauge in the prewar years. Thus, a long history of three-rail experience carried over to postwar production.

So refined and rugged were Lionel's designs that few changes were made during the postwar period. Only Super O and the change from an RCS to a UCS uncoupling track for magnetic uncoupling come to mind. But with such a long history of production, an abundance of packaging and minor design or color variations occurred. This is possibly the most fertile and least researched field in train collecting.

A variety of 26 and 260 Bumpers. The earliest ones are the 26s in gray and red with aluminum buttons. Next are the red 260s with die-cast housings and plastic buttons (shown with various boxes). Last is the all-plastic black 260, also available in a blister pack as B260.

	Gd	VG	Ex	LN

26 BUMPER, 1948–50

For O and O27 gauge and does not fit on Super O track. Die-cast bumper housing with spring-loaded unpainted aluminum energy absorber, along with four wide "feet." Uses bayonet-base L363 bulb and has a center-rail pickup with notch.

(A) 1948. Housing painted gray. Somewhat hard to find.

	Gd	VG	Ex	LN
	20	30	40	50

(B) 1949–50. Housing painted red.

	Gd	VG	Ex	LN
	9	15	20	30

31 CURVED TRACK, 1957–66

For Super O. Curved track section about 9″ long. Twelve sections form a 36″ outside-diameter circle. Price is per section.

	Gd	VG	Ex	LN
	—	—	2	4

31-7 POWER BLADE CONNECTOR, 1957–60

For Super O. Price is per dozen in original envelope. Same as 31-45 except packaged in a different envelope. Used for joining the center rails of adjacent Super O track sections.

	Gd	VG	Ex	LN
	—	—	1	3

31-15 GROUND RAIL PIN, 1957–66

For Super O. Price is per dozen in original envelope. Used for joining the two outer rails of adjacent Super O track sections.

	Gd	VG	Ex	LN
	—	—	1	3

31-45 POWER BLADE CONNECTOR, 1961–66

For Super O. Price is per dozen in original envelope. Same as 31-7 except packaged in a different envelope. Used for joining the center rails of adjacent Super O track sections.

	Gd	VG	Ex	LN
	—	—	1	3

32 STRAIGHT TRACK, 1957–66

For Super O. Straight track section 9″ long.

	Gd	VG	Ex	LN
	—	—	2	4

Note: Straight track seems to be less plentiful than curved. Outfits usually included 12 curved sections for Super O and eight sections for O and O27 gauge, but typically only one or three straight sections plus a remote-control track. Extra track, both straight and curve, was available for separate sale, but today the straight is less easily found.

32-10 INSULATING PIN, 1957–60

For Super O. Price is per dozen in original envelope. Same as 32-55 except packaged in a different envelope. Used for insulating the outer rails from each other in adjacent Super O track sections.

	Gd	VG	Ex	LN
	—	—	1	3

32-20 POWER BLADE INSULATOR, 1957–60

For Super O. Price is per dozen in original envelope. Same as 32-45 except packaged in a different envelope. Used for insulating the center rails from each other in adjacent Super O track sections.

	Gd	VG	Ex	LN
	—	—	1	3

32-25 INSULATING PIN

For Super O and O27 gauge. Part of the 1122-500 "O27" Gauge Adapter Set, which furnished the pieces necessary to mate

	Gd	VG	Ex	LN

Super O track with O27 gauge track. Available separately only as a service part. — — .25 .30

32-30 GROUND PIN
For Super O and O gauge. Part of O22-500 "O" Gauge Adapter Set, which furnished the pieces necessary to mate Super O track with O gauge track. Available separately only as a service part. — — .25 .30

32-31 POWER PIN
For Super O and O gauge. Part of O22-500 "O" Gauge Adapter Set, which furnished the pieces necessary to mate Super O track with O gauge track. Available separately only as a service part. — — .25 .30

32-32 INSULATING PIN
For Super O and O gauge. Part of O22-500 "O" Gauge Adapter Set, which furnished the pieces necessary to mate Super O track with O gauge track. Available separately only as a service part. — — .25 .30

32-33 GROUND PIN
For Super O and O27 gauge. Part of 1122-500 "O27" Gauge Adapter Set, which furnished the pieces necessary to mate Super O track with O27 gauge track. Available separately only as a service part. — — .25 .30

32-34 POWER PIN
For Super O and O27 gauge. Part of the 1122-500 "O27" Gauge Adapter Set, which furnished the pieces necessary to mate Super O track with O27 gauge track. Available separately only as a service part. — — .25 .30

32-45 POWER BLADE INSULATOR, 1961–66
For Super O. Price per dozen in original envelope. Same as 32-20 except packaged in a different envelope. Used to insulate the center rails from each other in adjacent Super O track sections. — — 2 5

32-55 INSULATING PIN, 1961–66
For Super O. Price per dozen in original envelope. Same as 32-10 except packaged in a different envelope. Used to insulate the outer rails from each other in adjacent Super O track sections. — — 2 5

33 HALF CURVED TRACK, 1957–66
For Super O. Half-curved track section 4½" long. — — 1 2

34 HALF STRAIGHT TRACK, 1957–66
For Super O. Half-straight track section 5¾" long. — — 1 2

36 OPERATING CAR REMOTE CONTROL SET, 1957–66
For Super O. Includes 90 Controller, two control blades, and three coiled wires. This track section contains the two rails used to energize the operating mechanism on operating cars such as the 3469 Operating Dump Car. Like New requires complete set in original box or envelope. 5 7 10 15

37 UNCOUPLING TRACK SET, 1957–66
For Super O. Includes 90 Controller, electromagnet on 11½" long track section, and two coiled wires. Used to operate magnetic couplers on all Lionel locomotives and rolling stock except those equipped with Scout or electromagnetic couplers. Like New requires complete set in original box or envelope. 6 8 12 18

38 PAIR OF ACCESSORY ADAPTER TRACKS, 1957–61
For Super O. A pair of straight sections, each 5¼" long. Has only two ties at each end, with a gap in the middle where ties would normally be. Used for adapting Lionel operating cars and accessories to Super O. Like New requires original box or envelope. 5 7 12 15

39 SUPER O OPERATING SET, 1957–66
This was the basic number of the envelopes containing all necessary small parts for Super O train sets. Each envelope had a part number, such as 39-5, 39-10, 39-25, etc., with content varying according to the needs of the particular set. Prices vary depending on content and condition, but always require the original envelope, since this is the collectible. The third volume of *Greenberg's Guide to Lionel Trains, 1945–1969* contains pictures and descriptions of many of these envelopes.

43 POWER TRACK, 1959–66
For Super O. 1½" long track section with ground and power terminals. Used to electrically connect the transformer to Super O track. Like New requires original box or envelope. 3 5 6 10

48 INSULATED STRAIGHT TRACK, 1957–66
For Super O. Straight track section 9" long that came in a box of six sections with six Power Blade Connectors. Box end states, "BE SURE TO SUPPLY ONE POWER BLADE / WITH EACH TRACK." To tell the insulated from the regular track section, look on the bottom and observe that there are no metal connections between the two outer rails on the insulated section. On regular Super O track, metal strips (to provide a magnetic path for Lionel's Magne-Traction feature) tie the outer rails together. Used to insulate one outside rail from the other for activating accessories when the train wheels made the electrical connection between these rails. This could substitute for a weight-activated switch, such as a 145C or 153C used with O and O27 track. Price is for a single piece of track; box of six sections is NRS. 4 6 9 12

49 INSULATED CURVED TRACK, 1957–66
For Super O. Curved track section approximately 9" long. See listing for 48 regarding box of six sections, use, and how to tell insulated from regular track. Price is for a single section. 4 6 9 12

112 PAIR OF REMOTE CONTROL SWITCHES, 1957–66
For Super O. One right-hand and one left-hand switch, each with an O22C Controller. The plain 112 was produced only during 1957. In this version, passing wheel flanges push down the contact springs above the track bed. Apparently this arrangement was not entirely satisfactory, because Lionel redesigned the

Clockwise from left: No. 130 60-Degree Crossing, three dealer packages of six insulated track sections (curves in larger boxes), No. 120 90-Degree Crossing, and four sections of Super O track. The inverted straight section (center left) is an insulated piece, while the one connected on its right is a regular piece.

	Gd	VG	Ex	LN

switch in 1958, designating it as 112R. That number and letter are found stamped on the switch's base. In the redesigned version, the contact springs are brushed by the backs of the passing wheel flanges, the swivel rails and springs are improved, and the motors have slightly larger housings. Both designs require two L19 bulbs per switch. S. Carlson Collection and comments. Like New requires the original box.

	Gd	VG	Ex	LN
	45	60	95	110

112-125 LEFT HAND SWITCH, 1957–60

For Super O. Separate-sale remote-control switch with O22C Controller. Like New requires the original box.

	Gd	VG	Ex	LN
	35	45	65	75

112-150 RIGHT HAND SWITCH, 1957–60

For Super O. Separate-sale remote-control switch with O22C Controller. Like New requires the original box.

	Gd	VG	Ex	LN
	35	45	65	75

112-LH LEFT HAND SWITCH, 1961–66

For Super O. Same as 112-125 (Lionel's service part number for the switch), but with a new designation, probably to make it easier for dealers to tell whether the switch was right-hand or left-hand without opening the box. Like New requires the original box.

	Gd	VG	Ex	LN
	35	45	65	75

112-RH RIGHT HAND SWITCH, 1961–66

For Super O. Same as 112-150 (Lionel's service part number for the switch), but with a new designation, probably to make it easier for dealer to tell whether the switch was right-hand or left-hand without opening the box. Like New requires the original box.

	Gd	VG	Ex	LN
	35	45	65	75

120 90 DEGREE CROSSING, 1957–66

For Super O. Like New requires the original box.

	Gd	VG	Ex	LN
	4	6	10	12

130 60 DEGREE CROSSING, 1957–66

For Super O. Like New requires the original box.

	Gd	VG	Ex	LN
	6	9	12	15

142 PAIR OF MANUAL SWITCHES, 1957–66

For Super O. The 1957 catalog shows illuminated direction indicators on the switches, but all known production uses an unlighted rotating signpost. One feature built into these switches, but not found in O42 manual switches, is a power interrupt to the center rail of the "open" direction. This is a safety device, but since the distance is so short it would only stop a very slow moving train in time to prevent derailment. However, by moving the insulating power blade a few sections away from the switch, this feature can be made more effective. Complications creating dead track sections can result from this procedure, but remedies are covered in the instruction sheets.

	Gd	VG	Ex	LN
	18	30	42	50

142-125 LEFT HAND SWITCH, 1957–60

For Super O. Separate-sale manual switch.

	Gd	VG	Ex	LN
	12	18	30	42

142-150 RIGHT HAND SWITCH, 1957–60

For Super O. Separate-sale manual switch.

	Gd	VG	Ex	LN
	12	18	30	42

142-LH LEFT HAND SWITCH, 1961–66

For Super O. A manually operated switch same as 142-125 (Lionel's service part number for the switch), but with a new designation, probably to make it easier for dealers to tell whether

Different O27 gauge remote control track sections and boxes. In the center foreground is a no. 1009 "Manumatic" section furnished with Scout outfits between 1948 and 1952.

	Gd	VG	Ex	LN

the switch was right-hand or left-hand without opening the box.

	12	18	30	42

142-RH RIGHT HAND SWITCH, 1961–66

For Super O. A manually operated switch same as 142-150 (Lionel's service part number for the switch), but with a new designation, probably to make it easier for dealers to tell whether the switch was right-hand or left-hand without opening the box.

	12	18	30	42

260 BUMPER, 1951–66 and 1968–69

Successor to the 26 and identical in size. Earlier production used a die-cast body that is painted red with a spring-loaded black plastic energy absorber. It is illuminated with an L363 bayonet-base bulb and has spring clips for electrical connection to the outside rails. In later years, unpainted black plastic replaced the die-cast body.

(A) 1951–57. Four wide "feet," center-rail pickup with notch, will not fit Super O track. S. Carlson comment.

	10	15	20	25

(B) 1958–65. Four narrow "feet," center-rail pickup without notch. This change was made, a year late, to accommodate Super O track, since the wide-footed version would not fit that track. S. Carlson comment.

	10	15	20	25

(C) 1966 and 1968–69. Black plastic bumper with black plas-tic energy absorber, center-rail pickup without notch. Came with outfit 11600 and also available for separate sale in Hagerstown orange and white box. To cut cost, the lamp and related hardware were removed. E. Trentacoste and I. D. Smith Collections. Like New requires the original box.

	20	30	40	50

(D) 1966. B260, the blister pack version of (C). Packaging is the real collectible, so only a Like New price is shown, indicating a pack that is shopworn.

	—	—	—	125

313-82 FIBRE PINS, 1940–42 and 1946–56

For O27 gauge. Price is per dozen in an original envelope. These were made of compressed fiber in the early days, either gray or black. Later they were molded nylon, either natural (white) or black. Catalog entry in 1956 says, "(New No. 1122-234)" following the 313-82 listing.

	—	—	1	3

313-121 FIBRE PINS, 1961–66 and 1968–69

For O27 gauge. Price is per dozen in original envelope. Same as 313-82 and 1122-234 except packaged in a different envelope.

	—	—	1	3

711 REMOTE CONTROL O72 SWITCHES, 1935–42

For O gauge. Pair of O72 wide-radius non-derailing switches with controllers. Prewar product, but listed here because of heavy use by postwar operators. See also 721 entry.

| | 90 | 100 | 195 | 225 |

721 MANUAL O72 SWITCHES, 1935–42

For O gauge. Pair of O72 wide-radius manually controlled switches. Prewar product, but listed here because of heavy use by postwar operators.

| | 65 | 80 | 110 | 125 |

760 O72 TRACK, 1938–42, 1950, and 1954–58

For O gauge. Box of 16 sections (making a 74″ outside-diameter circle) of O72 curved track, each section 14″ long. Same as O gauge track in height and construction, but the diameter of a circle of regular O gauge curve is only 31″. Before the "bigger is better" mentality set in, Lionel measured the diameter of a loop of track (except O27 gauge, which was always outside diameter) between the centerlines of the center rail. Hence the O72 designation. Note that reproduction track is available. Like New requires the original box.

| | 18 | 25 | 38 | 50 |

1008 UNCOUPLING UNIT, 1957–62

For O27 gauge. This plastic uncoupler clips to a straight section of O27 track. It works by spring-loaded blades that can be manually raised to pull down the uncoupling disc on AAR and archbar trucks. Cam action and the motion of the train combine to provide the force. In instruction sheets, Lionel called this a "CAM-TROL" Uncoupler.

"INSTRUCTIONS FOR OPERATING / LIONEL TRAIN OUTFITS" (sheet 1649-10, dated 6-61) explained, "To operate the 'Cam-Trol' uncoupler from a distance, tie a piece of strong thin twine to the 'Cam-Trol' lever, pass the string through the holes and around the pin provided for this purpose in the 'Cam-Trol' base . . . and bring it to your control position. A pull on the string will now move the lever and uncouple the car."

The "Cam-Trol" name does not appear in consumer catalogs, and the 1008 was included with only low-end sets. It is listed as a 1008 Uncoupling Unit in descriptions of these sets. In the 1957 catalog, the 1008 is listed under the heading, "ADDITIONAL ITEMS USED IN TRAIN SETS" and priced at $1.50.

| | — | — | 1 | 5 |

1008-50 UNCOUPLING TRACK SECTION, 1957–62 (uncataloged)

For O27 gauge. When the factory attached a 1008 to a section of O27 straight track, the assembly became a 1008-50! Included in inexpensive sets, but was not cataloged for separate sale.

| | — | — | 1 | 5 |

1009 MANUMATIC TRACK SECTION, 1948–52

For O27 gauge. The 1009 debuted with Scout sets in 1948 and came in those outfits only. Called "Manumatic" by Lionel, it amounted to a simple lever-and-platform arrangement that came installed on a slightly modified straight section of O27 track. Pressing the lever lifts the platform (called a "wedge" in the Scout set instructions), and it raises and disengages the coupler

heads on the special Scout trucks. Not cataloged for separate sale, but it is known in its own Classic box. Price is for just the track section. The box is an NRS collectible.

| | — | — | 1 | 5 |

1013 CURVED TRACK, 1933–42, 1945–66, and 1968–69

For O27 gauge. Curved track section 9½″ long. Also cataloged as 1/2 1013 for a half section. For 1966, four sections of this track were available as a B1013 blister pack, an NRS item.

| | — | — | .20 | .50 |

1013-17 STEEL PINS, 1946–60

For O27 gauge. Price per dozen in original envelope. A separate pin is used for joining each of the three rails in adjacent track sections. Same as 1013-42 except packaged in a different envelope.

| | — | — | — | .50 |

1013-42 STEEL PINS, 1961-66 and 1968-69

For O27 gauge. Price per dozen in original envelope. A separate pin is used for joining each of the three rails in adjacent track sections. Same as 1013-17 except packaged in a different envelope.

| | — | — | — | .60 |

1018 STRAIGHT TRACK, 1933–42, 1945–66, and 1968–69

For O27 gauge. Straight track section 8⅞″ long. Also cataloged as 1/2 1018 for a half section. For 1966, four sections of this track were available as a B1018 blister pack, an NRS item.

| | — | — | .40 | .75 |

1019 REMOTE CONTROL TRACK SET, 1938–42 and 1946–48

For O27 gauge. Includes an RCS-20 two-button Bakelite controller. Examples have been found with a brown controller and with black buttons, but most have red buttons in a black Bakelite controller housing. Track section includes two uninterrupted control rails with no center electromagnet. This item was discontinued and replaced by the 6019 when magnetic uncoupling was introduced.

| | — | — | 8 | 10 |

1020 90 DEGREE CROSSING, 1955–66 and 1968–69

For O27 gauge. Also available in 1966 as a B1020 blister pack, an NRS item.

| | — | — | 6 | 8 |

1021 90 DEGREE CROSSING, 1933–42 and 1945–54

For O27 gauge. There are several variations of this simple item over the years, but research has yet to be done on most of them.

| | — | — | 6 | 8 |

1022 MANUAL SWITCHES, 1953–66 and 1968–69

For O27 gauge. Price per pair. Like New includes the original box.

| | 10 | 15 | 20 | 25 |

1022LH MANUAL SWITCH, 1955–66 and 1968–69

For O27 gauge. Left-hand manual switch. Also available in 1966 as a B1022LH blister pack, an NRS item.

| | 2 | 8 | 12 | 15 |

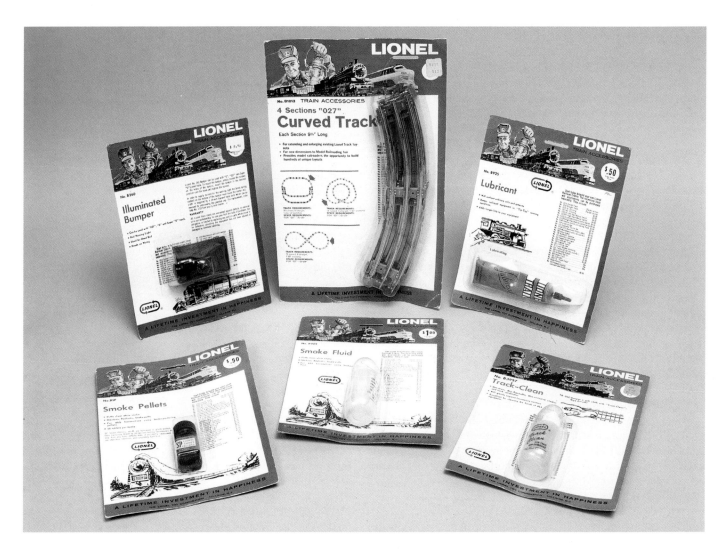

	Gd	VG	Ex	LN

1022RH MANUAL SWITCH, 1955–66 and 1968–69

For O27 gauge. Right-hand manual switch. Also available in 1966 as a B1022RH blister pack, an NRS item.

	Gd	VG	Ex	LN
	2	8	12	15

1023 45 DEGREE CROSSING, 1956–66 and 1968–69

For O27 gauge. Also available in 1966 as a B1023 blister pack, an NRS item. Like New includes original box.

	Gd	VG	Ex	LN
	—	—	5	7

1024 MANUAL SWITCHES, 1935–42 and 1946–52

For O27 gauge. Same moving rails as the 1121 remote control switches, circular metal red-and-green painted direction markers. Wide keystone-shaped aluminum and black plate reads, "No. 1024 / THE LIONEL CORPORATION / MADE IN U. S. / OF AMERICA." Cataloged for separate sale as 1024L and 1024R in prewar years, but sold only in pairs postwar. Price per pair. Like New requires an original box.

	Gd	VG	Ex	LN
	7	10	20	25

1025 ILLUMINATED BUMPER, 1940–42 and 1946–47

For O27 gauge. Black die-cast O26 bumper (not the same as 26 or 260) with L430(R) lamp, attached to a straight section of

A gathering of rare blister packs from 1966. With the exception of the smoke pellet bottle, the contents are common, but intact blister packs in decent condition are tough to find. Missing is a blister pack of straight track, one of the most difficult to find. The brown smoke bottle in the left blister pack is unique in size and color. J. Lampert Collection.

	Gd	VG	Ex	LN

O27 track. Packaged with track section attached. The same bumper attached to a section of O gauge track was cataloged as O25, though for some reason Lionel specified a higher voltage L431(R) lamp for the O gauge version.

	Gd	VG	Ex	LN
	6	10	15	20

1121 REMOTE CONTROL SWITCHES, 1937–42 and 1946–51

For O27 gauge. Each switch has two indicator lenses and a rounded motor cover. Pair has a single "dual" controller 1121C-60 with two levers and four indicator light lenses, two for each switch. Although externally identical to the 1122-100, these controllers differ electrically and are not interchangeable without modification. Switches came with bright or satin rail finish. They used L430 screw-base bulbs before 1949 and then changed to L431 bayonet-base bulbs. The controller used the same bulb, but made the change from screw to bayonet base for 1950.

| | Gd | VG | Ex | LN |

The prewar version has a metal switch cover box and metal controller cover with red-painted levers. Postwar production substituted molded black Bakelite for the two covers. Reliable operation but did not include a non-derailing feature. Right- and left-hand switches were also available and were supplied with an O22C Controller. Although the O22C will control the switch, the controller lamps will not illuminate. Price per pair. Like New requires an original box.

(A) Flat plastic direction indicator lenses on switches.

| | **11** | **20** | **35** | **45** |

(B) Protruding rubbery plastic direction indicator lenses on switches and rivet location on bottom differs from (A). The same lenses were also used on the later and most common version of 151 Semaphore.

| | **11** | **20** | **35** | **45** |

1122 REMOTE CONTROL SWITCHES, 1952

For O27 gauge. The addition of a non-derailing feature was the major reason a new switch was designed to replace the 1121. Early production switches each have a rotating direction indicator. There is a single controller, 1122-100, with two levers and four indicator light lenses to control the pair of switches. Five notches on switch box cover, insulated rails on outside with insulating break in rail so no separate insulating pins are needed. The moving rails are fastened to the drive rod with a large circular rivet.

An L53 Lamp for the direction indicator on each switch is mounted on a separate socket that plugs into a notch accessible through an arch-shaped hole in cover. Came first with swiveling directional indicators whose lenses have exposed surfaces that break easily. Later versions have recessed lenses. Flat frog point and wide frog rail. Operational and production problems led to a substantial redesign in 1953. See 1122E entry. R. LaVoie comments.

(A) Direction indicator with exposed lenses.

| | **11** | **20** | **35** | **40** |

(B) Later version. Direction indicator with recessed lenses.

| | **11** | **20** | **35** | **40** |

1122E REMOTE CONTROL SWITCHES, 1953–66 and 1968–69

For O27 gauge. Each switch has a rotating direction indicator and a single controller, 1122-100, with two levers and four indicator light lenses. Three notches on redesigned rounded switch cover, which allowed clearance for larger locomotives. (Lionel also sold this rounded cover to retrofit the older 1122 switches, and retrofit parts had the arched cutout for the light socket.) Light clip redesigned to be completely internal, eliminating the arched cutout and separate light socket.

Insulated rails were moved to the two inside short rails that branch from a rounded frog point, so separate insulating pins are required for 1122Es. The long curved and straight rails were made solid without any breaks, and a metal track insert was placed on the frog to prevent premature wear of the plastic base by wheel flanges.

Early versions have the moving rails fastened to the drive rod by a large clover-shaped rivet. The rack in the mechanism was redesigned, and the frog rail made much narrower. The bracket for the directional indicator was reinforced. Stamped "MODEL

When Lionel packaged the 1122LH Left Hand Switch in a blister pack in 1966, it gave it the number B1122LH. J. Algozzini Collection.

| | Gd | VG | Ex | LN |

1122(E)" on galvanized base bottom, this version provides more reliable operation than its predecessor did. R. LaVoie comments.

(A) Early version with moving rails fastened to drive rod by a large, clover-shaped rivet.

| | | **11** | **20** | **35** | **45** |

(B) Same as (A) except later production with moving rails fastened to drive rod by small circular rivet.

| | | **11** | **20** | **35** | **45** |

1122LH LEFT HAND SWITCH, 1955–66 and 1968–69

For O27 gauge. Remote-controlled left-hand switch with an O22C Controller. Although the O22C controls the switch, the controller lamps do not illuminate. Also available in 1966 as B1122LH blister pack with frame, an NRS item. Price assumes the controller is included.

| | **7** | **11** | **20** | **25** |

1122RH RIGHT HAND SWITCH, 1955–66 and 1968–69

For O27 gauge. Remote-controlled right-hand switch with an O22C Controller. Although the O22C controls the switch, the controller lamps do not illuminate. Also available in 1966 as B1122RH blister pack with frame, an NRS item. Price assumes the controller is included.

| | **7** | **11** | **20** | **25** |

1122-234 FIBRE PINS, 1958–60

For O27 gauge. Price per dozen in original envelope. Same as 313-82 and 313-121, but packaged in a different numbered envelope.

| | — | — | — | **1** |

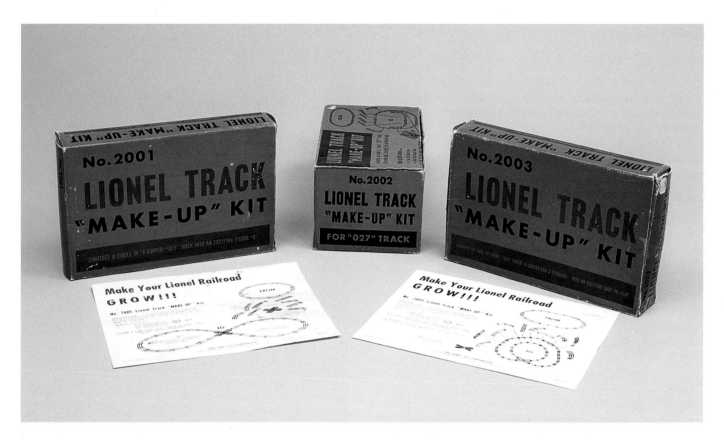

	Gd	VG	Ex	LN

1122-500 "O27" TRACK ADAPTER SET, 1957–66

For Super O and O27 gauge. Used for combining O27 and Super O track. Includes four 32-33 ground pins, two 32-25 insulating pins, and three 32-34 power pins. Price for complete set in original envelope. — — 1 3

2001 TRACK "MAKE-UP" KIT, 1963

For O27 gauge. Cataloged one year only as a package with everything the basic set buyer needed to convert a simple circle of O27 track (consisting of eight curves) into a figure eight. Includes four No. 1013 Curves, four No. 1018 Straights, and one No. 1012 90 Degree Crossing. These components were sold boxed together in one container, an Orange Picture box that did not age well with all the track pieces in it but is the collectible item. **NRS**

2002 TRACK "MAKE-UP" KIT, 1963

For O27 gauge. Printed on the Orange Picture box is the explanation, "For converting an oval of 'O27' track (8 curved, 2 straight) into an 'Oval-N-Oval'. Includes: 2 No. 1013 Curved, 4 No. 1018 Straight, 1 Pair of No. 1122 Remote Control Switches." Common components packaged in a collectible box that is very rare. **NRS**

2003 TRACK "MAKE-UP" KIT, 1963

For O27 gauge. Printed on the Orange Picture box is the explanation, "For converting an oval of 'O27' track (8 Curved, 2 Straight) into a 'Loop-to-Loop'. Includes: 8 No. 1013 Curved, 2 No. 1018 Straight, 1 No. 1023 45 Crossing." Also printed in black on the box is, "MAKE THIS EXCITING LOOP-TO-LOOP LAYOUT." Common components packaged in a collectible box that is very rare today. **NRS**

So rare are these 1963-only boxes that just one collection is known to include all three. The advertising flyers (a single-sided one for the 2001 and double-sided for 2002 and 2003) were included with many of the cataloged and uncataloged budget sets of that year.

	Gd	VG	Ex	LN

6009 UNCOUPLING SECTION, 1953–55

For O27 gauge. The 6009, 6029, and 6149 were Lionel's simplest and least expensive electric remote-control track sets. They came with low-end sets after Lionel discontinued its Scout sets and Manumatic uncouplers. The 6009 had only an electromagnet and came with a single-button 96C Controller. There are no control rails (like 6019 has) for energizing operating cars or electromagnetic couplers. See 6029 for differences with the 6009. — — 6 8

6019 REMOTE CONTROL TRACK, 1948–66

For O27 gauge. Provides control rails for powering operating cars and operating magnetic and electromagnetic couplers. Red or black (scarce) plastic housing around the top of the electromagnet in the center of the track unit. Uses a 6019-20 two-button controller that is identical to the RCS-20 and UCS-40 except for which of the four wires goes where. Wiring of mid-1950s versions often deteriorates. So far, 40 variations of the 6019-16 instruction sheet have been found!

(A) 1948. Nickel finish on track base. R. Hutchinson Collection. — — 7 10

(B) 1949–66. Same as (A) except black finish. — — 7 10

(C) 1966. Same as (B) except in a B6019 blister pack. **NRS**

These prewar and postwar boxes of large quantities of O27 and O gauge Track Clips are rare items. D. Corrigan Collection.

	Gd	VG	Ex	LN

6029 UNCOUPLING TRACK SET, 1955–63

For O27 gauge. Provides uncoupling function for magnetic couplers only, since there are no control rails. Came with a 90 Controller in the early years of production, and then with a less expensive 0190-25 single-button controller borrowed from the HO line. A small, undated instruction sheet, part number 6029-8, printed in black ink on 5½″ x 4¼″ white paper has been observed showing the HO controller.

The difference between a 6009 and a 6029 is that the former has no number on it and comes with a two-wire cable soldered to the track connections. Spade lugs are provided on the other wire ends for connection to a 96C Controller. For the 6029, one or both of the phenolic plates in the base has "PT. No (with the 'o' elevated and underlined) 6029" stamped into the material on the underside. There are two screw terminals instead of soldered wires underneath. Two coiled wires came with the track section for the operator to connect to the track and controller. Both 6009 and 6029 are listed in the 1955 catalog at the same $2.95 price.

	Gd	VG	Ex	LN
	—	—	4	8

6149 REMOTE CONTROL UNCOUPLING TRACK, 1964–66 and 1968–69

For O27 gauge. Similar to 6029 but without the base. Came with an 0190-25 HO single-button controller and two coiled wires. Nothing more than a standard piece of track with the magnet assembly in the center rail. There is only one screw for wire

attachment because the other lead from the magnet is permanently connected to the outer rails. The controller connects between the transformer center rail post and the magnet. One 4¼″ x 5½″ instruction sheet, part number 6149-17 dated 3/65 and printed black on white, has been examined. Like the 6029 instructions, they warn against holding the control button down for more than three seconds to avoid overheating the magnet. Also available in 1966 as B6149 blister pack, an NRS item.

			Ex	LN
	—	—	5	8

CO-1 TRACK CLIP, 1949

For O gauge. Price is per dozen (or more) in the original envelope. Included with O gauge outfits to lock track sections together, so the quantity furnished corresponded to the number of track sections included with the set. The 1950 catalog states that inclusion of these clips in sets was being discontinued due to material shortages. Although 1949 was the first year clips appeared in the catalog with their own number, it was not their first year. Dealer boxes of 50 and 100 have been observed labeled " 'O' GAUGE TRACK CLIPS" and are NRS. Small boxes containing CO-1 clips plus a lockon and even a tube of lubricant were commonly included with prewar sets.

				LN
	—	—	—	3

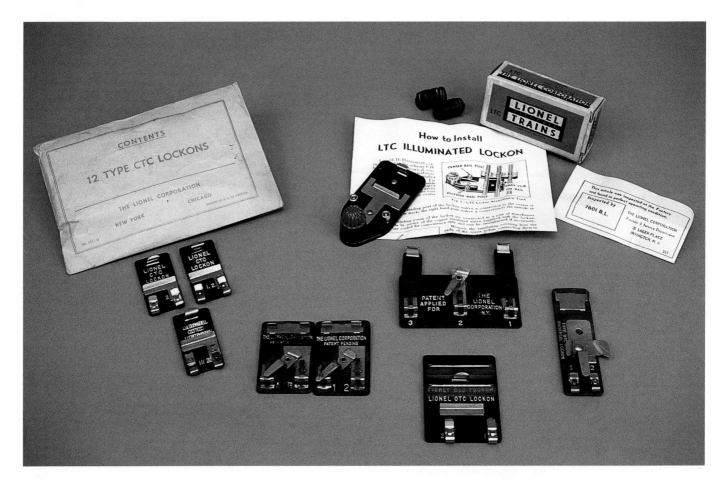

	Gd	VG	Ex	LN

Above: A variety of Lionel track lockons, both pre- and postwar. Note the double stamped CTC at lower left.

Above right: Rare packaging for the ubiquitous CTC Lockon. Twelve of these necessary items were commonly packed in a manila envelope, but these boxes of 12 and 36, and the master carton of 500, are seldom seen. Difficult as even one is to find, there are two variations of the 12 and 36 boxes! J. Lampert Collection.

Right: Lionel produced the LTC Lockon for 20 years with various packages. The only change to the LTC involved the method used to clinch the rivets. The wires (prewar at lower left) represent only a few of the coiled wire lengths and colors Lionel included with their various accessories over the years. M. Stephens Collection.

CTC LOCKON, 1947–66 and 1968–69

For O and O27 gauge. Included with all post-1945 train sets (except for Super O) and most locomotives, this is an essential piece of equipment for all but the permanent, hard-wired layout. It is used to connect the transformer to the track. Just snapping it onto the track provides electrical connection to the center rail and one outer rail. The track ties provide connection to the other outer rail. A few subtle changes were made in the CTC over the many years it was made, but none affect the value of this ubiquitous piece. A robust design, it is found either about Like New or broken and useless. — — — 1

LTC LOCKON, 1950–66 and 1968–69

For O and O27 gauge. A fancy CTC with an L1445 Lamp covered with a green lens that remains illuminated whenever power is applied. See CTC comments for the electrical function. Came in its own box, which is required for Like New. — — 5 15

011-11 FIBRE PINS, 1937–42 and 1946–60

For O gauge. In the early years, these were made of gray or black compressed fiber. In later years, natural (white) or black molded nylon was used. Price is per dozen in the original envelope. Same as O11-43 and TO11-43, except packaged in a different envelope. — — 1 2

	Gd	VG	Ex	LN

011-43 FIBRE PINS, 1961

For O gauge. Price is per dozen in the original envelope. Same as O11-11 and TO11-43, except packaged in a different envelope. — — 2 3

020 90 DEGREE CROSSING, 1915–42 and 1945–61

For O gauge. One of Lionel's longest running accessories, it dates back to the first days of O gauge. There are undoubtedly many variations, and those listed are only two observed examples of postwar production. As with most track items, the O20 is not widely collected so the variations have yet to be fully appreciated and chronicled.

(A) Black base, indented center with cross-shaped projection, solid metal rail connector under base, center held with visible rivet, red insulators, aluminum and black plate reads, "MADE

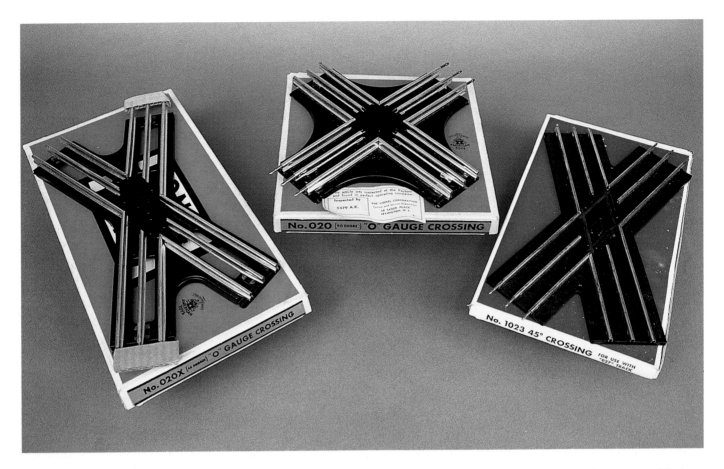

Left to right: 020X, 020, and 1023 Crossings. These rugged pieces are not difficult to find.

IN U. S. AMERICA / No. 020 / CROSSING / THE LIONEL CORP. / N. Y." R. LaVoie Collection.

| | 5 | 6 | 7 | 8 |

(B) Same as (A) except later version. Rail connector under base has punched circular hole, black insulators, no plate, larger center with square projection heat-stamped "No. 020 / CROSSING / MADE IN / U. S. OF AMERICA / LIONEL CORP. / N.Y." R. LaVoie Collection.

| | 5 | 6 | 7 | 8 |

020X 45 DEGREE CROSSING, 1917–42 and 1946–59

For O gauge. Another old-timer, but only two observed examples of postwar production are listed.

(A) Black base, brown Bakelite center, stamped "LIONEL CORP. / 020X / CROSSING / NEW YORK," red center insulation. R. LaVoie Collection.

| | 5 | 7 | 9 | 11 |

(B) Same as (A) except black Bakelite center and black insulation. R. LaVoie Collection.

| | 5 | 7 | 9 | 11 |

022 REMOTE CONTROL SWITCHES, 1938–42 and 1945–66

For O gauge. Also cataloged with this number from 1915-26 as a pair of unlighted manual switches. Postwar models have (compared to prewar versions) new curved control rails, new long curved rails, new auxiliary rails, a new long straight rail, and a new location for the screws that attach the bottom plate. When sold in pairs, came with two 022C Controllers, two lens hoods, and two constant-voltage plugs. Prewar identification plates read, "AUTOMATICALLY CONTROLLED / 1¼" GAUGE SWITCH"; postwar issues read, "LIONEL / REMOTE

CONTROL / NO. 022 / O GAUGE SWITCH." R. Gluckman comment.

| | 40 | 50 | 65 | 75 |

022-500 "O" TRACK ADAPTER SET, 1957–61

For Super O and O gauge. Set has all pieces for mating Super O with O gauge track. Includes four 32-30 Ground Pins, two 32-32 Insulating Pins, and three 32-31 Power Pins. Price is for complete set in original envelope.

| | — | — | 2 | 3 |

022A REMOTE CONTROL SWITCHES, 1947 (uncataloged)

For O gauge. Modified 022 switch issued during a period of critical materials shortages. As manufactured, the 022A excluded the following parts: terminal plate assembly 711-129, fixed voltage plug, contact plate 711-217, and fitted contact plate 711-37. The usual large stamped-metal bottom plate and the insulation piece above it were never installed. The metal identification plate was changed to read "022A."

These switches were non-derailing, but due to a shortage of 022C Controllers, Lionel substituted an 1121C-60 double controller, normally supplied with O27 remote-control switches. Each box is marked, "No. 022A / SUPERSEDES NO. 022 / NON-DERAILING REMOTE CONTROL / O GAUGE SWITCHES" on its ends. When materials became available again, the factory resumed installation of the missing parts and

For many years, controllers for 022 O gauge switches came in boxes inside the packages. They also were available for separate sale. Here are early and late postwar boxes for single controllers except for upper left, which is the usual component box for a pair of 022 switches. At lower right is a fixed-voltage plug.

Top and bottom views of the rare 022A cost-reduced version of the 022 Switch. Note the use of a single 1121C Controller in place of separate 022C Controllers, no bottom plate, and the "022A" on the number plate. Other features were omitted as well, such as provision for the fixed-voltage plug.

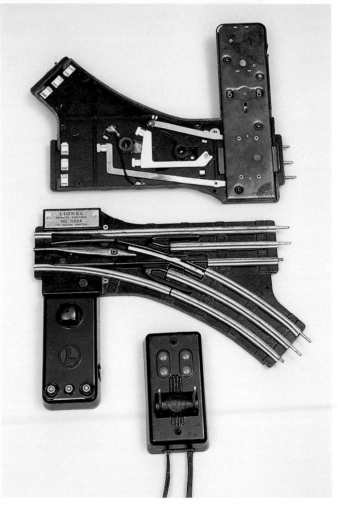

	Gd	VG	Ex	LN

renumbered the switches "O22." The first of these post-crisis identification plates were made of brushed lightweight aluminum instead of black-painted stamped steel.

Hard to find complete and boxed in original condition. Like New requires intact pair of switches, controller, and original box.

	70	85	115	225

022LH REMOTE CONTROL SWITCH, 1950–61

For O gauge. Left-hand switch with controller. Prewar version cataloged 1938-42 as O22L.

	15	20	35	45

022RH REMOTE CONTROL SWITCH, 1950–61

For O gauge. Right-hand switch with controller. Prewar version cataloged 1938-42 as O22R.

	15	20	35	45

Various O gauge remote control track sections and their boxes. The two at the top are RCS sections from 1948 and earlier. When Lionel introduced magnetic couplers, a UCS with an electromagnet (center) became necessary.

	Gd	VG	Ex	LN

O25 BUMPER, 1928–42 and 1946–47

For O gauge. An illuminated black O26 bumper with an L432(R) Lamp, attached to a piece of O gauge track. This was a late prewar carryover and is not the same as the 26 and 260. Packaged with the track section attached. The same bumper attached to a section of O27 straight track was cataloged as the 1025, though for some reason Lionel specified a lower voltage L430(R) Lamp for the O27 gauge unit.

	Gd	VG	Ex	LN
	7	15	20	30

O27C-1 TRACK CLIPS, 1949

For O27 gauge. Price is per dozen (more or less) in the original envelope. Included with all but the least expensive O27 outfits to lock track sections together, so the quantity furnished corresponded to the number of track sections included with the set. The 1950 catalog says inclusion of these clips in train sets was being discontinued due to material shortages.

The track clips were an Ives design and were available well before World War II. Lionel got the tooling when it bought the Ives assets, and the "IVES" name can be found stamped into some of these blackened steel clips. 1949 was the first year they appeared in the catalog with their own number, but it was not the first year for these clips. Dealer boxes of 50 and 100, labeled "O-27 TRACK CLIPS" without a part number, have been observed. These dealer packs are NRS.

	—	—	1	3

O42 MANUAL SWITCHES, 1938–42 and 1946–59

For O gauge. This pair of manually operated switches changed in 1950 from an L1447 screw-base lamp socket to an L1445 bayonet-base. Red die-cast operating lever, sometimes broken off but easily replaced. Also cataloged for separate sale as O42L and O42R from 1938–42, but only in pairs postwar. Prices are per pair.

	30	40	50	60

OC CURVED TRACK, 1915–42 and 1945–61

For O gauge. Curved track section 10⅞" long. Also cataloged 1934–42 and 1946–61 as ½ OC for a half section.

	—	—	—	2

OCS INSULATED O GAUGE CURVED TRACK, 1933–42 and 1950

For O gauge. Same as OSS, but curved instead of straight. Both outside rails are insulated from the ties, so either or both can be used as sense rails for activating signals, throwing switches, etc. No information available on packaging. **NRS**

OS STRAIGHT TRACK, 1915–42 and 1945–61

For O gauge. Straight track section 10" long. Also cataloged 1932–42 and 1946–61 as ½ OS for a half section.

	—	—	—	2

OSS INSULATED O GAUGE STRAIGHT TRACK, 1933–42, 1946, and 1950

For O gauge. A special straight track section 10″ long with both outside rails insulated from the ties, so either or both can be used as sense rails for activating signals, throwing switches, etc. An instruction sheet, Form OCS-16 (dated 11-50) was issued, and two variations have been found. No information on packaging.

NRS

OTC LOCKON, 1955–59

For O and O27 gauge. A special lockon-type contactor with two short control "rails." Made to supply power to the longer operating cars, such as the 3562 Operating Barrel Car and 3359 Twin Dump Car that were too long for a standard remote-control track section. The contactor was made the correct height for O27 gauge, and it included O gauge extension rails.

— — — 5

OC-18 STEEL PINS, 1946–60

For O gauge. Price per dozen in the original envelope. They were also packaged 36 to an envelope. Same as OC-51 and TOC-51, except packaged in a different envelope.

— — — 1

OC-51 STEEL PINS, 1961

For O gauge. Price per dozen in the original envelope. They were also packaged 36 to an envelope. Same as OC-18 and TOC-51, except packaged in a different envelope.

— — — 1

RCS REMOTE CONTROL TRACK, 1938–42 and 1946–48

For O gauge. Has two uninterrupted control rails with no center electromagnet. Will not operate magnetic couplers or plunger-actuated cars such as the 3464 operating boxcars. Includes RCS-20 two-button controller. Replaced after 1948 by the UCS section. Thirteen versions of the RCS-8 instruction sheet have been observed.

(A) Controller with red push buttons.

— — 9 12

(B) Controller with green push buttons. B. Spivock Collection.

— — 20 30

TO11-43 FIBRE PINS, 1962–66 and 1969

For O gauge. Price per dozen in the original envelope. Molded nylon in white or black. Same as O11-11 and O11-43, except packaged in a different envelope.

— — — 2

TO20 90 DEGREE CROSSING, 1962–66 and 1969

For O gauge. There is no significant difference between O20 and TO20. Starting in 1962, Lionel renumbered all its O gauge track items by placing a "T" in front of the old number. Thus "OC" curved track for O gauge became "TOC" and so forth. This may have been to clarify that the "O" in O22, etc., was a letter, not a numeral, a distinction that affected the placement of the item in parts lists.

2 4 6 8

TO22-500 O TRACK ADAPTER SET, 1962–66

For O and Super O gauges. Has all pieces to mate Super O with O gauge track. Same as O22-500, except redesignated and packaged in a different envelope. Price is for a complete set in the original envelope.

— — — 3

TOC CURVED TRACK, 1962–66 and 1968–69

For O gauge. Curved track section 10⅞″ long. Same as OC but cataloged under Lionel's new designation. Cataloged 1962–66 as ½ TOC for a half section.

— — — 2

TOC-51 STEEL PINS, 1962–66 and 1969

For O gauge. Price is per dozen in the original envelope. Also came packaged 36 to an envelope. Same as OC-51 and OC-18 pins, except redesignated and packaged in a different envelope.

— — — 1

TOS STRAIGHT TRACK, 1962–66 and 1968–69

For O gauge. Straight track section 10″ long. Same as OS but cataloged under the new designation. Cataloged 1962-66 as ½ TOS for a half section.

— — — 2

UCS REMOTE CONTROL TRACK, 1949–66 and 1968–69

For O gauge. Red or black (late) plastic housing around top of electromagnet in center of track unit. Includes UCS-40 two-button controller, which is identical to the RCS-20 except for the nomenclature on the bottom plate. Has control rails on each side of center electromagnet, so it will operate electromagnetic and magnetic couplers, and activate all operating cars. Instructions for the UCS and 6019 track sections were combined in the 6019-16 sheets.

— — 12 15

UTC LOCKON, 1936–42 and 1945–46

For O and O27 gauge. Fits O27, O, and Standard gauge track. See entry for the CTC on this item's common electrical function. Replaced by the CTC Lockon soon after the war, when Lionel discontinued Standard gauge track.

— — 2 3

CHAPTER 9

Transformers and Controllers

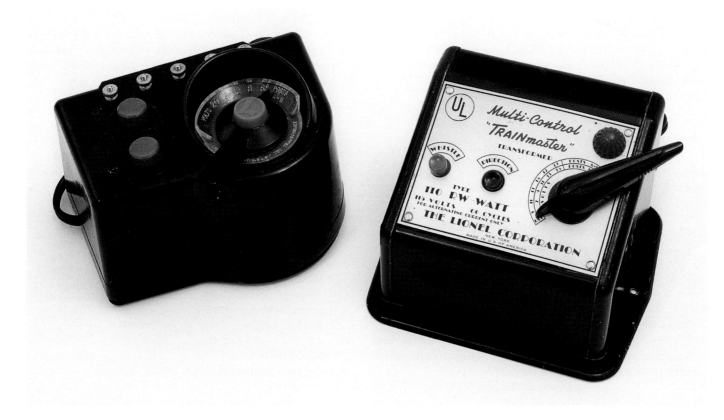

Lionel cataloged an enormous variety of transformers in the postwar era. The LW and RW were among the most popular and reliable. Large numbers can still be found to provide power to a layout or for accessories.

The transformers and controllers described in this chapter, while necessary, are not as glamorous or exciting as the trains themselves. As more collectors shelve and store their treasures, and as operators discover more modern power supplies, many fine Trainmaster transformers have become useful only as boat anchors. Low-cost, sophisticated electronic sensors, undreamed of in Lionel's heyday, render obsolete the clever mechanical switches and controllers of yesterday. Only the mighty ZW and, to a lesser extent, the KW retain their esteem in the eyes of today's hobbyist, attesting to their excellent design. And they were made before extensive government regulations, which seem to preclude reproduction today.

All the same, Lionel Trains are more than just another hobby that competes with television and all the other diversions and duties of life. They evoke nostalgia, an escape to our youth, happy memories of times gone by that can be briefly recaptured through the magic of these treasures from our past. Somehow, though, it seems that modern "improvements" to our toys dilute their magic. Although technological advances can improve operation, the simple design of the mechanical switches and transformers is easier to understand and appreciate than cutting-edge electronics.

Lionel's engineers were clever and used their talents to design exceptionally durable products. The items are so well designed that, when required, repairs and maintenance are usually simple. This elegance of design and quality of construction can be appreciated even more today, in our disposable society. Because this has not been an active area of collecting for most, it is an area ripe for research and discoveries.

88 CONTROLLER, 1938–42 and 1946–50

Pressing the button on the 88 Controller interrupts the circuit that is normally "on." This switch was designed for use with transformers like the R, V, and Z that did not include an integral direction reverse button. The 88 is identical in appearance to the 96C Controller, a switch that is normally "off." The 88 was packaged for separate sale in a Classic box. A dealer box of 12 No. 88 Controllers has been observed, made of grayish paperboard with a Lionel Trains logo in red and blue on one side only. As with most dealer packages, this desirable collectible is an NRS item. An 88 in a clean, individual box with intact flaps at least doubles the price.

(A) Binding posts on 1″ centers, rivet between posts.

| | — | — | — | 7 |

(B) Binding posts on ½″ centers, later production.

| | — | — | — | 7 |

90 CONTROLLER, 1955–66

Introduced in 1955, the 90 replaced the metal-case 96C Controller supplied with 1954 production 3562 Operating Barrel Cars and accessories of earlier vintage. In the later years of its production, a 90 was included in Super O remote control track sets. Early versions have a black Bakelite case, and all versions have a large red button embossed with the circled "L" logo. Later versions changed to a molded black thermoplastic case. Included with many accessories and available (but not cataloged) for separate sale in a manila envelope, part number 90-31, printed in the usual black ink and containing the controller and four 81-32 Connecting Wires.

(A) Earliest version includes stainless-steel clip with window cut to expose flat surface above button. This window is intended to hold a printed label identifying controller function. Clip attaches to bottom of plastic case with indentations on either side that fit into cutouts molded into lower edge of long sides of case. Later models lack cutouts and clip.

| | — | — | 7 | 16 |

(B) Same as (A) except no clip, to reduce cost.

| | — | — | 6 | 8 |

(C) Same as (B) except cutouts removed at base of each long side. | | — | — | 6 | 8 |

(D) Case redesigned and changed to injection-molded plastic (not as rigid and fracture-prone as Bakelite). Has raised plastic "No. 90 CONTROL"; raised lines molded on top surface above button.

| | — | — | — | 6 |

91 CIRCUIT BREAKER, 1957–60

The 91 Circuit Breaker produced from 1930 to 1942 had a die-cast design that differs from the plastic-case unit considered here. The 91 produced in 1957 has the coil of an electromagnet connected in series with the load (a train, accessory, or whatever). As the load draws more current, this current also

The 88 Controller is a normally "on" switch that is used for direction control with transformers lacking a built-in control, such as the V and Z.

The 91 and 92 Circuit Breakers were intended to supplement inexpensive transformers that lacked internal circuit breakers. The 92 uses the same case as the 90 Controller, but has a different number and a circuit breaker.

passes through the coil, increasing the magnetic pull of the iron core. An armature positioned nearby holds a spring-switch closed. The current from the transformer passes not only through the coil, but also through the contacts of the spring switch on its way out to the load. When the current reaches a certain level, the armature is pulled against the iron core of the electromagnet. This releases the spring-switch and stops the current flow.

When the contacts are open, an L53 Lamp connected across the switch contacts turns on, illuminating the red warning lens. Only 0.1 amp is required to light the lamp, which is all that flows through the circuit. The amount of current required to trip the breaker can be adjusted from about 1 to 6 amps with a screw that changes tension on the armature. The switch must be reset manually using the red reset button on top, which also contains the warning lamp.

Two instruction sheets are known to exist, both part number 91-37. The early one, dated 10-57, is printed in blue ink on white; the late one, dated 11-59, is in black on white. The 91 was packaged in a Late Classic box and included large aluminum terminal nut connectors. Like New requires a nice original box and instruction sheet. Dimensions: 4¾" long, 1⅜" wide.

| | 12 | 18 | 24 | 30 |

92 CIRCUIT BREAKER CONTROLLER, 1959–69

Simpler and cheaper than the 91, the 92 Circuit Breaker Controller has the added versatility of being a reversing button as well, as indicated by its name. Circuitry of the 92 is enclosed in a case identical to that used by version (D) of the 90 Controller, only with different graphics. Circuit breaker function depends on a heated bimetal switch. The heater coil wraps around a switch arm made of two dissimilar metal strips bonded together. Electrically, the heater is connected in series with the switch contacts, which in turn are in series with the load (a train, accessory, or whatever).

As the current to the load increases, the heater warms the bimetal arm. Different expansion rates of the two metals cause the arm to bend until the contacts open and break the circuit. Heating the bimetal arm takes time, so even with the heavy current flow of a short circuit in the load, the breaker will not act for as long as a few seconds. How quickly the breaker functions depends on how much heat was generated from normal operation before the short occurred.

The 92, unlike the 91, is a self-resetting breaker. Once the contacts open, current ceases to flow to the load and the heater winding. This allows the bimetal arm to cool and straighten, which closes the contacts and starts the cycle again. Unless the short circuit is removed or the transformer turned off, the circuit breaker will cycle on and off every few seconds indefinitely. The instruction sheet for the 92, printed black on white, has part number 92-22 and is dated 11-59.

(A) Packaged for separate sale in a manila envelope, part number 90-26, with black printing. This envelope contained a 92 Controller and two 81-32 Connecting Wires, but no instruction sheet. Prices shown are primarily for the original envelope.

| | — | — | 9 | 18 |

(B) Packaged for separate sale in a small Classic box with an instruction sheet. Prices are primarily for the original box.

| | — | — | 9 | 18 |

(C) B92, the blister package of 1966. These came with the controller packaged right side up (button down) or upside down, so there are two variations! The 92 is common, so the price is for an original, intact blister pack. | — | — | — | 125 |

96C CONTROLLER, 1938–42 and 1945–54

Although the 96C was never cataloged for separate sale and no individual packaging has been reported, it served as an important part of such accessories as the 30 and 38 Water Towers, 313 Bascule Bridge, and early 3562 Operating Barrel Cars. Like the 88 described above, the 96C has a two-piece stamped steel case, with a control button that is usually red (brown, green, and black are also known). Unlike the 88, a normally closed switch, the 96C has a normally open circuit that is closed by pressing the control button. The two binding posts of the 96C are positioned

on 1" centers, same as those found on early production versions of the 88. | — | — | 5 | 7 |

145C CONTACTOR, 1950–60

First introduced for the 145 Automatic Gateman, this contactor is a single-pole single-throw (SPST) switch, meaning it performs only a simple on/off function. It is normally off. When the 145C is properly installed and adjusted, the weight of a train on the overlying track turns it on. After the train has passed, spring tension returns the switch to the off position. In comparison, the 153C Contactor, described later, is a single-pole double-throw (SPDT) switch. It connects one contact (pole) to either of two others, depending on which of the two possible switch positions (the double-throw part) is selected. A 153C can substitute for a 145C by using terminals 2 and 3. However, a 145C cannot perform all the functions of a 153C.

It is not known why Lionel discontinued the 41 Contactor before World War II, only to bring back essentially the same thing as the 145C in 1950. Several accessories included a 145C. Each time a new product was introduced, the 145C instruction sheet was revised to include a reference to the new item. No fewer than 26 different printings and 23 printing dates have been reported on instruction sheets for the 145C. The first variations have part number 145-40 and are dated 6-50. For the 1-54 printing only, the number becomes 145-51. In the next printing, 1-55, the part number changes to 145-56, a number that remains through the final issue, dated 4/65. Somewhere around 1957, one issue of 145-56 was published with only "8-1" where the date should have been.

Although usually packaged in an envelope and included with an accessory, the 145C was available in a Classic box for separate sale, probably as early as 1951. It was not listed separately in the catalog until 1955. These contactors are so rugged that one in Good condition with some rust may still be operational.

| | — | — | — | 3 |

147 WHISTLE CONTROLLER, 1961–66

Rather than using a rectifier to convert alternating current (AC) to direct current (DC), the 147 Whistle Controller uses a regular size D battery. DC voltage is required to activate the horn or whistle relay in Lionel equipment, so the 147 connected its DC battery in series with the normal AC track current. To avoid tripping a train's reverse mechanism (E-unit) while the battery is switched in and out of the circuit, the 147 uses a fast-acting snap-type switch. Because the battery has a certain amount of internal resistance, this controller is only a marginal substitute for transformers with an integral whistle control.

When the control button is pressed, the AC voltage drop across the battery (plus the extra load of the whistle motor in the case of a whistle) causes a train to slow. Transformers with integral whistle control include a booster coil to compensate for the load of the whistle motor and do not create additional resistance in the rectifier system used to produce the DC whistle control current.

Although listed in the catalogs as a component of several train sets, this item was never cataloged for separate sale. Be sure to inspect for damage from a leaking battery before purchasing this item. | — | — | 4 | 15 |

148-100 DOUBLE POLE SWITCH, 1957–58

This single-pole double-throw (SPDT) switch (for an explanation, see the 153C listing below) was included with the 148 Dwarf Signal and made available for separate sale in its own manila envelope. Instructions for the 350 Transfer Table also refer to the 148-100, since it is useful in at least one extension arrangement. The switch may have a black or a red slide control. Prices are for the switch alone; having a separate-sale envelope in decent condition merits a premium.

		Gd	VG	Ex	LN
		—	—	5	25

153C CONTACTOR, 1940–42, 1946–66, and 1968–69

This single-pole double-throw (SPDT) weight-activated switch was developed for the 153 Block Signal. The SPDT designation means one terminal contact (the single-pole part, which is terminal 3 in the case of the 153C) is connected to either of two other terminals (hence, double-throw), depending on which way the switch is thrown. Terminals 3 and 1 are the ones normally closed (electrically connected to each other) on a 153C. When the weight of a passing train activates the switch, terminal 3 loses its connection to 1 ("opens"), and it connects to terminal 2.

When used in conjunction with the proper insulated rail sections and the necessary electrical connections, a 153C can control two trains on the same track. The 153C does not require the use of any signal to operate two trains, since the control function is in the switch itself. Signals just add realism to the operation. If only one set of contacts is used, a 153C can perform a simple on/off function. Using its full capability, it can control red and green signal lights as well as train stop-and-start functions.

This versatility led Lionel to discontinue the 41 weight-activated on/off switch shortly after it introduced the 153C in 1940. Consequently, the 45 Automatic Gateman and 152 Crossing Gate came with a 153C beginning in 1940, although they required only an on/off contactor.

In the postwar period, a separate instruction sheet for the 153C was issued to show how to connect several accessories (45 Automatic Gateman, 152 Crossing Gate, 151 Semaphore, and 153 Block Signal). This sheet served as the only instruction material for all of them. After the 145C (a simple weight-activated on/off switch like the discontinued 41) was introduced in 1950, the 153C instructions covered only the 151, 153, and, in later years, 353 Single Target Block Signal.

The first two issues of the separate instructions for the 153C had part number 153C-18 and are dated 3-46 and 11-46. The first issue had the words "and service department" blanked out for the Chicago Showroom; the second removed these words altogether. The part number then changed to 153C-22 for the issues of 8-47, 3-48, 7-48, 4-49, 6-49, 10-49, 2-50, and 5-52. Lionel changed the part number to 153C-23, starting with the issue of 1-51. Chronologically, the next issue is dated 5-52, but that part number is 153C-22 again. Then, for the 8-53 issue, part number 153C-23 returned and remained through the issue of 3-60, with issues of 2-54, 4-55 (both black and blue ink versions known), 2-56, 2-57, and 2-58 in between.

Although Lionel eventually discontinued the 153C-23 instruction sheet, instructions for the 153C were revised and expanded to a six-page sheet (part number 452-13, dated 4-61). Instead of focusing on the 452 Gantry Signal, it has the same title as the 153C-23 sheets. Beside the 452, it covers the 163 and 353 Block Signals and 151 Semaphore.

A 153C Contactor and various boxes. This weight-actuated single-pole double-throw (SPDT) switch was the "brains" behind several signals and accessories.

	Gd	VG	Ex	LN

Beginning in 1954, the 153C Contactor is listed for separate sale in the catalogs under the heading, "Replacement Parts." However, it was available in its own separate-sale box probably as early as 1951, when a category entitled "Little Extras You May Need" began to appear in the catalogs. This entry stated that the listed items "and others" were available from Lionel dealers. A 153C box with a printed OPS label is known, so separate-sale packaging existed at least by 1952.

		Gd	VG	Ex	LN
		—	—	—	5

167 WHISTLE CONTROLLER, 1940–42 and 1946–57

A ubiquitous item, this inexpensive controller is available with several interesting and collectible variations. It debuted in 1940 as a simplified replacement for the earlier 65, 66, 67, and 166 Whistle Controllers. At that time, the whistle was new and controllers had not yet been installed in most transformers. Even to the end, Lionel supplied a multitude of budget transformers with no whistle control. Consequently, the 167 was useful to operators who chose to add a locomotive equipped with a whistle or horn before upgrading their transformer.

There are undoubtedly variations in the 167's internal works over the years, but for our purposes and that of most collectors, only the commonly observed variations in the case and base are of interest. Two red (sometimes black or maroon) control buttons protrude through the black Bakelite case of all 167s. The stamped-steel base frames may be cadmium-plated (very dull silver-gray appearance) or nickel-plated (bright, shiny appearance), or they may have a blackened finish.

Numerous instruction sheets were issued over the years, starting with 167-29, dated 8-39, which is available in versions with the numbers 70.X and 65.X. The "X" following the number probably indicates a print quantity in hundreds, but this is only speculation. Some instruction sheets are also found with an "M" following a similar number, possibly indicating the quantity in thousands. Based on the printing date of the initial instruction sheet, the 167 may have been available in late 1939. The 167-29 instruction sheet part number persisted for issues of 1-40, 3-41, 4-42, 10-45, and two printings of 1-46, the latter printed with and without the Chicago and San Francisco Service Stations. All 167-29 sheets are light blue with dark blue printing.

With the addition of a built-in circuit breaker, the instruction

	Gd	VG	Ex	LN

sheet for 167 was renumbered as 167-55, most likely in late 1946. The first, undated version of the 167-55 instruction sheet was followed by issues dated 4-47 and 9-47, the last of the 167 sheets printed on light blue paper with dark blue printing. Judging by other accessories that spanned this period, Lionel began the switch to white paper in 1948. What is probably the first version of the 167-55 printed on white paper with dark blue ink is undated. The final three reported issues of the instruction sheet are dated 2-50, 6-53, and 8-54. For the first few issues, a "C" (for circuit breaker) is printed after "167" in the title of the instructions; this letter is omitted from the last issues.

It appears that the same situation with the "C" suffix occurred with the number stamped on the metal base plate of the controller. The boxes for the 167 reflect the packaging changes made over the period it was offered. In the following listings, "T shape" refers to the inverted and raised T-shaped area that surrounds both buttons and runs between the "REVERSE" and "WHISTLE" labels to the first step that forms the top edge of the two labels. "Dummy button" refers to a raised round shape $\frac{5}{16}$" in diameter and about $\frac{1}{8}$" high, molded in the case and centered between the control buttons.

(A) Earliest prewar version with no round ejector-pin marks in the four corners of case top. Each control button has raised collar around its hole in the case, but there is no T shape. Each of the two terminals is recessed in a U shape molded in the case, and there are no visible hex nuts under the terminal nuts. Instead, hex nuts are recessed into case. In all other versions observed, terminal is on the case surface and hex nuts are visible under terminal nuts. Black base plate. — — **10** **15**

(B) 167X version meant for OO gauge and cataloged in 1941–42. Has "X" rubber-stamped on each end of box behind "167" and behind this number on base plate actually stamped with a punch into the metal. Recessed terminals and collar around holes for control buttons both omitted. First appearance of T shape. No ejector-pin marks on case top. Black base plate. — — **10** **25**

(C) 167S, known postwar version built for added current draw of smoke locomotives in 1946. Has "S" rubber-stamped behind "167" on each end of box (examples also observed stamped on only one end). Two $\frac{1}{4}$"-diameter depressions on base positioned symmetrically between two "top" base screws. (Only three screws used to attach the base, two on "top" and one on "bottom.") Midway between these depressions, "S" stamped with punch. Base has black finish with grainy appearance. Case has T shape. For the first time, four round ejector-pin marks appear in four corners of case top. This is the only version observed with the base plate depressions. — — **10** **25**

(D) Same as (C) except no "S" and ejector-pin marks. Base plate black with normal appearance. — — **10** **15**

(E) First appearance of dummy button and open front. The latter refers to vertical front edge (control button side) of controller. Previously this surface was part of the case, but beginning with this version, the case mold is changed so an upturned extension of base plate is visible. According to the Lionel Service Manual, cutaway on case front was done so control-button activated "pile-up" switch (attached to case, not base) could be serviced without removing it from case. Case has T shape, ejector-pin marks, and base is nickel-plated.

| | — | — | 10 | 15 |

(F) Same as (E) except no ejector-pin marks on four top case corners.

| | — | — | 10 | 15 |

(G) Same as (E) except black base plate with "C" stamped in with punch behind "167." The "C" designates a 167 with a built-in circuit breaker. After the first year or two of this change, the "C" was dropped. No ejector-pin marks.

| | — | — | 10 | 15 |

(H) Same as (E) except with cadmium-plated (dull silver-gray) base with no "C" punched in behind "167" and no ejector-pin marks.

| | — | — | 10 | 15 |

364C SWITCH, 1959–64

This single-pole double-throw (SPDT) switch (see 153C listing) was available as early as 1948 but only cataloged for separate sale as listed. There are various colors and shades of the base plate (underside of the switch), some stamped "PART NO. 364C" or "364C," others not marked. Most have only two terminal screws, though some have three or four (or at least have extra contact pieces even when the screws are not installed).

Several variations in the 364C stem from the switch housing and the base it shares with the 148-100 four-pole switch and the 390C switch used in conjunction with wiring reverse loops for two rail HO gauge layouts. The 390C Controller typically has a red slide switch, rather than the black typical for the 364C, but a red slide also sometimes appears in the 364C. The only way to distinguish the separate-sale 364C from the one that came with accessories, such as the 3656 Operating Cattle Car, is to find it in its separate-sale manila envelope (part number 364-206). Two different printings of this envelope have been observed. Like New requires a switch with a separate-sale envelope. A serviceable switch, without the envelope, is worth much less.

| | — | — | 7 | 15 |

390C SWITCH, 1960–64

This versatile double-pole double-throw (DPDT) switch (see 153C listing) was first illustrated in the HO section of the 1959 catalog before its usefulness brought it to the O gauge section in 1960. For HO, its main use is in reversing loops, where the hot and ground leads on this two-rail track must be reversed as the track comes back on itself. The slide on the 390C is almost always found in red. Like New requires the separate-sale manila envelope in decent condition.

| | — | — | 9 | 25 |

413 COUNTDOWN CONTROL PANEL, 1962

Simply a modification (the gantry control was removed) of the controller from the 175 Rocket Launcher, repackaged for separate sale. It can be used to control any device requiring a push "on" switch. The panel is molded in gray plastic decorated with black lettering. The face of the panel contains a red dial, countdown set lever, start button, and fire button. The underside of the panel has two electrical wiring attaching posts through

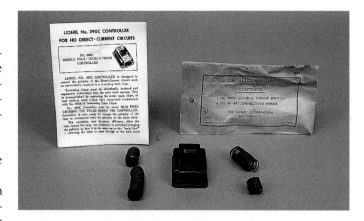

A 390C Switch. Although the envelope refers to six wires, only four were enclosed.

| | Gd | VG | Ex | LN |

which the circuit (between the two posts) is completed by depressing the fire button. As with the 175, the countdown controller is a crude timer and has no effect electrically. Like New requires the original box.

| | 40 | 55 | 70 | 95 |

ECU-1 ELECTRONIC CONTROL UNIT, 1946–50

Not offered separately, but included with all Electronic Control Train Sets. Has a vacuum tube and electronic circuitry that generates a unique frequency signal for each of its 10 buttons. Miniature receivers in each special car of these sets can be tuned to respond to one of these frequencies. Typically, each car, tender, or locomotive included an "Electronic Control" decal on each side whose color matched the color of its control button. ECU-1 connects electrically between the transformer and track; frequency signals are transmitted through the wiring and the track.

| | 22 | 40 | 65 | 90 |

TRANSFORMERS

Transformers are usually purchased to operate trains and accessories. So if a transformer is not in operating condition, it has little, if any, value. Several of the larger models, such as the KW, V, VW, Z, and ZW, still hold some value for their handles, plates, and terminal nuts, even if the internal components are burned out or rusted. Operators are finding that the smaller transformers, usually available quite reasonably, are handy for powering lamps and as individual power supplies for accessories.

Today, we in the United States and Canada are used to standard 110-volt, 60-cycle AC power in all our homes and places of business. But it was not always so. Even until well after World War II, many parts of Canada and the northern United States used 125-volt, 25-cycle AC. Before the war, DC was used in some parts of New York City, and battery power was used in many rural areas where electric lines had not yet reached. In Europe, 220-volt, 60-cycle power is the standard.

Since Lionel aimed to sell its products to a national and international market, it had to provide appropriate power sources for every market. Thus you will find some transformers in the following listing that were made specifically for the export and the 25-cycle markets. These are quite rare, but the lack of interest in collecting transformers makes for some attractive prices when one of these unusual versions turns up.

In the listing that follows, Good, Excellent, and Like New assume that a transformer is in operating condition. Note,

Among the transformers supplied with inexpensive 027 gauge outfits were (left to right): the 1043, 1012, 1039, and 1014.

however, that even a transformer in operating condition may have an unsafe electrical cord. Before using any electrical device that may be 40 or more years old, be sure to have it completely checked, and repaired if necessary, by a qualified service technician. Values for the larger, more popular transformers have held their value relatively well over the years, but they face increasing competition from more modern and, in some cases, more powerful power supplies.

All transformers listed here contain a circuit breaker (to protect against overloads or short circuits) unless specifically stated otherwise. Where a "power on" lamp and/or a "short circuit" lamp is built into the transformer, it requires an L51 bulb, with the exception of the LW, SW, TW, and Model R of the ZW. Lamps for these are noted in the listings. Only a "throttle" (voltage control) is included unless noted that a separate direction control or whistle control is included. The direction control is a button or lever for interrupting current, thus cycling the E-unit (Lionel's name for its forward-neutral-reverse current switching device that controls the direction of the locomotive).

To activate the whistle, later Lionel transformers included a separate button or lever that activates special circuitry in the transformer to impose a direct current (DC) voltage on the normal alternating current (AC) voltage that powers the locomotive motor. This DC voltage activates a relay in the locomotive or tender, thus closing contacts that connect the whistle motor to the normal AC track voltage or connect the horn in diesel or later electric-outline locomotives to the battery that powers the horn. Lionel's first postwar electric, the 2332 GG1, used a "sound box" that responded to AC voltage to simulate a horn.

Many of the smaller transformers did not include a separate instruction sheet. Instead, operation and electrical connections were covered in the general outfit instruction sheet.

	Gd	VG	Ex	LN
1010, 1961–66				
35 watts, direction control. Replaced 1016.				
	8	12	20	25
1011, 1948–52				
25 watts. Not offered for separate sale but included with all "Scout" train sets.				
	8	12	20	25
1011X, 1948–52				
25 watts. Same as 1011 except made for 125-volt, 25-cycle power. An observed example included a rare instruction sheet, part number 1011X-13, dated 8-49.				
	8	12	20	25
1012, 1950–54				
35 watts.				
	7	9	19	25
1014, 1955				
40 watts. Handle colors red, black, or silver.				
	11	15	30	35
1015, 1956–60				
45 watts.				
	8	12	32	40
1016, 1959–60				
35 watts.				

	Gd	VG	Ex	LN
(A) 1959, no direction control button.	6	12	30	40
(B) 1960, has direction control button.	6	12	30	40

1025, 1961–66 and 1969
45 watts. Replaced 1015.

	12	18	30	40

1026, 1961–64
25 watts. Originally included with set 1123, one of three very low-end sets shown only in the 1961 advance catalog. Probably came with most of Lionel's introductory offerings of the time.

	5	7	12	18

1032, 1948
75 watts, direction and whistle controls.

	30	40	60	75

1032M, 1948
75 watts, direction and whistle controls. Same as 1032 except designed for the Mexican market, which used 125-volt, 50-cycle power.

	5	15	35	55

1033, 1948–56
90 watts, direction and whistle controls. One of Lionel's most popular and reliable small transformers.

	40	55	75	85

1034, 1948–54
75 watts, direction control. Sold only with outfits without a whistle and not available for separate sale. It was designed for 115-volt, 60-cycle power, but could be used with 150-volt, 60-cycle power.

	28	35	55	65

1035, 1947
60 watts.

	—	5	10	20

1037, 1946–47
40 watts, 5 to 17 volts.

	10	15	28	35

1041, 1945–46
60 watts, direction and whistle controls. This, the 1042, and the 1241 were the first Lionel transformers with built-in circuit breaker, direction, and whistle controls; they introduced the "Multi-Control" designation.

	12	20	35	45

1042, 1947–48
75 watts, direction and whistle controls. This, the 1041, and the 1241 were the first Lionel transformers with built-in circuit breaker, direction, and whistle controls; they introduced the "Multi-Control" designation.

	12	20	35	45

1043, 1953–58
50 watts, black case.

	12	20	35	50

1043-500, 1957–58
60 watts. Ivory case with gold-plated speed control handle, binding posts, and usually the case mounting screws, although these are found in black as well. Black metal base. Made espe-

The 1033 Transformer, shown with three variations of its box, was included in many 027 sets and was also available for separate-sale.

	Gd	VG	Ex	LN

cially for the 1587S Lady Lionel set, but also found in some uncataloged sets. Of interest is the fact that the Lionel Service Manual only shows a 50-watt 1043, but 1043-500 is clearly marked 60 watts.

	55	75	115	150

1043M, 1953–58
50 watts. Same as 1043 except designed for the Mexican market, which used 125-volt, 25-cycle power.

	5	15	45	75

1044, 1957–66 and 1968–69
90 watts, direction and whistle controls. A redesign of the 1033, it has a new look to the control panel.

	30	40	65	75

1044M, 1957–66
90 watts, direction and whistle controls. Same as 1044 except designed for the Mexican market, which used 125-volt, 50-cycle power.

	5	25	75	95

1053, 1956–60
60 watts, whistle control. Has a range of 8 to 17 volts, once the throttle control is moved from the "off" position.

	18	22	40	50

1063, 1960–64
75 watts, whistle control. Basically the same as 1053 except higher wattage.

	18	25	55	65

1063-100, 1961
75 watts, whistle control. Can be distinguished from 1063 by its green whistle control button, compared to the usual red for 1063. According to the Lionel Service Manual, "No. 1063-100 Transformer was produced in 1961 (and was) used with whistling outfits provided with 'Scout' type locomotive which has a tendency to reverse when regular whistle-control circuits are used to operate the whistle." It goes on to describe changes in the normal whistle control and associated resistor to fix this problem.

	5	25	55	65

Lionel developed a number of transformers for foreign markets, including (clockwise from upper right) the RW250 (sealed and opened boxes), RX, and 1011X.

	Gd	VG	Ex	LN
1073, 1961–66 60 watts.	20	25	55	65
1144, 1961–66 75 watts, direction control.	—	5	25	35

1232, 1948
75 watts, direction and whistle controls. Same as 1032 except made for the European market, which uses 220-volt, 50- or 60-cycle power.

	Gd	VG	Ex	LN
	10	35	75	125

1241, 1947–48
60 watts, direction and whistle controls. Same as 1041 except designed for 220-volt, 60-cycle power.

	Gd	VG	Ex	LN
	5	25	65	95

1244, 1957–66
90 watts, direction and whistle controls. Same as 1044 except designed for the European market, which uses 220-volt, 50- or 60-cycle power.

	Gd	VG	Ex	LN
	5	25	65	95

	Gd	VG	Ex	LN
A, 1947–48 90 watts.	20	25	45	55

A220, 1947–48
90 watts. Same as A except made for use with 220-volt, 50- or 60-cycle power.

	Gd	VG	Ex	LN
	20	25	45	55

	Gd	VG	Ex	LN

AX, 1947–48
90 watts. Same as A except made for use with 110-volt, 25-cycle power.

	Gd	VG	Ex	LN
	20	25	45	55

KW, 1950–65
190 watts, direction and whistle controls. Two throttle controls can operate two trains independently, on separate track circuits. Shares a whistle control between the two independent voltage controls so that both whistles cannot be operated at once. Separate direction control button for each voltage control. Includes a fixed 14-volt connection for operating switches or accessories. After many hours of operation, the carbon rollers on this, the V, Z, VW, and ZW must be replaced. Rollers and rivets are readily available. Instead of a "KW" prefix, the parts for this transformer use "20." Thus the instruction sheets are part number 20-97, printed in blue ink on white paper, with dates of 9-50, 6-51, 10-51, 6-53, 6-54, 3-55, 12-55, 1-57, 5-57, 6-58, 7-59, and 10-60.

(A) 1950–56. Coil and lamination assembly not riveted, no stamping on base underside.

	Gd	VG	Ex	LN
	—	155	195	225

(B) 1957–65. Same as (A) except riveted coil assembly, stamping "KW (C)" on bottom plate.

	Gd	VG	Ex	LN
	—	155	195	225

(C) 1953–58 (exact years uncertain). Same as (A) or (B) except with an approval decal on the base plate underside. Cleveland and Los Angeles evidently had electrical codes that required approval for Lionel's larger transformers before they could be sold in those cities. Some KW and ZW transformers can be found with the appropriate decal signifying approval by one of these cities. Only one decal from Cleveland has been observed, but at least two decals, for different years and with different designs, are known for Los Angeles. Either "C" or "LA" is rubber-stamped in black somewhere on the box label of the few observed examples.

	Gd	VG	Ex	LN
	—	175	225	275

LW, 1955–66
125 watts, direction and whistle control. Has a green "power on" light in the center of the voltage control, which uses lamp L53, and separate large buttons for the direction and whistle controls. Parts for this transformer use the prefix "22." Known instruction sheets, all part number 22-86, are dated 5-55, 12-55, 5-57, 1-58, 6-59, 6-60, and 3/65. All are printed in blue ink on white paper except the 6-60 and 3/65 sheets, which use black ink on white paper.

	Gd	VG	Ex	LN
	—	125	140	175

Q, 1946
75 watts, 6 to 24 volts.

	Gd	VG	Ex	LN
	—	—	65	75

R, 1939–42 and 1946–47
Two independent circuits with two voltage controls, each supplying 6 to 24 volts.

(A) 1939–42 and 1946. 100-watt version.

	Gd	VG	Ex	LN
	—	50	80	110

(B) 1947. Same as (A) except faceplate has "110 watts." Instruction sheet dated 6-47.

	Gd	VG	Ex	LN
	—	50	80	110

R220, 1946–47
100 watts. Same as R (A) except made for use with 220-volt, 60-cycle power.

	Gd	VG	Ex	LN
	—	50	80	110

	Gd	VG	Ex	LN

RW, 1948–54
110 watts, direction and whistle controls. Ten printings of the RW-43 instruction sheet are known.

	—	55	85	110

RWM, 1948–54
100 watts. Same as RW except made for 125-volt, at least 50-cycle power. Included instruction sheet RWM-10, printed black on white paper and dated 4-48.

	—	55	85	110

RW250, 1948–54
100 watts. Same as RWM except made for 220- to 250-volt, at least 50-cycle power. — 55 85 110

RX, 1947–48
100 watts. Made for 115-volt, 25-cycle power, it can also be used with 150-volt, at least 40-cycle power and with 220-volt, at least 60-cycle power. — 75 125 175

S, 1947
80 watts, direction and whistle control. Cataloged as 75 watts, but the instruction sheet (part number S-47, dated 8-47) specifies 80 watts. — 20 35 50

S220, 1947
80 watts. Same as S except made for 220-volt, 60-cycle power. — 30 45 90

SW, 1961–66
130 watts, whistle control. Two voltage controls for two-train operation, but has a whistle control for one throttle only. The "Power On" lamp requires an L12 bulb. Of interest is the part

The TW (left) and SW (right) are less common than some other postwar transformers, but are good values for operators whose layouts have many accessories.

	Gd	VG	Ex	LN

numbering system for this transformer. Instead of "SW" as the prefix, Lionel used "25." The known instruction sheets are all part number 25-36, dated 9-61 (both black and brown ink versions on white paper) and 4/66 (black ink on white paper).

	—	75	120	130

TW, 1953–60
175 watts, whistle control. The "Power On" lamp requires an L53 bulb. Unique among all Lionel transformers in that it has separate primary and secondary coils for the train control and for constant voltage (to power switches, accessories, etc.) Essentially a "transformer within a transformer." All other Lionel transformers that provided one or more fixed voltage connections have one primary coil and just use taps off one or more secondary coils to provide fixed voltage sources. Instead of "TW" as the prefix, Lionel used "21." The instruction sheets are all part number 21-80, printed in blue ink on white paper, with dates of 9-53, 8-54, 12-55, 1-57, 5-57, 5-58, and 6-59.

(A) 1953. Has terminal post B. — 100 145 175
(B) 1954–60. Same as (A) except no terminal post B.

	—	100	145	175

V, 1939–41 and 1946–47
150 watts. Provides four independent voltage control circuits, so four trains can be operated independently, on four different track circuits. However, the two circuits with smaller control knobs were intended for accessory operation. Many operators use one or more 167C controllers to provide whistle and direction controls when they use this or an R or Z transformer.

	—	120	145	150

VW, 1948–49

150 watts, direction and whistle controls. Both "Power On" and "Short Circuit" lamps are included. Provides four independent voltage control circuits, with whistle and direction controls for only two of them. The other two voltage controls were intended for operating accessories, but they can be used for train control if desired. This and the ZW share the same case and look identical, but the power available is quite different. Later Electronic Control Sets included a VW, and it was available for separate sale as well. Even inoperative units have value for their parts, many of which are interchangeable with ZW models.

—   125   150   175

Z, 1938–42 and 1945–47

250 watts. Both "Power On" and "Short Circuit" lamps are included. Provides four independent voltage control circuits, 6 to 24 volts each, so four trains can be operated independently, on four different track circuits. However, the two circuits with smaller control knobs were intended for accessory operation. Many operators use one or more 167C Controllers to provide whistle and direction controls when they use this, an R, or a V transformer. Some prefer this to the ZW due to its higher voltage output.

—   175   225   250

Lionel included a 150-watt VW Transformer in its Electronic Control Sets in 1948 and 1949. During those same years, the 250-watt ZW was cataloged. Both "Trainmasters" were available for separate sale.

	Gd	VG	Ex	LN

ZW, 1948–66

250 or 275 watts, whistle and direction controls. Both "Power On" and "Short Circuit" lamps are included. Provides four independent voltage control circuits, with whistle and direction controls for only two of them. The other two voltage controls were intended for operating accessories, but they can be used for train control if desired. This and the VW share the same case and look identical, but the power available is different.

(A) 1948–49. 250 watts. Not as desirable as later models that have an extra 25 watts. However, even inoperative units have value for their parts, most of which are interchangeable with later models.

—   75   125   175

(B) 1950–56. 275 watts. Earlier examples have Bakelite circuit breakers, which hold up much better than the later wafer type. Replacement Bakelite circuit breakers are available for about $10. Original box merits a premium.

—   150   250   300

Five of the box variations Lionel used for the 275-watt ZW Transformer between 1950 and 1960. M. Stephens Collection.

	Gd	VG	Ex	LN

(C) 1957–66. 275-watt, ZW(R) version. Externally, this appeared unchanged, but Lionel made substantial changes to the internal construction, largely it appears to provide easier assembly. These units, at least for the first few years, were rubber-stamped "ZW(R)" on the bottom of the base plate. Probably the most desirable of all Lionel transformers, unless the higher voltage of the Z is required. Original box merits a premium.

	—	200	250	325

(D) 1953–58 (exact years uncertain). Same as (B) or (C) except with an approval decal on the base plate underside. Cleveland and Los Angeles evidently had electrical codes that required approval for Lionel's larger transformers before they could be sold in those cities. Some KW and ZW transformers can be found with the appropriate decal signifying approval by one of these cities. Only one decal from Cleveland has been observed, but at least two decals, for different years and with different designs, are known for Los Angeles. Either "C" or "LA" is rubber-stamped in black somewhere on the box label of the few observed examples. Rates a substantial premium for the correctly overstamped box, with the stamp matching the city of the bottom decal on the transformer.

	—	250	300	375

These 275-watt ZWs were marked specially for Los Angeles, as shown by the "LA" stamped on each box and the decals affixed to the transformers. A similar decal for Cleveland has also been observed. M. Stephens Collection.

CHAPTER 10

Miscellaneous and Replacement Accessories

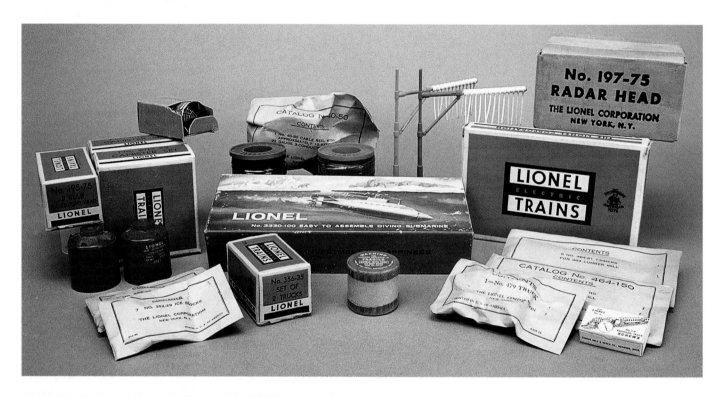

The range of replacement parts offered by Lionel was incredible! In the center is the 3330-100 separate-sale Operating Submarine Kit. Starting with the 394-37 Rotary Lens Housing (front center) and moving clockwise: 356-35 Baggage Trucks; 352-29 Ice Blocks; 264-150 Set of Timbers; two of the many canister variations, including the rare black rubber-stamped on red; 195-75 extra light bank and extension poles for the 195 Floodlight Tower; two box variations of the 6112-75 Set of Four Canisters; 394-37 Rotary Lens Housing in later unmarked square box; 40-25 Four-Conductor Wire Reel; 40-50 Three-Conductor Reel with another in a sealed envelope at rear; two shades of orange for the 3424 Telltales; 197-75 Radar Head; 3424-100 separate-sale set of two telltales and track clips; two different packages of 464-150 Lumber; and 479 Replacement Truck (the envelope is mislabeled 6326-16). The tiny box of track screws at the lower right, labeled "For / LIONEL / NO. 6," was made by Sharon Bolt & Screw Co.

Who would have thought that Lionel's mighty locomotives, majestic passenger cars, and rugged freights would still be available in quantity today, while accessories like replacement bulbs, extra coal and logs, and bottles of smoke pellets would be so scarce—at least in the packaging that made them uniquely Lionel? In many ways, miscellaneous and replacement accessories are the most fun to collect. Like buried treasure, these items are often hidden at train meets or in the last box of miscellaneous items purchased in a train deal.

With collectors appreciating the fun of collecting these items, demand for them increases and prices rise.

While distressing to some, this trend preserves items that might be forgotten or discarded. Learning about the vast array of peripherals Lionel made can be great fun, but with a little more effort one can collect a display of tiny containers that perhaps brings back memories of long-ago visits to hobby shops and hardware stores.

More than in any other chapter, the value of the items listed is based on their packaging. Most of these items are readily available or have modern equivalents that are all but indistinguishable from originals. It is those tantalizing manila envelopes with black printing and the magical orange, blue, and white miniature boxes that make the contents so fascinating.

Because the box is the main collectible in many of the following entries, the condition listed is primarily for the box. And, since most of these boxes are small, the flaps usually suffered greatly when they were opened. In perhaps most cases, these boxes are found with missing or torn flaps. Like New indicates a box that shows some shop wear, but has complete, intact flaps and is otherwise undamaged in appearance.

Lionel Replacement Lamps

Rather than scatter them throughout this chapter, all "collectible" lamps have been gathered in this section. Such lamps, by definition, must be packaged in the original Lionel container. Packaging, rather than the lamps themselves, is primary here.

Over the years, Lionel used three numbers to refer to its lamps: "old number," "part number" or "stock number," and "catalog number." Listings in this chapter use the number Lionel put on its packaging. For lamps supplied during the late prewar period and postwar up until 1953, this is the "old number." Although the lamps were sometimes made especially for Lionel, most were industry standards. Whenever Lionel released a new lamp (meaning first Lionel application), it gave that lamp a number corresponding to the item that first used it. Thus the Q-90 first appeared on the Type Q transformer, the 152-33 on the 152 crossing gate, and so on.

Starting in 1953, Lionel adopted industry standard numbers for its lamps, but with the twist of having the number uniquely Lionel. Thus the industry standard 432 lamp became the 432-300 Lionel stock or part number, replacing the 28-3 "old number," and so on. The first part of the number is the industry designation, and the -300 makes it a Lionel part number. Clear lamps are -300, red are -301, green are -302, frosted white are -303, and yellow are -304.

Over the late prewar and early postwar periods, Lionel furnished 40 different verified lamp part numbers individually packaged in tiny boxes. These in turn were sold to dealers in boxes of 12 bulbs. As with most Lionel packaging, the box design varied from year to year, and sometimes lot to lot, so over 100 variations of the individual bulb packaging are known. Here is a collection of many, but by no means all, of the dealer packs for these individually boxed bulbs. Note the OPS price label on the upper left box, dating it to 1952. J. Lampert Collection.

This system lasted only a year at most. By 1954 the parts list shows a catalog number, which is just the industry number preceded by an "L" (for Lionel). Thus the L1445 superseded 1445-300 (which had replaced 2026-58). Lamp colors are shown in parentheses behind the number in the catalog number; L430(R) is a red 430 lamp.

"Lionel Replacement Lamp" charts issued for the Lionel Service Manual continue to show all three numbers in each issue after 1953, which was when replacement lamps were first offered in industry standard packages of ten lamps. Lionel's boxes had their own graphics, which make them collectible, but otherwise the box and interior paperboard lamp carrier are industry standard. Individual boxed lamps appear to have been discontinued after 1952. Beginning a year later, lamps were available individually only from the 123 Replacement Lamp Assortment or the ten-lamp packs intended for sale to retail dealers.

The 123 was not the first postwar Replacement Lamp Assortment. A predecessor, the 122, was introduced in 1948 in a box with a paper-hinged plain orange cover that contained individually boxed lamps. For 1949, the same box contained a different assortment of individually boxed bulbs. Starting in 1950, a cardboard carrier filled with separate lamps occupied the box that now incorporated graphics on the lid. Using various cardboard carrier designs, this packaging format continued until 1953, when the 123 replaced the 122.

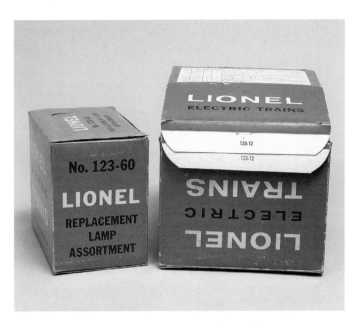

Two views of the 123-60 Lamp Assortment that contained a dozen of the ten-pack bulb boxes. Note the two different colors of the 123-12 box part number printed on the lid flap of the two boxes at right. Variation collectors live for this! J. Lampert Collection.

Lionel's first smoking steam locomotives in 1946 used the heat from a special bulb that also served as the headlight. An 18-volt bulb, no. 703-10, was designed for the 703 Hudson (cataloged but never produced) and specified for the 726 Berkshire. For the 671 and 2020 Steam Turbines, a 12-volt bulb, no. 671-75, was specified. The 12-volt bulbs must have proved unsatisfactory, because the packaging was overstamped for 18 volts and the part number changed to 703-10. Shown are examples of dealer display cartons of a dozen of each of these variations. J. Lampert Collection.

The 123 Replacement Lamp Assortment continued the cardboard lamp carrier, again in different patterns, as the mix and quantity of lamps varied. Lionel's final lamp master carton was the 123-60, a dealer display containing an assortment of the ten-pack lamp packages, including some meant for Lionel HO gauge products.

All the variations of the 122 and 123, originally intended for dealers, are scarce and desirable collectibles.

Packaging variations of the individually boxed lamps and the ten-packs are too numerous to list. However, the lamps in this chapter are categorized by four major types of packaging:

individually boxed lamps, master cartons containing 12 individually boxed lamps, ten-lamp packages, and display assortments.

Individually Boxed Lamps

In addition to smoke lamps, the following lamps are found in individual Lionel boxes, one lamp to a box. Note that all of these were probably also available in a dealer pack of 12 individually boxed lamps. This master carton was usually made with a lid that folds into a pop-up counter display. Such displays are eagerly sought by collectors and can easily double the price of the boxed lamps. For all these lamps, the tiny Lionel box must be present and in good shape to be worthy of purchase. All the following have been observed in orange, white, and blue Classic boxes, but some may be prewar lamps not made in postwar production.

Three box types are known for individually boxed lamps: (1) a box closed conventionally (two inner flaps and an outer flap with printing) on each end without the word "Tested" in script; (2) the same type of box with "Tested"; and (3) a box having a large flap that pushes up into one end to hold the bulb while leaving the lamp base accessible. These last boxes have a tiny punchout hole in the printed cover. By pushing out the center of the hole (which would devalue the box today!) and connecting power to the exposed lamp base, the lamp can be tested without opening the sealed box. All boxes of the third type have the word "Tested." Although not confirmed, it appears that the boxes with two conventional ends without "Tested" are prewar; the same boxes with "Tested" are early postwar. Boxes with only one conventional end soon replaced the latter.

The correct way—but not the obvious way—to open a "one-end" box is to remove the staple that secures the base retainer flap to the box side. Lionel glued the top shut on the conventional end.

Here in numerical order (except Q-90 at the end) are all the known individually boxed bulbs: 012 (12-volt lamp and signal case); 27-3, 27-6, 28, 28-3 (clear); 28-6 (red), 29-3, 39-3, 40, 40-3, 47-40, 47-73 (both 47s include a metal lantern), 63-11, 64-15 (12-volt and 14-volt versions); 0072-70, 79-23, 151-51, 152-23 (6-8-volt and 8-volt versions); 152-33 (12-volt and 14-volt versions); 153-23 (red, screw base); 153-24 (green, screw base); 153-48 (green, bayonet base); 153-50 (red, bayonet base); 154-18, 156-13, 165-53, 210 (18-volt lamp and signal case); 315-20, 394-10 (dimple bulb for beacon); 408-45, 616-13, 636-13, 717-54, 752-9, 2026-58, 2420-20, and Q-90.

Many of these bulbs come in two or more box variations that stem from the box type as well as the printing on the box. Also, 64-26 (12-volt) is found on one or more lamp charts, but its existence is uncertain.

Lower values for more common bulbs in small boxes, higher for special shapes, larger bulbs, and the 47-40 and 47-73 with lantern. In Excellent condition, values range from 1 to 20; Like New examples range from 5 to 45.

671-75 SMOKE LAMP, 1946

This special bayonet-base 12-volt lamp was built for the smoke unit of the 1946 versions of the 671 and 2020 steam turbine locomotives. The bulb has a small "pan" depressed in the glass. Installation in the locomotive smoke generator leaves this pan positioned just below the smokestack. The pan holds the special 196 Smoke Pellet while heat from the bulb vaporizes it and creates smoke. A puffer mechanism in the locomotive provides synchronized drafts of air to move smoke up and out the stack.

Three of the earliest postwar dealer lamp assortments. Left: The version from 1948 that included four larger boxes containing special bulbs for the lampposts. Right: In 1949, these gave way to more of the smaller bulbs in this assortment. Neither box had any printing on the lid. Center: Starting in 1950, the box lids were printed as shown. Beginning in 1953, the number changed to 123. J. Lampert Collection.

	Gd	VG	Ex	LN

Either because 12-volt lamps tended to burn out too quickly or because Lionel wanted to standardize replacement smoke lamps, the 671-75 was changed to an 18-volt bulb and the master cartons were renumbered 703-10 (described below). To use up existing 671-75 boxes, the "12v" markings on the end flaps were overstamped "18V." Lamp boxes without the 18V overstamp are harder to find and bring a modest premium over the prices shown. — — **15** **35**

703-10 SMOKE LAMP, 1946
Identical in appearance to the 671-75, the 703-10 is an 18-volt bulb created for the 703 Hudson locomotive cataloged for 1946, but never manufactured. Lionel's lamp application charts indicate this lamp was intended for use on 1946 model 726 Berkshire locomotives only. The 703-10 is less common than the 671-75, since 671-75 dealer cartons were overstamped 703-10 and both the bulb boxes and their dealer cartons were overstamped for 18 volts. — — **30** **45**

Ten-Pack Lamps
These industry-standard-size packages, usually containing ten lamps, are orange with distinctive blue and white Lionel graphics. They qualify as "picture boxes" because of the locomotive front and bulb illustrations. Contents are listed on one end flap only, with "LIONEL TRAINS / miniature lamps" and the circled "L" on the other end. This package replaced individually boxed bulbs starting in 1953. Although the 1953 Replacement Lamp Chart in the Lionel Service Manual shows only the "NEW STOCK NUMBER" of the form 431-300, all boxes so far observed have the "catalog number" of the form L431. Interestingly, a few boxes have been observed without the "L" preceding the number. In the

following listing, every lamp has the "L" before the number, except for those originally printed without it:

L0214, L0961, L12, L12(R), L12(G), L13, 19, 19(R), 19(G), L47, L50, L50(R), L50(G), L51, L52, L53, L53(R), L53(G), L55, L57, L131, L191, 216, L257, L363, L363(R), L363(G), L402, L430, L430(R), L430(G), L431, L431(R), L432, L432(R), L432(G), L451(W), L452(W), L461, L797, L799, L1402, L1402(R), L1441(W), L1442(W), L1445, L1447, L1447(Y), L1449, L1449(R), L1456, and L1446(R).

This listing reflects lamps included in Lionel's charts, as well as independent observations. However, not all the listings have been confirmed. L402 is an example of a lamp packed six to a box rather than the usual ten, since it is a special lamp with wire leads rather than a screw or bayonet base.

Values are primarily for the box in nice condition. Lamps and their paperboard carrier can be obtained from the more readily available GE and other brand ten-packs. More expensive lamps are the less common numbers in pristine boxes. In Excellent condition, values range from 3 to 10; Like New examples range from 5 to 50.

122 LAMP ASSORTMENT, 1948–52
For 1948 and 1949, this paperboard display box had no graphics on its orange, paper-hinged cover. For 1948, it contained an assortment of 60 individually boxed bulbs; for 1949, an assortment of 66 boxed bulbs. A larger number of bulbs were

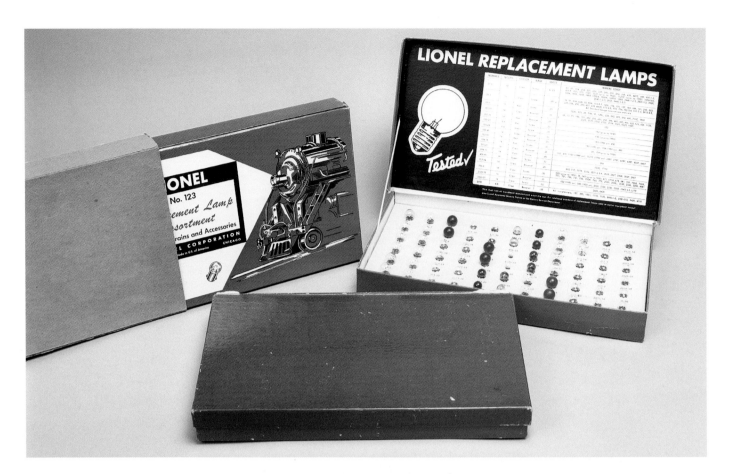

Three versions of Lionel's dealer lamp assortments. Left: Brand-new 123 with original shipping sleeve from 1953–59. Center: A 122 Lamp Assortment from 1948–49 with unmarked cover. These contained individually boxed bulbs. Right: A 122 Lamp Assortment with a cardboard carrier for the bulbs, introduced in 1950. J. Lampert Collection.

possible in the same box in 1949 due to deletion of the large street lamp bulbs 39-3 and 40-3. Lionel's 1949 Price List illustrates a 1948 assortment yet lists the contents of the 1949 assortment and refers to it as 122-9.

For 1950, the box construction remained the same, but graphics and the display number (122) were added to the cover. Instead of individually boxed bulbs, the interior contained a paperboard carrier with a yellow background and dark blue lettering. Sixty individual bulbs (more or less) of the various types were pressed through holes in this carrier. All 122s include a bulb application chart printed inside the cover that can be used to determine the vintage of the assortment. Further research is required in this area, but as many as five variations of the 122 may exist, one for each year. They vary in the type and number of the bulbs, as well as in the pattern of the display and the listings on the application chart. **NRS**

123 LAMP ASSORTMENT, 1953–59

Like the 122, this assortment is contained in a paperboard box with orange paper covering and a fragile paper hinge. More graphics adorned the cover, and inside are more than 40 bulbs of the various types, all pressed through holes in a yellow paperboard carrier. Although the 123 is similar to the 122, Lionel probably changed the number to highlight the move to industry standard bulb numbers.

Further research is required, but there may be as many as seven variations of the 123, one for each year, for the same reasons mentioned in 122 above. Price can vary tremendously, depending on the condition of the box. With a little effort, original-vintage bulbs can be found to replace missing bulbs. Brand-new examples of this display have been found in a white or cardboard-color paperboard sleeve used to protect the box in shipping. **NRS**

123-60 REPLACEMENT LAMP ASSORTMENT, 1960–63

Listed in Lionel's advance catalogs but not a consumer item, the 123-60 is rare. The collectible part is the orange, thin-paperboard box whose lid was made to form a pop-up display. An application chart is printed on one side of this outer box. Inside are 12 boxes of the regular ten-packs (packages of ten bulbs with Lionel graphics listed elsewhere in this section). A detailed listing of the contents is given on page T-11 of the 1963 Advance Catalog. Included are L19, L51, L53 (two boxes), L57, L191 (two boxes), L432R, L432G, L1445, L1447, and L216. **NRS**

0209 SIX SMALL BARRELS, 1930–42 and 1946–50

This is an individually boxed set of six natural-color wood barrels that each measure 1⅜″ high and just under 1″ in diameter at any of the four bands encircling them. These bands are positioned top and bottom, with the other two more closely spaced near the center. Prewar production included rare pull-apart barrels. These appear identical to the solid barrels, but a pulling twist separates the two halves just below one of the center bands, revealing a hollowed-out interior. A few 2452 gondolas, especially those with the 1945 set 463W, have been found with these barrels. Examples of the solid barrel missing the top band but of correct height have been observed and are factory errors.

The box is difficult to find in decent shape. Tiny flaps made it hard to open without nearly destroying the end. Refer to the

Dealer packs of 40 Hook Up Wire. Gray reels (left) are less common than orange. There is a printing style difference on the tape band around each reel. Generally, two reels of each color came in the box.

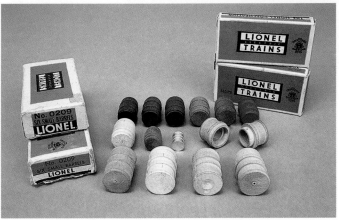

Barrels came in all sizes and many colors at Lionel. Note the missing top band on the barrel at the lower right and the prewar take-apart barrel packed with 2452 Gondolas in 1945. The rare red barrels came with some 3562-1 Barrel Cars. An oil drum from the 455 Oil Derrick is in the center.

	Gd	VG	Ex	LN

entry for 362-78, which contains smaller barrels that replaced the 0209 with the introduction of the 362 Operating Barrel Loader.

(A) Box containing rare pull-apart barrels. Barrels are almost indestructible, but parts can be lost. Even a poor box with nice barrels is worth acquiring. Separate barrels of the take-apart variety should be purchased whenever found.

			45	65

(B) Box containing usual solid barrels. Little if any added value for barrels, so price is determined by condition of box.

			10	25

	Gd	VG	Ex	LN

40 HOOK UP WIRE, 1950–51 and 1953–63

An orange, though sometimes gray, reel contains about 50 feet of 18-gauge plastic-coated solid conductor wire. Original wire colors are white, maroon, blue, and yellow. Examples from the first years of production have a piece of cellophane tape wrapped around the filled reel to secure the wire. This tape is printed in black block letters with four lines of lettering, starting with "CAT. NO. 40." Two print styles have been observed on this tape. Usually the four-line graphic repeats every 5 inches or so along the tape, but one example has only a single print on the entire overlapping wrap. In later years, clear, unlettered cellophane tape replaced the printed tape to secure the wire in the reel.

The word "LIONEL" in raised letters appears twice on each side of each reel. Original reels were undecorated, but after 1969 General Mills and its successors have used the original tools to produce more of these reels, which sometimes are found with "LIONEL" colored on top by black heat-stamping or ink. A Like New orange reel must include the original printed tape wrap. Double the value for a gray reel with original tape. Clear or no tape diminishes the value considerably.

			10	40

40 HOOK UP WIRE DEALER DISPLAY, 1950–51 and 1953–63

The display was illustrated (although not exactly as produced) in the 1950 catalog and several later ones and was available for several years. This rare display box with dark blue or black graphics may contain any of the reel and wire color variations

described in the listing for the 40 Hook Up Wire. The box lid folds in the middle and provides a pop-up background for the wire reel display. Examples whose lid has not yet been folded increase the value.

The box liner that holds the eight reels in place, while usually dark blue, can also be orange or plain cardboard color. Prices are for the complete box with liner. Add the value of each reel of wire included according to its condition and completeness. Wire colors in the display vary and are easily interchanged. Note that the box, alone, is greatly devalued by the absence of its original liner. Unscrupulous vendors have tried to make cardboard liners by cutting out the slots for the reels and spray-painting the color. Original liners had the slots die-cut and the color printed on. Look closely at the liner, including the underside, for evidence of paint overspray and knife-cut slots.

Five variations of this display have been observed. The outer box may be printed in blue or black, the background may be orange on both cover and box ends or orange with plain cardboard box ends, or the whole box may be plain cardboard with just blue printing. Add to this the three known lining colors (blue, orange, and plain cardboard) and the two reel colors (orange and gray), and quite an assortment of combinations can be made! Prices shown are for an orange box, orange ends, a blue liner and

In 1955, a longer version of the 160 Bin was introduced for the 3359 Twin Bin Dump Car. Separate-sale boxes for the short bin had long been known, but the existence of a special Classic box for the long version was totally unexpected! J. Lampert Collection.

	Gd	VG	Ex	LN

printed tape on orange reels. Other variations add to the value, sometimes substantially.

| | — | 150 | 300 | 500 |

40-25 CABLE REEL, 1955–57 and 1959

These orange reels are most collectible when located in an original manila envelope with typical black printing. It is probably useless to collect without the envelope, as the approximately 15 feet of black four-conductor wire can be wound on any reel to duplicate the original contents. Cataloged as 20 feet of wire in 1955 and with 15 feet thereafter, but probably always was 15 feet. Prices shown require the original envelope and reflect primarily its condition.

| | — | — | 125 | 275 |

40-50 CABLE REEL, 1960–61

Same comments as for the 40-25, except the 40-50 contains approximately 15 feet of black three-conductor wire.

| | — | — | 125 | 275 |

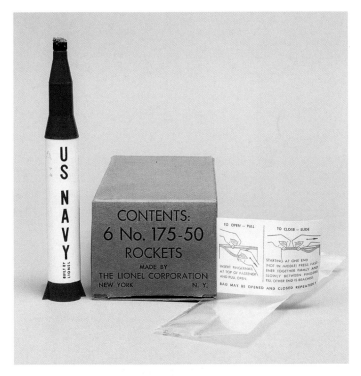

Dealer carton of six, separate-sale 175-50 Rockets. Each of the rockets came packaged in its own plastic bag, with an instruction sheet on how to operate the closure on the bag! Resealable plastic bags were just coming into use at the time. Note the deteriorated foam pad on the nose of this brand-new rocket, typical for this item. J. Lampert Collection.

160 UNLOADING BIN, 1952–55

Although available before World War II and well past 1955, the years listed indicate when this common item was cataloged for separate sale. It is not easy to find one in its own separate-sale box. With a little effort, however, you can find a multicolored, short 160 to put beside your common short and long black bins. Multicolored 160s were made by using up scrap Bakelite (molded material cannot be recycled), so each one is different. With considerably more effort and a bit of luck, you can find a brown (the natural color of Bakelite) short 160 or a metal 160! The price shown is for a short black 160 in its original separate-sale box. The bin itself is readily available: $1 or $2 for a black one and maybe $5 for multicolored.

(A) Short (about 7″ long) and most common variety in black. Like New requires one in its original separate-sale box. To add spice to your treasure hunt, there are two boxes to look for: one with an OPS price printed on the box, and the more common version without it.
— — — 150

(B) Same as (A) except bin has multicolored specks mixed with black. These Bakelite bins are brittle, so only Excellent and Like New are listed.
— — 2 5

(C) Same as (A) except molded in solid brown Bakelite. Probably made only in a small batch about 1948. Note that other Bakelite items in this period, such as the RCS Controller and 022 Switch Controller, are also known in brown. A solid dark wine-red example has been observed and is NRS.
— — — 25

(D) Short steel bin. Identical to the aluminum tray on the 3459 Automatic Dump Car except not punched for the tilting gear pieces. Apparently, the original plan was to make the 3459 tray out of steel. But when an initial sample was filled with a load of coal, it was too heavy for the solenoid to dump it! So the material was changed to aluminum, and trays already produced went out as 160s with the initial production 3459s. Most show rust through their black oxide finish. An original boxed 3459 including this bin has been observed, but most are found loose and are barely recognized as Lionel. However, if you look closely at the 1947 catalog, you will see both this bin and the standard 160 pictured. T. Schumacher Collection.
— — — 100

(E) Long (about 8¼″), introduced in 1955, and made of black injection-molded plastic rather than the compression-molded Bakelite used on short 160s. It is somewhat flexible and less prone to break than Bakelite bins. The material change was undoubtedly a cost savings for Lionel, if only because runners from the mold and damaged bins could be recycled (ground up and reused in the molding machines). This version was made longer to accommodate the increased length of the 3359 Twin Bin Dump Car, although it is not long enough to handle both bins without moving the car. An example of this bin in an original Classic box has been found! The box was not even known to exist before and is, of course, NRS.
— — — 3

164-64 SET OF 5 LOGS, 1952–58

These tiny boxes contain plain natural color (white) or (1954 and later) stained brown logs. A box with perfect flaps is rare due to the small size of these features. The box may have the 1952 OPS price printed on one side, but is usually found without it. Since the logs are common, the prices are for the box, full or empty!
— — 45 125

44-80 MISSILES, 1959–60

Four spare 44-40 missiles intended for use with the 44, 45, 448, 6544, and 6844 launchers. The missiles are common and are available in almost indistinguishable reproductions. However, all reproductions examined are about ⅛″ shorter than an original. Watch for broken or cracked fins.

The 44-40 missiles have a metallic weight inside that can be seen through the tail. The same missile was used without the weight for the "Littlejohn" rocket on the 6820 Flat Car with Missile Carrying Helicopter. These weightless missiles, Lionel part number 6820-10, are discussed in detail in the first volume of *Greenberg's Guide to Lionel Trains, 1945–1969*.

The essential piece of the 44-80 set is its tiny original manila envelope with black printing (part number 44-81). Top price requires an intact envelope with four original missiles.
— — 10 35

55-150 TIES, 1957–60

A manila envelope, part number 55-1, with standard black printing contains 24 spare ties for the 55 Tie-jector. Ties, also useful as scenic items, can be reproduced, although their octagonal shape is somewhat challenging. The envelope is required to authenticate this accessory, in addition to being the most collectible element. A crisp envelope still sealed with the original staple and containing its original ties may command a significant premium. Prices shown reflect the condition of the envelope.
— — 20 35

Dealer cartons of smoke pellets. Top center is the 196, used only with smoke-lamp locomotives in 1946. These came in a clear plastic "pail" with a bail handle. The other items are various vintage SP pellets. Note the OPS label on the carton at right, dating it to 1952. Almost unknown is the black bristle brush in the center. It was furnished with 1946 smoking locomotives to brush residual smoke powder down to the bulb.

	Gd	VG	Ex	LN

175-50 ROCKET, 1958–60

Separately sold rockets for use with the 175 Rocket Launcher and 6175 Flat Car with Rocket are invariably found, even brand new, with a deteriorated or missing foam tip. When new, they came in a resealable bag with a small instruction sheet for the bag and not the rocket! The challenge is to find the dealer pack of six individually bagged rockets. This is an olive paperboard box with black printing on only the end flaps, an NRS item. Prices are for the rocket; Like New requires the original resealable clear plastic bag and instruction sheet.

	Gd	VG	Ex	LN
	—	—	50	125

182-22 STEEL SCRAP, 1946–49

Not cataloged for separate sale, this rare item was included with new 182 Magnet Cranes. Cloth bag similar in size to that used for 207 Artificial Coal, with similar serif lettering, red printing, and red drawstring. Contents appear to be H-shaped punchouts from forming O gauge track ties. Prewar 165 Magnet Cranes included a similar bag of the same type of "scrap," with a 165-83 part number.

NRS

195-75 8-BULB FLOODLIGHT EXTENSION, 1957–60

A standard bank of eight lamps from the 195 Floodlight Tower individually packaged with two extension posts in a Classic box. The box and posts are the collectibles. Plugging the extension posts onto a 195's existing posts provides support and electrical contact for mounting the second lamp bank above the original. The extra head can also be used without the extensions if it is mounted back to back with the existing head. In fact, up to three extra banks can be used with a single 195 to create a monster light source with 16 bulbs shining front and rear!

The usual box is the Classic orange, white, and blue, but a box with a brighter, glossier orange and a lighter, brighter blue (like other boxes from about 1958) is known. Like New requires a decent box and the two posts.

	Gd	VG	Ex	LN
	—	—	25	75

196 SMOKE PELLETS, 1946–47

Approximately 100 smoke pellets are stored in a sealed, clear-plastic container. Intended for use only in lamp-type smoke units, which were installed in 1946 versions of the 671, 726, and 2020 locomotives. An unfortunate characteristic of these pellets, unlike SP pellets, is that they sublimate, like mothballs. So the container, which resembles a miniature lunch pail with a black oxide-finish wire bail to keep the lid tightly shut, has a thin rubber seal between the case and removable top. An identifying Lionel marking is noticeably absent; all that's there is "KEEP TIGHTLY CLOSED" in raised letters molded into the cover.

Lionel literature warned against using 196 pellets in heater-type smoke units. The chemicals in 196s attack the nichrome heater wire and destroy it. SP pellets can be used in lamp-type units, but performance is unsatisfactory because the lamp does not get hot enough to vaporize the pellet.

Prices do not depend upon the presence of the smoke pellets, and these prices are doubled if the correct pellets are still there. Beware of those who put SP smoke pellets in a 196 container and try to pass it off as an original! Old 196 pellets are prone to

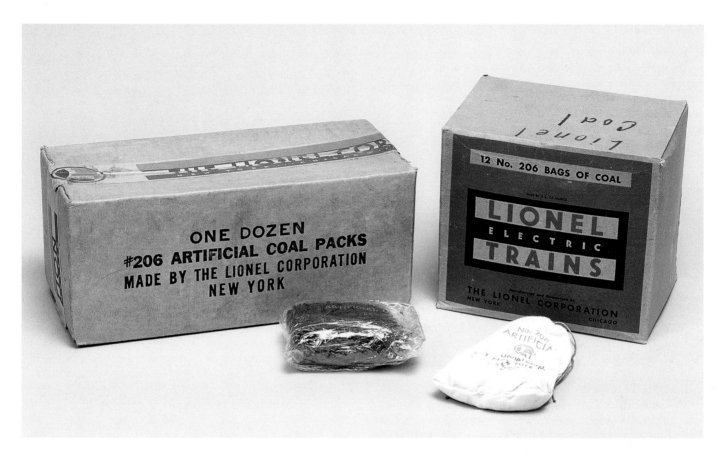

| | Gd | VG | Ex | LN |

disintegrate and even when intact show a fuzzy surface. SP pellets are more robust and tend to present a smooth surface, even when broken. One dealer package containing 12 of these 196 plastic pails has been observed and is NRS.

| | — | — | 75 | 150 |

197-75 RADAR HEAD, 1958–60

A separate-sale replacement for the antenna on the 197 Rotating Radar Antenna. The horn is the most vulnerable part, but the antenna is also fragile. The antenna appears in both a chrome (actually vacuum-metallized) finish and a later argent (silver-painted) finish. Of most interest is the cardboard box with black printing, sealed with paper tape, used to package the antenna. Two printings of the box, each with a different style, are known. The box is the most collectible element, with or without an antenna. Prices shown include the antenna.

| | — | — | 85 | 175 |

206 ARTIFICIAL COAL, 1938–42 and 1946–59

Artificial Coal is commonly found in a white cotton cloth bag with orange-red printing and a closely color-matched drawstring in the top. When full, the bag contains about ½ pound of the ground-up, black Bakelite scrap that Lionel used as coal. This was the separate-sale bag of coal, while the 207 (containing about ¼ pound of coal) was typically included with all operating cars and accessories that handled coal.

Before World War II, the 206 was packaged in a clear cellophane bag with orange printing. This wrapper was not durable, especially for sharp-cornered items like coal. Examples are so rare that few even know such a package exists, although it appears in prewar catalogs, and are NRS. Prices are for the cloth bags, with

Many Lionel accessories and cars used the ground Bakelite Lionel supplied for coal, so a ready supply of extra coal was an essential for Lionel dealers. On the left is a sealed box of 12 prewar cellophane packages, while the box on the right contains a dozen of the common 206 bags. A box of this size and type is also known for such items as lampposts, but its use for bags of coal is something never before seen in the author's many years of collecting! J. Lampert Collection.

| | Gd | VG | Ex | LN |

the highest going to clean bags with bold printing and their matching drawstring. If they still contain coal, so much the better!

(A) Common version with "Corporation" in the Lionel data. Sans-serif lettering, except "Made in / U.S. of America" in serif, ¾"-diameter circled "L."

| | — | — | 10 | 15 |

(B) Less common version with "Corp." in the Lionel data. Serif lettering, ¾" circled "L," lettering, drawstring more red than orange. Probably prewar.

| | — | — | 10 | 15 |

(C) Same as (B) except sans-serif lettering for all but "Made in . . ." and orange-red drawstring.

| | — | — | 10 | 15 |

(D) Same as (C), except ¹³⁄₁₆-diameter circled "L" and much broader strokes in serif lettering (most noticeable in "No. 206" line, which is nearly ¼" longer than usual).

| | — | — | 10 | 15 |

207 ARTIFICIAL COAL, 1938–42

Similar to 206, except it always has "Corp." rather than "Corporation" in the red lettering. The bag is considerably smaller, containing only about ¼ pound of coal. Although uncataloged for separate sale in the postwar years, this item was typically included with all operating coal cars and accessories throughout this period. Lionel HO gauge operating dump cars came with HO size coal in a clear plastic bag with yellow lettering numbered 0207.

There are a number of interesting variations in the 207 bag, as there are in 206s. Price is for the bag, full or empty, and the condition of the printing. On all variations, the circled "L" is ¾" in diameter, and "Made In U.S. of America" is always in serif lettering, even when the other words are sans-serif.

(A) Dark red, almost brown serif lettering. Probably prewar. — — 7 15

(B) Same as (A) except orange serif lettering. Probably prewar. — — 7 15

(C) Same as (B) except sans-serif lettering about ¼" high in "Artificial," the word "Coal" is about ⅞" long. — — 7 15

(D) Same as (C) except lettering is ⁵⁄₁₆" high in "Artificial" and slightly less than ¼" high in "N" (for "No. 206"), the word "Coal" is about ⅞" long. — — 7 15

(E) Same as (C) except lettering in the word "Coal" is about 1" long. — — 7 15

(F) Bag whose bottom is almost identical in width to a normal 207 but whose height is typical of the taller 206. Found with a 497 Coaling Station. **NRS**

264-150 SET OF 12 BOARDS, 1957–59

This set contains 12 of the 264-11 Timbers, packaged for separate sale in a 4⅜" x 1⅞" manila envelope with black lettering and part number 264-151. One observed example has "CATALOG No. 264-150" rubber-stamped across the top. This is not the same as the 6264-8 envelope (containing 12 timbers and 8 posts) included with the relatively rare separate-sale 6264. Since the boards are easily reproduced, the value is in the envelope. Add a modest premium for a crisp example still sealed with the original staple. — — 50 75

352-55 SET OF 7 ICE CUBES, 1955–57

Several examples have been observed in a manila envelope, part number 352-60, with contents listed only as "7 No. 352-29 ICE BLOCKS." None have the catalog number 352-55 shown anywhere. Printing on the larger envelopes (part number 352-45) that came with 352 Ice Depots originally listed eight ice blocks, but "8" has been covered with an X and "5" has been stamped in its place. It would be interesting to hear if anyone has found a 352-45 envelope without this modification. The 352-44 instruction sheet dated 10-55 warns that no more than five cubes should be loaded into the car to prevent jamming its ice compartment.

Ice blocks have been reproduced. Originals have rounded edges, an air bubble in the approximate center, a faint parting line about ¹⁄₃₂" down from one surface, and a large round ejector pin mark on the opposite surface. These cubes are not easily damaged but are easily lost. Thus, prices shown reflect condition of the envelope, but the envelope must include all seven original cubes. — — 50 85

356-35 SET OF 2 TRUCKS, 1952–56

A small Classic box contains two baggage trucks (usually one orange and one dark green) for use with the 356 Operating Freight Station. The trucks are described in detail under the listing for the 356 in Chapter 2. They have been reproduced, with the original Lionel nomenclature on the bottom. Here the primary item of value is the box itself.

(A) Usual box has "356" (not "356-35," the number on each

These common baggage trucks for the 356 Operating Freight Station came with an uncommon lithographed tin load during the earliest production of this accessory. M. Stephens Collection.

end flap) printed on all four sides. Price includes set of trucks, quite common by themselves. — — 50 85

(B) Later box without any number on four sides. — — 50 85

(C) Box from 1952, same as (A) but with the OPS price on one side. Very difficult box to locate. — — 75 125

362-78 SET OF 6 BARRELS, 1952–58

These brown-stained wooden 1¼" high barrels replaced the larger 0209 barrels starting in 1952, with the introduction of the 362 Operating Barrel Loader. Evidently, the smaller barrels worked better with the vibrating ramp of the loader. Several different shades of brown are known, and there are some slight variations in shape. Lionel also made a few red stained barrels. These were most likely included with early production of the black 3562-1 Operating Barrel Car, introduced in 1954. One such example has been observed with all red barrels. With the cream-color ramp and black body shell, it makes a very attractive car!

Of particular interest is the tiny Classic box that contains the set. The same box was available for separate sale and, because it was included with new loaders and new barrel cars, is not particularly hard to find. What appear to be the same barrels were cataloged as the 5158 for a set of 12 in the road-racing section of the 1963 catalog. Condition shown is for the box. — — 10 20

394-37 ROTATING BEACON CAP, 1954–60

This fragile plastic and foil-thin metal cap was intended for use with the heat-operated 394 Rotating Beacon. Since the caps are often missing or irreparably damaged on otherwise decent 394s, the caps are as valuable as the round containers with lift-off lids used to package them. Original caps have "LIONEL" in raised letters embossed on the tiny tabs projecting down on each

The separate-sale boxes of these 460-150 Two Trailers are the collectibles; their contents are common. Note the difference in the "FRUEHAUF" label color.
J. Algozzini Collection.

	Gd	VG	Ex	LN

side. Look-alike reproductions and competitors' products are blank. Original cartons have a gray cardboard tube section with a thin red or gray paperboard lid at the top and bottom. The bottom is glued to the tube, and the removable top has a Lionel label. Also observed packaged in a tiny unmarked conventional brown paperboard box. Prices shown assume a cap and its carton in comparable condition.

	—	—	15	35

450L SIGNAL LIGHT HEAD, 1952–58

Packed in a tiny Classic box, the 450L is a complete spare signal light head for the 450 Signal Bridge or 452 Gantry Signal. It includes a twin lamp socket with red and green lamps, wires, a mounting screw, and a plastic snap-on hood. As with most boxes produced in 1952, this one can be found with an OPS price printed on one side, but most have no price. Condition is for the box; Like New requires complete contents.

	—	—	50	90

460-150 TWO TRAILERS, 1955–57

A unique separate-sale box contains two spare trailers for use with the 460 Piggyback Transportation Set. Trailers furnished with new 460s were packaged in the box, nestled in the box liner. Original contents of the 460-150 usually are green vans with black or silver background Fruehauf labels and "LIONEL TRAINS" signs. White vans with "duals" (two tires on each end of the axle) and gray vans have also been reported as original contents. But the vans are easily obtained, and it is this scarce separate-sale box that is eagerly sought. Information on Lionel's extensive assortment of vans appears in the first volume of *Greenberg's Guide to Lionel Trains, 1945–1969*.

	—	—	200	300

	Gd	VG	Ex	LN

464-150 SET OF 6 BOARDS, 1956–59

These are the flat boards that emerge from the left side of the 464 Operating Lumber Mill as 164-64 logs disappear into the right side. Spare boards are easily duplicated, so the collectible element is the manila envelope, part number 464-151, with black printing containing six No. 464-51 Timbers for 464 Lumber Mill. This is not the same envelope that came with the 464. Price and condition are for the envelope.

	—	—	50	85

479(-1) LIONEL TRUCKS, 1955–57

This single railcar truck was cataloged as 479 in 1955, and by the correct service part number of 479-1 in 1956–57. The truck has a plain bar end design with no coupler or center pivot stud and was available as a service item. Lionel included three of them as the load for the 6362 Railway Truck Car and packaged them individually for separate sale in a small manila envelope with black printing. Condition and price are for the envelope alone, as the trucks are easily found.

	—	—	60	110

480-25 CONVERSION COUPLER, 1950–60

A separate-sale magnetic coupler sold to convert Scout and prewar couplers to remote control operation. A single coupler was packaged in a manila envelope with black printing except in 1952, when a pair of couplers was cataloged. An envelope has been observed with "two" in the title and others with the "two"

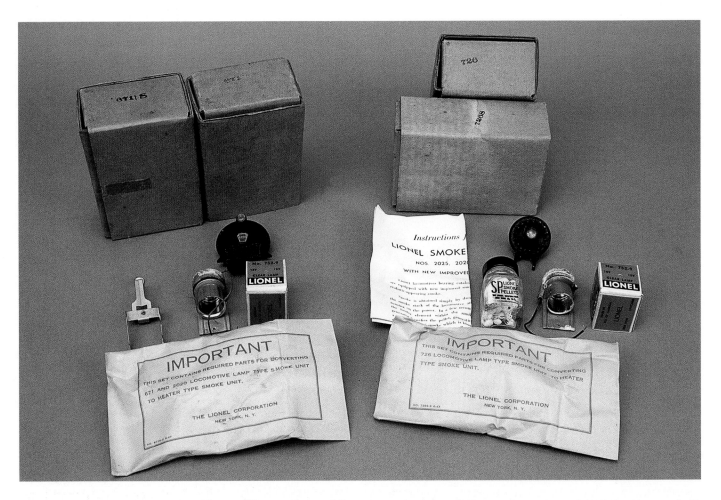

Owners of 671, 726, and 2020 steam locomotives made in 1946 could not use the SP Smoke Pellets Lionel introduced a year later. To resolve the situation, Lionel made the 671S (left) and 726S kits to convert the older bulb-type smoke units.

	Gd	VG	Ex	LN

blanked and "one" substituted. Also of interest is an envelope with "480-25" on top with "Assembly No. 480-32" on the second line. After 1960, the catalog and envelope designations changed to "480-32."

All these envelopes contained a part number 480-23 instruction sheet, which is known in 21 variations! Only one of the two versions dated 9-60 refers to 480-32; all the others, including the last edition, dated 4/65, refer to 480-25. The couplers were apparently borrowed from the inventory used to build railcars in production, so they would typically include the finger tab incorporated about 1955 to facilitate manual uncoupling. This feature was discontinued a couple of years later, and the contents of 480-25 followed suit.   —   —   —   **10**

480-32 CONVERSION MAGNETIC COUPLER, 1961–66 and 1968–69

See comments for 480-25, as the 480-32 appears to be a renumbering of the 480-25, with no apparent difference in the coupler. It usually comes in the same manila envelope, but in the quantity "one." Only a 480-23 instruction sheet dated 9-60 or 4/65, or the undated 5½" x 8½" sheet, should be included with the 480-32. Many examples in a white envelope with the later Lionel twin arrow logo have been observed. All these have the number 480-32 and contain a 4/65 instruction sheet.   —   —   —   **10**

671S CONVERSION KIT, 1947–49

Not cataloged but available to Lionel Service Stations for converting bulb-type smoke units in 1946 versions of the 671

and 2020 locomotives to the later heater-type unit. All components necessary for the conversion, including a new boiler front and a bottle of SP smoke pellets, came packed in a plain brown tuck-flap corrugated box approximately 3⅛" x 4¾" x 2" high. The lid or ends are stamped "671S" in black ink with the same serif figures used to mark the locomotive. A list of kit contents and installation instructions are on the 671S-2 instruction sheet, dated 11/47, included in the kit.   —   —   **50**   **90**

726S CONVERSION KIT, 1947–49

Similar to the 671S, the contents of this kit are tailored to 1946 models of the 726 and include a 726S-4 instruction sheet dated 11/47. The cardboard box is stamped "726S" or "726" and contains a manila envelope, part number 726S-3, dated 8-47 and printed in red, which holds some of the small parts. Details of the 671S and 726S kits are included in Section LOC-SU, pages 7 and 8, of the Lionel Service Manual.   **NRS**

909 SMOKE FLUID, 1957–66 and 1968–69

This special liquid smoke fluid was intended for use with the 6557 Smoking Caboose and such locomotives as the 243, 746, and 1872. Only the 2-fluid-ounce size was cataloged for separate sale. It comes in a clear plastic squeeze bottle, 3⅞" high, with

	Gd	VG	Ex	LN

blue printing on the front and back. A smaller, ½-fluid-ounce size in a 2⅟₁₆″-high bottle was included with all smoking units and not intended for separate sale. Except for size, the bottles appear almost identical.

A rare dealer display box of 12 large bottles has also been observed. This paperboard box with inner divider and a pop-up lid forms a nice though not durable counter display when opened and folded in half. Of course there is a variation! The "hat logo" of the Toy Manufacturers Association may be present or missing from the flap; all examples are NRS. The prices shown are for a large squeeze bottle and cap, with or without fluid. The quality of the printing on the bottle sides determines condition.

| | — | — | 20 | 40 |

B909 SMOKE FLUID, 1966

The same 2-ounce bottle as the 909, but packed in a blister pack on a white paperboard card printed in orange and blue and punched for hanging on a display rack. The blister packaging was only produced in 1966 — — 100 285

Note: Lionel also made tiny capsules of smoke fluid to include with its cheaper locomotives and sets—especially uncataloged outfits—offered during the 1960s. These are the same size as the oil and grease capsules (not the tubes) described below in the Note under the 926. The color is blue, rather than the orange used for lubricants. The typical packaging is a "sandwich" of thin Kraft paper on one side and cellophane on the other. Examples of a single capsule and of three capsules in the package have been observed. This is a highly desirable collectible to some, but very difficult to find unless you get a brand-new set or locomotive and remember to save this seemingly insignificant item.

925 LIONEL LUBRICANT, 1934–42, 1946–66, and 1968–69

This 2-ounce tube of grease was cataloged continuously from 1934 until 1969, with the sole exception of the 1945 abbreviated catalog and 1967, when there was no catalog. Some variations exist in tube printing and top design. Early production has a screw-on metal cap and a short nozzle; later postwar tubes have a needle nozzle with a push-on cap in black or dark blue. Red caps are occasionally seen, but they are from A. C. Gilbert Co., which used the same red cap for its American Flyer lubricant.

Dealer displays contain 12 tubes of lubricant, and several variations of this NRS display are known. Another unusual packaging of the 925 is a test-tube-shaped, hard plastic tube with bottle-size screw-on lid. These tubes were probably available to service stations for repacking gearboxes, but no Lionel promotion of this NRS item has been observed to date.

Prices are for a full 2-ounce squeeze tube, Like New or better. This lubricant should no longer be used on your trains. Modern automotive wheel-bearing grease containing molybdenum disulfide (MoS_2) is a far superior lubricant that will not harden over time. — — — 10

925-1 LUBRICANT, 1950–66 and 1968–69

Same lubricant as the 925, but packaged in a 1-ounce tube that uses the same push-on cap. One tube was included with each of the various maintenance kits Lionel cataloged and was not offered for separate sale. The printing on these tubes changed over the years. — — — 5

Rare though the Orange Picture box display of 12 bottles of 909 Smoke Fluid is, the display on the right is even rarer! It and the single bottle blister pack date to 1966. J. Lampert Collection.

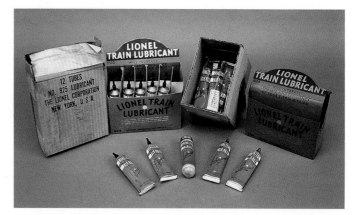

Lionel 925 Lubricant packaging and dealer displays. At left rear is a display of 12 tubes and its shipping carton. On the right is a bulk pack of tubes with no display, and a closed dealer display of earlier vintage than the one on the left. Variations of individual packages are arrayed in the foreground. Note the unique "test tube" package at front center.

	Gd	VG	Ex	LN

926 LIONEL LUBRICANT, 1942 and 1955–56

The smaller 926 tube contains approximately ½ ounce of the same grease found in the 925. Although cataloged for only the three years shown, this size tube was available over the entire postwar period and may date back to 1934, when 925 was introduced. It was typically included with each new locomotive. There are some interesting variations in the printing and cap design. On the back of one prewar example is a printed statement extolling the virtues of the lubricant, followed by "U O MFG. CO PATENT 1,902,635." Examples with a Lubriplate advertisement on the back also are known. Price shown is for a full tube, Like New or better, with the usual blank white back.

| | — | — | — | 2 |

Note: Although not cataloged for separate sale, some interesting lubricant packages were included with locomotives and train sets. First are sealed orange plastic tubes with blue printing containing oil or lubricant. A whitish tube with blue printing is also known for the lubricant. To release the contents, the end of the tube is cut off with scissors and the tube serves as a one-time applicator. These tubes were packaged loose in locomotive

boxes. In train sets, they came either packed separately in their own envelope or with other small items in a larger envelope.

In the 1960s, Lionel also packaged oil and lubricant in small capsules that were similar in shape to the capsules of smoke fluid American Flyer used, although not as large. Because of their small size, the Lionel capsules were typically packaged inside a "sandwich" of clear cellophane on one side and a Kraft paper backing on the other. Since these tubes were meant for one-time use and are so small, they have a low survival rate.

927 LUBRICATING AND MAINTENANCE KIT, 1950–59

All variations contain a can of track cleaner, six small emery boards, a metal-handle brush with black bristles, two orangewood sticks, a white wiping cloth with hemmed edges, and a wooden tamper to push smoke pellet residue down the stack without damaging the smoke unit heater. With the introduction of the 3927 Track Cleaner Car in 1956, Lionel discontinued orange cans of 927-3 Track Cleaner, which is flammable, and introduced nonflammable 3927-75 Track Cleaner in a blue can. Warnings indicated that only cleaner contained in the blue can should be used with 3927. So beginning in 1956, 927 Maintenance Kits also included the blue can.

The box with its snap-lock lid is one of the interesting variations. In 1950 the front edge of the box is about ¼ or so higher than in following years and staples are visible on this part. 1952 kits can be identified by the OPS price label printed on the cover. No example has been observed with the pocket for the instruction booklet inside the lid, as illustrated in the catalog. Instead, the booklet was placed on top of the contents.

Booklets tend to measure 4″ x 5″, although some examples of the 1954 edition are 4⁹⁄₃₂″ x 5⁵⁄₁₆″, which is too wide to fit under the lid without bending down the edge. They are part number 927-14, although the 1956 edition changed to 927-19. Editions are determined by the copyright date on the booklet's back

927 Maintenance Kits from various years. The copyright labels found on the rear of the instruction booklets help date individual kits. Note the height of the front box lip on the kits at center rear from 1950 (kit on center left is earliest production, as seen by its paper labels). Cleaning fluid cans are typically packaged on the left side of the box, but liners are easily rearranged, as shown by the 1950 kit at the far left.

	Gd	VG	Ex	LN

cover. Editions for 1950, '52, '53, '54, and '56 have been observed.

The earliest 1950 production included a 927-3 orange can of track cleaner that has a paper label instead of the usual lithographed can. Similarly, the 927-7 oil vial has a paper label instead of the common printed glass. In early 1956 production, when the blue can was introduced, it also had a paper label! Evidently the lithographed cans were not ready in time. The 3927-75 Track Cleaner is water-based, so it rusts through the can from the inside and then evaporates. Consequently, it is rare to find a blue can of cleaner with anything inside.

Since the oil vial was not affected by the change to a nonflammable cleaner, it remained unchanged. However, two different ridge patterns are found around the edge of the caps of oil vials, and these caps have been observed in blue, black, purple, and maroon.

Tubes of 925-1 lubricant in 927 kits share a common nozzle cap with the 925 and are known in black or blue. Red nozzle caps have been observed, but these are borrowed from A. C. Gilbert Co., which used the same cap, only red, on one of its lubricants! Like New requires a complete kit in a nice box with the booklet and a clean wiping cloth.   —   —   **30**   **75**

927-3 LIONEL CLEANER, 1955

Although part of the 927 Maintenance Kit for several years, this item was cataloged for separate sale only in 1955. Highly effective, this cleaner in the orange can is, unfortunately, flam-

| | Gd | VG | Ex | LN |

mable. When the 3927 Track Cleaning Car debuted in 1956, a nonflammable substitute had to be introduced. The product selected received part number 3927-75 and was put in a blue can. Lionel included a warning tag with new 3927 Track Cleaning Cars and put additional warnings in the instructions that only the new cleaner should be used with 3927.

The entry for 927 mentions the paper label and lithographed can variations of the 927-3. Also observed is a dealer display of 12 cans in a thin orange paperboard carton with pop-up display lid. It is not durable, making it rare enough to be NRS. Like New is for a single lithographed can with screw-on cap in nice condition, whether full or empty.

| — | — | — | 10 |

927-90 LIONEL LUBRICATING OIL, uncataloged 1963

A tiny orange plastic capsule of oil was found in the small parts envelope of an uncataloged O27 outfit from 1963 with a plastic 200-series locomotive. The 927-90 was undoubtedly included with many sets and perhaps separate-sale locomotives of this period. The capsule came sealed in a cellophane package with dark blue printing and illustrations depicting how to open the capsule and use a thumbtack as a stopper. Assembly no. 1103-20, a manila envelope with part number 1103-21, also contains the same cellophane package. But in the envelope contents, the oil capsule is listed as 927-85. So 927-90 is probably the part number for the assembly of the capsule and cellophane.

| — | — | — | 35 |

Front: Rare 928 and 5159 Maintenance Kits. Rear: Nonflammable 3927 Track Cleaner in a blister pack and dealer packages of flammable 927-3. MPC kit in center used original Lionel components in new packaging.

| | Gd | VG | Ex | LN |

928 MAINTENANCE AND LUBRICANT KIT, 1960–63

Essentially a low-cost version of the 927 with a flimsy window box and paperboard liner, this kit is difficult to find in nice condition. Less extensive than the 927, it included only an unmarked needlenose oiler, an eraser-like Lionel Rail Cleaner (known with two different styles of printing), a 925-1 tube of grease, and a blue can of 3927-75 Track-Clean. In place of a booklet, a 928-13 instruction sheet was provided in either of two issues. The 8-60 issue is printed in black on pink paper, while the 3-62 issue is printed in black on green paper.

| — | — | 40 | 60 |

950 U.S. RAILROAD MAP, 1958–66

Produced for Lionel by Rand McNally, this colorful 52″ x 37″ map showed all the major American railroad routes of the time. Heralds of many of these roads decorate the border. Two different dealer cartons of six rolled maps have been observed and are NRS, though the maps are fairly common. Some came folded as part of a catalog offer or other promotion, or were included in an uncataloged train set. Those offered for separate sale were rolled inside a cardboard tube that was wrapped spirally with tape printed with the "950" and Lionel nomenclature. Prices are for the map, rolled or folded. A substantial premium is warranted for an original tube.

| — | — | 60 | 85 |

The author's son Matthew poses in an assembled 970 Ticket Booth. This cardboard structure is the only known "child size" Lionel item since its prewar stove.

	Gd	VG	Ex	LN

970 TICKET BOOTH, 1958–60

Shipped disassembled, this all-cardboard booth is trimmed in green and red and has a simulated blackboard in front, a green roof with a "LIONELVILLE" sign, and a clock on the roof that indicates "7:08." Came packed flat in a carton labeled "3592-1" and manufactured by United Container Corporation, Philadelphia ("United for Strength"). Quite an unusual item for Lionel, as this was actually large enough for a child to play inside. Included an 8½" x 11" white instruction sheet, "LIONEL TICKET OFFICE," showing how to assemble the booth. It has no part number or date, but does indicate, "Designed and Produced / by / COLOR PROCESS CO., INC. / Phila. 4, Pa." Dimensions: 11" x 22" base, 46" high when assembled.

— — 150 200

1640-100 PRESIDENTIAL KIT, 1960

This desirable kit was made to accompany set 1640W for the presidential election year 1960. It was also cataloged as a separate-sale item. Paper signs for both major political parties, Secret Service, and the press corps, along with a cellophane bag of unpainted Plasticville figures, were included in a unique orange

	Gd	VG	Ex	LN

box with black printing and lift-up lid. Double-sided adhesive was also supplied that could be cut into thin strips and used to hold the signs onto passenger cars. When found, the box for this kit is usually missing some of its original contents. Prices are for a complete kit. — — 200 350

3330-100 OPERATING SUBMARINE KIT, 1960–61

Identical components were included in this separate-sale kit and with the 3330 Flat Car with Operating Submarine Kit. The only unique inner packaging with the 3330 was the clear plastic bag of small parts. For the separate-sale kit, all the submarine parts were packaged in a unique picture box with lift-off lid. Kit includes a 3330-107 instruction sheet dated 8-60. Two versions of this sheet are known, distinguished by different Lionel Service Department addresses. — — 200 350

3356 OPERATING HORSE CAR, 1956–57

Unlike the 3656 Operating Cattle Car, the 3356 Operating Horse Car did not include a car box within the set box. Instead, this car was packed in a partition of the liner in the 3356 Operating Horse Car and Corral box. However, Lionel did print a special Classic box (similar in size to a 6464 boxcar box) for the separate-sale car. Price is for the rare box, since the car is easily acquired. — — 250 400

3356-2 HORSE CAR CORRAL, 1956–57

This separate-sale item originally contained not only the corral, but also (unlike the separate-sale cattle car platform) a box of livestock (horses). Any corral will do, but the unique box is rare. Price reflects the condition of the Classic box, with or without contents. — — 250 400

3356-100 FIGURES FOR HORSE CAR, 1956–59

A separate-sale, Classic box contains nine black horses identical to those included with the 1956–60 version of the 3356 Operating Horse Car. The 1964–66 reissue of this accessory included horses packaged in a plain off-white box, completely undecorated except for blue printing on each of the two opening sides.

(A) Usual Classic box containing nine black horses. This is the version cataloged for separate sale. Condition is for the box. — — 20 60

(B) Plain box, never cataloged for separate sale, included with the 1964–66 reissue of 3356. — — 35 85

3366-100 FIGURES FOR CIRCUS CAR, 1959–60

A Classic box contains nine white horses for the 3366 Circus Car. All observed examples are the glossy orange that appears on several Lionel boxes of this period. Condition is primarily for the box, although these white horses can be difficult to find. Prices assume all nine are present. — — 50 125

The 1640-100 Presidential Kit was included with the 1640W passenger outfit in 1960 and was also cataloged for separate sale.

A gathering of some of the rarest accessory boxes in Lionel collecting! Although the contents are common, these separate-sale boxes are eagerly sought though seldom offered for sale. J. Lampert Collection.

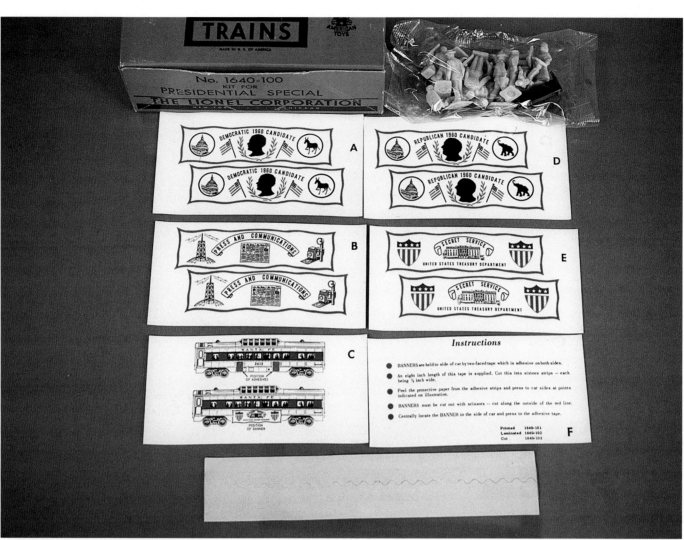

	Gd	VG	Ex	LN

3424-75 LOW BRIDGE SIGNAL, uncataloged

A Classic box identical to that of the 3424-100 except for marking. Contents are one telltale, its mounting clip and twin-blade grounding contacts for O and O27 track. Two box variations have been observed, one originally printed as a -75 and the other a standard 3424-100 box, factory re-marked by blanking out "-100" and printing "-75" beside it. Both original instruction sheets for the 3424 Brakeman Car offer the opportunity to send $1.35 to the Lionel Service Department for this item. It may also have been included in one or more uncataloged sets, but no confirmation has been received. **NRS**

3424-100 LOW BRIDGE SIGNAL SET, 1956–58

A separate-sale Classic box of parts that was also included with each 3424 Brakeman Car. To be complete, the set must include two telltale poles (each with 12 telltales), two pole-mounting track clips, two each of the twin-blade O and O27 grounding contacts, and a 3424-95 instruction sheet printed in blue on white paper. Two versions of the instruction sheet are dated 8-56 and 5-57. The later one includes instructions for mounting the telltales on Super O track. Both dark orange (usual color) and much lighter "faded" orange telltale poles are known. The same variation shows up in other unpainted orange molded items of this era, such as the 6816-100 Bulldozer and 6519 Allis-Chalmers Car. — — **35** **50**

3454-51 MINIATURE PACKING CASES, uncataloged

Not a cataloged item but a very desirable collectible. There is no assembly number printed on the envelope, as there would have been had it been offered for separate sale. The number 3454-51 is the envelope part number, printed in black in the lower left-hand corner of the manila envelope. It contains one no. 3454-47 Instruction Sheet and an unspecified number of no. 3814-53 Miniature Packing Cases. These are the "Baby Ruth" cubes, most commonly found in brown but also known in red

A common flat car but an exceedingly rare box! Cataloged only in 1955, no example of the separate sale box had ever been reported until Barry Keener discovered one at a recent auction. B. Keener Collection.

	Gd	VG	Ex	LN

and black. One of these envelopes came with each 3854 and 3454 Automatic Merchandise Car. Several versions of the instruction sheet are known, and one of the changes is the number of packing cases included. Earlier examples of this envelope may exist with the number of cases printed on it, but none has been reported. Prices are for a nice envelope with all the contents. — — **50** **100**

3460 FLAT CAR, 1955

In one of the most exciting "finds" in postwar collecting, Barry Keener purchased this previously unverified separate-sale item at an auction. Of particular interest is that a unique Classic box was printed just for this accessory. Its end flaps are hinged along the long dimension of the box ends, but the end flap printing is parallel to the short dimension. This was not Lionel's usual practice, and the fact that it would print a special box for this one-year-only item, yet overstamp a common gondola box for the 6342 Culvert Car, which it cataloged for two years, is most unusual! As its $5.95 original price might suggest, trailers were not included with the car. Extra trailers were cataloged for separate sale as the 460-150. The 3460 car itself is common and was included with the 460 Piggy Back Transportation Set. **NRS**

3462-70 MAGNETIC MILK CANS, 1952–59

Although available from the initial introduction of the 3462 Operating Milk Car in 1947, these cans were not cataloged for separate sale until 1952. By then, only the last of three versions of this box was available. When originally issued in 1947, the box was 3¼" long and contained seven cans "For Use With 3462 Operating Milk Car."

This box variation is long enough for more cans, and a mint

example has been observed with a bit of paper to keep the cans from rolling back and forth. Fairly soon after introduction, judging by the rarity of long boxes, the box was shortened to 2¹⁵⁄₁₆″. But it still contained seven cans and mentioned only the 3462 in the "For Use" statement.

Later, for reasons of economy or because seven cans used at once jammed the mechanism, the content was changed to six cans with no change in the box. In support of the theory that seven cans may have been too much for the mechanism, all the instruction sheets through 1950 stated that the unloading chute could hold seven cans and warned against trying to force more into it. Starting with the sheet dated 11-51, this number was reduced to five.

When the 3472 with magnetic couplers was introduced in 1949 (first 3472-11 instruction sheet is dated 2-49), the statement on the box was changed to "For Use With 3462 and 3472 Operating Milk Cars." When the 3482 superseded the 3472 in 1954, the milk can box stayed the same, as far as is known. No examples mentioning 3482 have been reported.

Such a tiny box is difficult to open without damaging the conventional end flaps. Despite the huge number of milk cars produced over the years, original, undamaged milk can boxes are difficult to find.

(A) Early version, about 3¼″ long with statement "For Use With 3462 Operating Milk Car." Originally contained seven cans.

			25	55

(B) Same as (A) except 2¹⁵⁄₁₆″ long. May contain six or seven cans.

			20	50

(C) Late version, 2¹⁵⁄₁₆″ long with statement "For Use With 3462 and 3472 Operating Milk Cars." Originally contained only six cans.

			20	50

3462P MILK CAR PLATFORM, 1952–55

Any milk car platform will do, but it takes the box to authenticate this rare separate-sale platform. Early platform framework was painted a glossy eggshell color, while a flatter, truer white was used for most production and is correct for this box. 3462P is the number for all milk car platforms, whether the car was a 3462, 3472, 3482, or 3662. This number and the Lionel nomenclature are stamped into the metal base on the platform bottom. Plating on the adjustable platform floor is thin, and it is rare to find an original with no trace of discoloration. Reproduction floors are better plated but are much too shiny.

The same platform with a different paint job became the 3672-50 Platform for the 3672 Operating Bosco Car. However, the 3672-50 was not cataloged for separate sale. Some Bosco examples have been observed with "3462P" and the Lionel nomenclature stamped into the metal on the bottom side of the base, while others have no stamping at all. Prices for the 3462P reflect the box condition, as the platform is common.

		50	100	200

3530-50 SEARCHLIGHT WITH POLE AND BASE, 1956–57

Accessories for the 3530 Generator Car Set (cataloged from 1956 to 1958) were also available in a Classic box, available for separate sale only. Unlike the accessories for the 3424 Brakeman Car, the contents of the 3530-50 were contained by a box liner when sold as part of the 3530 set. Consequently, the separate-sale box is much harder to find than a 3424-100. Complete

contents include the searchlight with a magnet in its red base, two-conductor green cable, and a telephone pole with a simulated transformer on its base, molded in black or blue.

In recent years, two examples have been reported with a molded yellow base and transformer! Both reportedly were included in set 2291W, a 1956 Rio Grande F3 outfit. An aluminum tube runs up parallel to the pole, carrying the green cable so that it can be strung over to the 3530 car and plugged into the receptacle in the car roof. The box is the primary collectible, though the contents are not easily found by themselves. Prices include the box and contents with either common transformer color.

		150	250

3656-34 SET OF 9 CATTLE, 1952–58

Although first cataloged in 1952, these tiny Classic boxes of cattle date from the 1949 introduction of the 3656 Operating Cattle Car. From the beginning, one of these boxes of cattle was included with each car. Very early cattle have a rounded ridge on their base that extends around the front and about three-fourths of the way back along each side. Later and more common are cattle whose bases have plain sides. Most cattle are black, but a few show some brown or other color that appears to have crept in as an impurity. Brown cows are reproductions, as are some black ones that are almost indistinguishable from original.

Five variations in the Classic box have so far been identified: (1) an almost red box from 1952 with the OPS price printed on one lid, (2) orange box with "3656" on the four sides, (3) same except for "3656-34" on the sides, (4) same except for no number on the sides, and (5) same except the glossy orange of 1958 vintage. Prices are for boxes with all nine original cattle figures. A premium is warranted for the early cattle with side ridge, the glossy orange box, and the almost red OPS box.

		25	45

3656-150 CORRAL PLATFORM, 1952–55

A later design corral platform with cream-yellow movable gates in a Classic box. This separate-sale accessory did not include cattle or an instruction sheet and is difficult to locate in decent condition. The box, of course, is the collectible and is very rare. **NRS**

3662-79 NON-MAGNETIC MILK CANS, 1955–59

The catalog number is evidently for the assembly of the envelope, cans, and instruction sheet. The cans themselves are 3662-60, and the small manila envelope they are packaged in is 3662-80. This is the same envelope included with the 3662 Operating Milk Car of this vintage. No Classic box or manila envelope from 1955–59 has been reported that contains just the milk cans or has the 3662-79 number. However, a plain white envelope rubber-stamped "3662-79" in ¹³⁄₁₆″-high black numerals and containing only the milk cans was originally included with the 1964–66 reissue of the 3662.

The cans are of completely different construction from the 3462-70 and contain no magnet. Operation of the 3662 is much slower than that of earlier milk cars, so no magnet is required to keep the cans upright on the platform. Since the cans are common, prices are for the envelope; Like New requires a full complement of seven cans.

		20	35

3672-79 SET OF SEVEN CANS, 1959–60

Set includes seven nonmagnetic cans, identical to those for the 3662 except painted yellow and stamped "BOSCO" in red. Original cans are hard to find, and the value of a 3672 Operating Bosco Car is greatly affected by their presence or absence. Unmarked reproductions are difficult to distinguish from originals.

Original cans came packaged in a small manila envelope, part number 3672-7, along with a 3662-81 instruction sheet printed in black on white paper and dated 5-59. There is no unique instruction sheet for the 3672. Since the cans are quite scarce, even a poor-quality envelope with a couple of cans is worth buying. Like New requires a nice, complete envelope with all seven original cans. **50 90 150 240**

3927-50 25 WIPING CYLINDERS, 1957–60

A package of 25 white cotton cylinders similar to those dentists use, but somewhat larger in length and diameter. They are wrapped with a band of dark blue paper as wide as the cylinders are high, so that only the ends of the cotton rolls are visible. Some are more tightly wrapped than others are, so the wrapped rolls fit snugly in some boxes, while in others there is considerable space to spare.

They came packaged in a round, orange cardboard container with a dark blue lift-off lid and matching bottom glued in place. Printed on the orange is a rectangular white label with dark blue stick lettering. Two printings are known with different-sized background and lettering. Round boxes of wiping cylinders were shipped to dealers in cartons of 24. Like New requires the box and contents to be complete and in Like New condition.
— — **10 30**

3927-75 TRACK-CLEAN, 1956–66 and 1968–69

Introduced concurrently with the 3927 Track Cleaner Car, this nonflammable detergent in a blue can replaced the 927-3 (the orange can of flammable cleaner). It was not nearly as effective as the flammable version but is the only safe thing to use with the 3927. Sparks from the cleaning car pickup roller could easily ignite cleaner from the orange can. Probably a water-based detergent, 3927-75 seems to readily rust through and escape, even from never-opened cans. Examples of cans still sealed in their blister packs have been observed empty, showing just a trace of the fluid's escape path.

The cleaner is commonly found in a dark blue lithographed can. However, like the 927-3, it can also be found in a can with a paper label. This version has a distinctly lighter blue background color than the lithographed can and has been found in a 928. A dealer package identical to that for the 927-3 except picturing the blue can has been observed and is an NRS item.

(A) Common version with dark-blue lithographed can.
— — **10 20**

(B) Less common version with lighter blue label printed on paper and wrapped around the can to form the label.
— — **25 50**

B3927 TRACK-CLEAN, 1966

Not specifically cataloged, but a separate-sale item in 1966, when Lionel tried blister packaging on a number of items. The blue can is the standard lithographed version, but the blister pack that turns it into a B3927 is the collectible. New cans still sealed in the blister have been found empty, showing only the slightest trace of the escaping fluid's path. — — — **275**

4080 TRAIN AND ACCESSORY MANUAL, 1966 and 1968–69

A 36-page, 8½" x 11" illustrated booklet titled, *How to Operate Lionel Trains and Accessories*. This is the same title, after 1952, on the 8½" x 5½" booklets last issued in 1960 and commonly included with each train set. According to the 1966 and later catalogs, this booklet was available from Lionel Service Stations or directly from its Service Department. It was first issued, but not cataloged, in 1965 with a yellow cover, a 9/65 date, a 1965 copyright, and no ZIP Code for Lionel. For 1966 and later, the cover was redesigned in orange and white, all dates were removed, and the Service Department address included a ZIP Code. — — **15 30**

5159 MAINTENANCE AND LUBRICANT KIT, 1964–65

First appearing in the slot-car section of the 1963 catalog, this item replaced the 928 in the train section a year later. Three different packagings have been observed, but the vintage is not certain. The first is a window box identical to the 928 except for the number. Second is a blister pack (see B5159 entry below), and third is a small cardboard box sealed with paper tape and rubber-stamped "5159." All appear to have the same content as the 928, except for the Track-Clean container and the instruction sheet. The 6-2927 blister pack of 1970–71 contains components labeled with the original Lionel nomenclature.

(A) Window box identical to 928, with same contents, including a lithographed blue can of Track-Clean. Instruction sheet differs from that in 928s observed, but details could not be determined from the new example observed.
— — **30 60**

(B) Small thin cardboard box, white on inside with brown straw pattern printed on outside. Box opens down middle of top, which has narrow overlapping between halves. Sealed with a wrap of paper tape. Rubber-stamped "5159" on tape wrap. Same content as 928, but Track-Clean is in plastic squeeze bottle and instruction sheet is 5159-22, dated 3/65, and printed in black on white paper. — — **30 60**

5159-50 MAINTENANCE AND LUBRICANT KIT, 1966 and 1968–69

No examples with "-50" have been observed, so packaging is not certain. Possibly this refers to the small cardboard box version described in the 5159 above. **NRS**

B5159 MAINTENANCE AND LUBRICANT KIT, 1966

A blister pack not specifically cataloged but available in 1966. Contains an unmarked needlenose oiler, a squeeze bottle of Track-Clean, an eraser-like abrasive Rail Cleaner, a 925-1 tube of grease marked "For Model Trains And Racing Cars," and an instruction sheet that looks like the one in the 5159. Details could not be obtained from the sealed pack observed.
— — — **175**

6112-25 CANISTER SET, 1956–58

This is a separate-sale set of four canisters in a Classic box. Usually, the dark red canisters are rubber-stamped "LIONEL / AIR ACTIVATED / CONTAINER," followed by two weight lines and "61125" in white. However, the set may contain white canisters with black heat-stamped lettering or red canisters with white heat-stamped lettering. But the separate-sale box is the collectible, since the canisters are identical to those furnished with several gondolas. Red canisters with black rubber-stamped lettering have been observed but are rare and typically appear with gondolas and not canister sets.

| | | — | — | 25 | 50 |

6342 CAR and 7 CULVERT SECTIONS, 1956–57

Although the car is common, the separate-sale box is rare. When included with the culvert loaders and unloaders, the car was packaged in the box liner. In 1957, consumer catalogs ordered from Madison Hardware included an extensive price list, but the 6342 was not on it. Yet several examples have come to light, all in 6462 gondola boxes of 1956–57 vintage factory re-marked "6342." Contrary to the catalog description, none of the observed examples has culverts! This item should not be confused with the relabeled, perforated-style Picture box shown with the 348, which is not a separate-sale box of the mid-1950s.

NRS

6352(-25) ICE CAR, 1955–57

Of interest here is the rare separate-sale Classic box, identical to a typical 6464 boxcar box of that vintage except for the end printing. When included with the 352 Ice Depot, the set box liner provided a space for the car, so no car box was required. All separate-sale boxes observed are marked "6352-25," but the catalog listings use only "6352."

NRS

6414-25 FOUR AUTOMOBILES, 1955–58

A Classic box containing four premium automobiles packaged two to a cardboard sleeve. The same sleeves were used for packaging these autos in the 6414 Automobile Transport Car. The autos usually found are the common red, white, yellow, and turquoise versions, referred to as "premium" because of their chrome bumpers and clear plastic window inserts. This accessory is seldom found complete in less than Like New condition because it is nearly impossible to extract the cars without destroying their cardboard sleeve. The box flaps are usually torn or missing, since their small size makes opening the box difficult without damaging it. Condition is primarily for the box. Prices are for a complete box with autos still in their sleeves. More information on the automobiles appears in the first volume of *Greenberg's Guide to Lionel Trains, 1945–1969*.

| | | — | — | 375 | 700 |

6511-24 SET OF 5 PIPES, 1955–58

These thin, silvery plastic pipes were included with the 6511, 6477, 6311, and 6121 flatcars. The pipes have been reproduced in improved material, so the color and thickness readily distinguish them from originals, which are prone to lengthwise cracks. They were packed five abreast in a Classic box for separate sale. As with most of these miniature boxes, the flaps are easily torn on the first opening. Prices are for the box, but all five original pipes without cracks or dents must be included for Like New.

| | | — | — | 120 | 210 |

6650-80 MISSILE, 1959–60

This is a replacement or spare missile for the 6630, 6650, 6823, 443, and 470. There are two "stages," or main body parts, to the missile, which can be separated with a gentle twisting. Both halves are known in red and in white. Authentic examples have been found in all combinations except all red, but an all-red example is easily assembled. All color combinations typically have a dark blue, flexible rubber tip on the top stage. Several examples with a red tip have been observed that look original, but seem to have come from Madison Hardware. Reproduction tips, which do not appear as well done as originals, are available. Unmarked reproductions of the missile are readily available. They tend to be slightly shorter than originals, and the fins appear slightly thicker.

Original separate-sale packaging consists of a cardboard tube with a second short section of a slightly larger-diameter tube that fits over the open end of the primary tube as the lid. The tube ends are metal, and the lid has the part number on an attached sticker. What appear to be the identical tubes, but without the Lionel sticker, are available from Madison Hardware. Prices require the original tube packaging with Lionel label.

| | | — | — | 150 | 220 |

6800-60 AIRPLANE, 1957–58

Usually found as the load on a 6800 Flat Car with Airplane, the black-and-yellow Beechcraft Bonanza model was also offered for separate sale in a Late Classic box. This model is known in black over yellow (black top half of fuselage and yellow bottom half) and vice versa. The wings usually reversed the colors of the fuselage, but since they are removable, a matching combination is easily assembled. The propeller, which is not easily removable, should match the color of the lower fuselage. Both orange-yellow and lemon yellow shades of plastic are known. More information on the plane appears in the first volume of *Greenberg's Guide to Lionel Trains, 1945–1969*.

It is the box and not the airplane that is the collectible. It came only with the separate-sale model and was not included in the box with the flatcar. Either version of the airplane could be found, but of the many authentic examples observed, only the black-over-yellow version has appeared. Prices are for a box with an original airplane.

| | | — | — | 175 | 380 |

6801-60 BOAT, 1957–58

This individually packaged plastic speedboat normally came as a load on the 6801 Flat Car with Boat. There are three regular-production versions of the boat: white hull with brown deck and no printing on the cabin floor, blue hull with white deck, and yellow hull with white deck. The last two versions have Lionel nomenclature in raised letters molded into the cabin floor. Excellent reproductions of these boats have been made, and they do not have printing on the cabin floor. More information on the boat appears in the first volume of *Greenberg's Guide to Lionel Trains, 1945–1969*.

All the authentic boxed separate-sale 6801-60 Boats observed contain a model with a brown deck, which is the one that most closely matches the reproductions! But the Late Classic box marked "6801-60 / BOAT" is the collectible. It came only as a

	Gd	VG	Ex	LN

Left and center are two different sides of the boxes for the Allis-Chalmers promotional models made for them by Lionel. At right is Lionel's packaging for the same items. The 'dozer and scraper were furnished as loads for the 6816 and 6817 flatcars, respectively, as well as for separate sale. In the foreground is the late, lighter orange version of the 6816-100 Bulldozer. J. Lampert Collection.

separate-sale package and was not included in the box with the flatcar. Prices are for a box with an original boat inside.

		—	—	165	360

6816-100 ALLIS-CHALMERS TRACTOR DOZER, 1959–60

This is the individually boxed version of the orange plastic bulldozer normally found as the load on a 6816 Flat Car with Bulldozer. The separate-sale box, which was not included with the flatcar, is of interest. Two types, both rare, are known. The one intended for sale through Lionel dealers is an Orange Picture box common to this era. It is just large enough for the model and contains nothing else. Lionel also packaged this model as a promotional item for Allis-Chalmers in a box identical in size but with different graphics. More information on the bulldozer appears in the first volume of *Greenberg's Guide to Lionel Trains, 1945–1969.* **NRS**

6817-100 ALLIS-CHALMERS MOTOR SCRAPER, 1959–60

This is the individually boxed version of the orange plastic earth scraper normally found as the load on a 6817 Flat Car with Earth Scraper. The separate-sale box, which was not included with the flatcar, is of interest. Two types, both rare, are known. The one intended for sale through Lionel dealers is just a plain

	Gd	VG	Ex	LN

off-white color with no graphics at all. Only the part number and Lionel nomenclature are printed on the end flaps. Lionel also packaged this model as a promotional item for Allis-Chalmers in a box identical in size but with graphics similar to those on the Allis-Chalmers bulldozer box. Of course, a motor scraper (Lionel called it an Earth Scraper) is pictured instead of a bulldozer. Both boxes contained an instruction sheet, 6817-130, dated 11/59 and printed in red on buff color paper. More information on the scraper appears in the first volume of *Greenberg's Guide to Lionel Trains, 1945–1969.* **NRS**

6827-100 HARNISCHFEGER TRACTOR SHOVEL, 1960

Although this model and the crane in the following entry are even more elaborate and fragile than the two Allis-Chalmers models listed above, the Lionel boxes for them are not as difficult to find, since the separate-sale boxes were also included within the flatcar box. Individual crane and shovel boxes

| | Gd | VG | Ex | LN |

departed from the usual Lionel orange, white, and blue color scheme and adopted Harnischfeger's black and yellow colors. Harnischfeger used Lionel's models for promotional purposes and may have subsidized the tooling.

Lionel made a display board with Super O track for the flatcar and crane. The flatcar is mounted to the board via two screws through the bed of the car. A special shipping box has been observed containing the display board, car, and crane. This NRS item likely was for presentation to Harnischfeger executives and their best customers.

Examples of Harnischfeger's individual promotional box have recently been observed! They appear identical to Lionel's, but lack "6827-100" and the Lionel nomenclature. Two variations of the promotional box have been observed, each with slightly different text on the outside! Both versions are NRS items. More information on the shovel appears in the first volume of *Greenberg's Guide to Lionel Trains, 1945–1969*. Prices are for a Lionel box containing a complete, original shovel.

| | — | — | 150 | 275 |

6828-100 HARNISCHFEGER MOBILE CONSTRUCTION CRANE, 1960

See comments for 6827-100 above. Separate Harnischfeger promotional boxes without Lionel's numbers and nomenclature

Not only did Lionel package the 6827-100 Shovel and 6828-100 Crane for its own use (the two boxes on the left), but it also made promotional models for Harnischfeger. Note the absence of Lionel's name and item number on the two boxes on the right. J. Lampert Collection.

| | Gd | VG | Ex | LN |

have been observed for the crane. They are NRS items. More information on the crane appears in the first volume of *Greenberg's Guide to Lionel Trains, 1945–1969*. Prices are for a Lionel box containing a complete, original shovel.

| | — | — | 150 | 275 |

SP SMOKE PELLETS, 1947–66 and 1968–69

Starting in 1941 and continuing after the war until 1947, Lionel cataloged a line of chemistry sets. Only a few items spilled over into the train line, but the brown glass bottles used for storing chemicals are an example. An SP label was applied, and Lionel's supply of chemical bottles suddenly had another use. It was apparently short-lived, since these bottles are fairly rare and no display carton for them has yet surfaced. Of course, it would be no challenge if the round, brown bottle did not have a variation or two, so Lionel provided it with two different cap designs. For die-hard collectors, the mold numbers on the bottom of each bottle offer an as-yet-unknown series of variation.

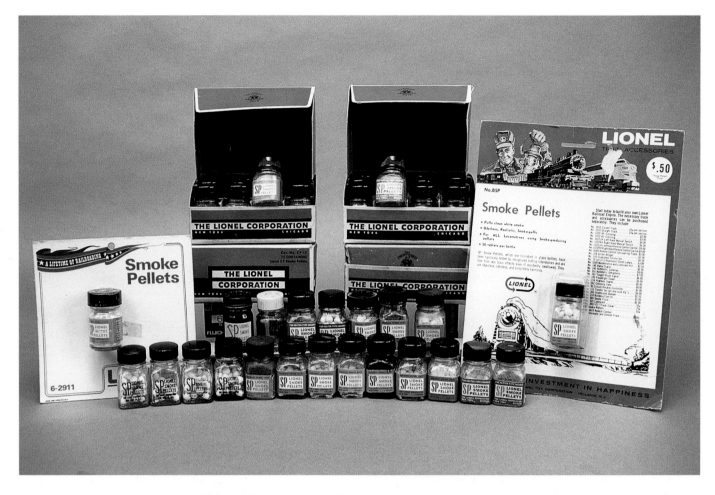

	Gd	VG	Ex	LN

But this bottle is only the beginning. Round and square, short and tall, plastic and metal caps, the list goes on and on. Prices are for a typical square bottle with a full complement of approximately 50 pellets and an intact label. Although pellets that have become pulverized in the bottle from rough handling still work fine in the smoke generator, they detract from the value of a bottle. **— — 20 35**

SP SMOKE PELLETS DEALER DISPLAY (uncataloged)

SP dealer displays, as with other dealer displays, were not typically listed in consumer catalogs, but they are highly collectible items. They probably were available every year from 1947 to 1969, just as SP bottles were, and a surprising number of these displays have survived. Prices are for just the empty display box, complete with lid and dividers, in clean, intact condition. Several variations of the box are known, including examples from 1952 with an OPS label. If the bottles are there, add value according to their quantity and condition and the number of pellets included in each one. **— — 125 225**

SP Smoke Pellets feature a host of label variations, bottle shapes and colors, cap designs, and packaging. The white-capped bottle is from Lionel's supplier but is intended for another use.

	Gd	VG	Ex	LN

TS-162 COUPLER ADAPTER, 1949

This adapter came out in November of 1949, several months after Lionel introduced the TT-100 Coupler Adapter. The latter was Lionel's answer for those who had prewar trains that had become obsolete with the introduction of knuckle couplers. However, coupler height varied considerably between various series of prewar cars, and the TT-100 is best suited for the 600 and 2600 series. As a result, Lionel introduced the TS-162 for the higher 800 and 2800-series couplers.

First mentioned in the Lionel Service Manual as revised in November 1949 and probably available for a few years after, the TS-162 had a "step" down in the tang leading to the dog-bone that mated with a knuckle coupler. Its purpose was to compensate for the greater height of the high-series couplers. Probably came in a package of 50 or 100 pieces, but there have been no reports of this packaging. Price is for one adapter in decent shape. **— — — 1**

These rare SP Smoke Pellets and 3927-75 Track-Clean dealer display boxes featured colorful illustrations. D. Corrigan Collection.

	Gd	VG	Ex	LN

TT-100 COUPLER ADAPTER, 1949

Although it did not appear in the consumer catalog, this handy item was made available through Lionel Service Stations and was Lionel's answer for those who had prewar trains that had become obsolete with the introduction of knuckle couplers. A simple nickel-plated steel stamping, this adapter fits "permanently" over the tang in the prewar coupler and has a dog-bone shape that engages the knuckle.

First introduced in the Lionel Service Manual pages dated 1-49 as "... recently designed," this model "A" Coupling Adapter had no restriction on the type of prewar coupler it was suited for. However, coupler height varied considerably between various series of prewar cars, and the TT-100 is best suited for the 600 and 2600 series. Several months later, Lionel introduced the TS-162 for the higher 800 and 2800-series couplers.

"NOTE-ORDER IN LOTS OF ONE HUNDRED," states the Lionel Service Manual. Sure enough, a manila envelope with black printing has been observed with contents listed as "100 TT-100 COUPLER ADAPTERS." Definitely an NRS item! Price is for a single adapter in decent shape.

— — — 3

	Gd	VG	Ex	LN

(No Number) LIONEL OFFICIAL RULE BOOK, 1952–53

Since it was unusual for Lionel to catalog a paper item for sale in the consumer catalog, this book is considered an accessory. The usual source for this 4³⁄₁₆″ x 6⅛″, 16-page booklet with a dark blue cover was the 1952 catalog offer included in many Lionel advertisements of that year. But for a dime, *Official Book of Rules for Model Railroading* could be purchased direct from Lionel.

— — 5 15

(No Number) LIONEL TRACK LAYOUTS, 1966 and 1968–69

An 8½″ x 11″ four-page folder in black and white showing suggested layouts for O, O27, Super O and HO track. It represents the only mention of Super O or HO in catalogs after 1966. First issued in 1962 as part of the dealer promotional package, this publication remained unchanged in content. Versions with and without the ten-cent price on the cover are known. The catalog says that it is available for the asking, but suggests sending ten cents to cover postage and handling.

— — 2 5

Index